The Practice of Justice

The Practice of
JUSTICE

A Theory of Lawyers' Ethics

William H. Simon

HARVARD UNIVERSITY PRESS
Cambridge, Massachusetts
London, England
1998

Library of Congress Cataloging-in-Publication Data

Simon, William H.
  The practice of justice / William H. Simon.
    p.   cm.
  ISBN 0-674-69711-1 (alk. paper)
    1. Practice of law—United States—Philosophy. 2. Legal ethics—
United States—Philosophy. I. Title.
  KF300.S55 1998   97-40929
  174′.3′0973—dc21   CIP

For Gary Bellow

Contents

The Practice of Justice

1

Introduction

An Anxious Profession

No social role encourages such ambitious moral aspirations as the lawyer's, and no social role so consistently disappoints the aspirations it encourages.

Many young people go to law school in the hope of finding a career in which they can contribute to society. They tend to come out with such hopes diminished, and the hopes often disappear under the pressures of practice. Late in their careers, especially if they achieve worldly success, they often recall their hopes with nostalgia and regret. We owe to this late-career experience a booming literature of books, after-dinner speeches, and bar association reports decrying the ethical poverty of law practice.

Some of this literature attributes ethical disappointment to recent developments in practice or theory. Practice has become more bureaucratic in some ways, more commercial in others. The claims of legal thought to autonomy, coherence, and authority have been challenged from both left and right. Yet we know that the experience of ethical disappointment, and indeed the literature of late-career lamentation, long antedate these developments. The current critiques are simply the latest peak in a cycle at least a century old. The volume of complaint has fluctuated, but complaint has been with us constantly.[1]

We find a similar expression of anxiety about the lawyer's role, expressed at a fairly steady rate over the years, in popular culture. The heroic portrayals of lawyering consistently excise important features of both official and empirical versions of the lawyer's role. Perry Mason's clients are always innocent. Dramatic portrayals that purport to treat lawyers more realistically are usually ambivalent or downright disparaging about the role. Dickens's Jaggers and Tulkinghorn look more grotesque the more faithfully they serve their clients.

So an explanation of the moral anxiety associated with lawyering should look to conditions more longstanding than recent developments in organization and jurisprudence. My explanation focuses on a structural tension in the lawyer's role that has always been present but has become more acute during the past century. The core of the explanation is this: the dominant conception of the lawyer's professional responsibilities weakens the connection between the practical tasks of lawyering and the values of justice that lawyers believe provide the moral foundations of their role. This conception often requires that the lawyer take actions that contribute to injustice in the circumstances at hand. Of course, these actions are supposed to facilitate a greater justice in a more remote sense. But the remoteness of the ultimate moral payoff of the lawyer's conduct is a problem. At best the situation demands of the lawyer an exacting moral asceticism. Her immediate experience implicates her in violations of the values to which she is most fundamentally committed; the redeeming beneficial effects occur somewhere outside of her working life, perhaps invisibly. So in a way most readily associated with religious norms, the lawyering role demands a deferral of the ethical gratification of experiencing the good to which one's right conduct contributes.

The problem becomes more serious once we have reason to doubt the connection between the vividly perceived injustice of the here and now and the greater justice expected elsewhere and later. The connection can't be observed. It is a matter for theory, and theory has made it harder for lawyers to believe that their immediate injustices are really necessary to a more remote good.

Thus there is truth in the suggestion that developments in legal theory contribute to the moral anxiety of the lawyer role. But the familiar accounts of the contribution of theory are misleading. As it happens, the important theoretical developments long predate the past two decades; they extend back beyond the beginning of the century. Moreover, the problem is not that legal theory has made people cynical about values. Cynicism is not necessarily a threat to the dominant conception of professional responsibility. If I am right, the key source of moral anxiety is the perceived tenuousness of the connection between the concrete immediate injustices of practice and the remote justice that is supposed to redeem them. An increase in cynicism would have no major effect on this experience. Cynicism would reduce our confidence in the redemptive power of remote justice, but it would also make us comparably more indifferent to short-term injustice.

The important developments in legal theory are not those that encourage skepticism about justice, but those that challenge the idea that justice in the abstract requires deliberate injustice in the here-and-now. And the most important of these is the century-long critique of formalistic, categorical or "mechanical" judgment. For the central problems of the lawyer's role stem from the tendency of the dominant conception to define its responsibilities in terms of formalistic, categorical, and "mechanical" norms.

The revolt against formalism in legal thought has carried the day in nearly every legal field other than that of lawyering itself. Nearly everywhere else, modern jurisprudence teaches that the hallmark of legal judgment is complexity: its commitment is to vindicating general principles while taking account of factual particularity. In this view legal judgment is characteristically contextual. Alone, the modern jurisprudence of professional responsibility presupposes or prescribes categorical judgment. There is no justification for this difference. The classic critiques of categorical judgment apply with exceptional force to the field of lawyering.

Through a remarkable act of intellectual segregation, the categorical practices of conventional legal ethics have enjoyed relative immunity from these critiques. But lawyers who have absorbed the critiques of formalism and who are accustomed to operating under regimes of contextual judgment in other areas cannot be completely insensitive to the deficiencies of categorical judgment here. Indeed, striking rhetorical lapses in professional responsibility doctrines occasionally suggest that the proponents could not possibly believe what they are saying.[2]

In these circumstances, the lawyer's anxiety and disappointment are readily explained. The norms of practice require her to take actions that frustrate the values to which she is supposed to be committed. The ideological rationales that are supposed to make this experience tolerable are weak and ineffectual.

The argument here resonates with the traditional critique of lawyering in popular culture. The main thrust of this lay critique has always been that lawyers in their conventional practices contribute knowingly to injustice. Though lawyers like to attribute lay hostility to lawyers' ethics to jurisprudential naiveté, the opposite is closer to the truth. The lay public has always been relatively less handicapped than the profession by the jurisprudence of formalism. The better lay portrayals of lawyering reflect a jurisprudential understanding superior to the profession's own pronouncements on the subject.

The Moral Terrain of Lawyering

The kind of moral decisions that implicate the profession's most fundamental commitments to legality and justice are those that arise from conflicts between client interests on the one hand and third-party and public interests on the other. Consider some examples.

The Innocent Convict. In about 1914 Arthur Powell, a Georgia lawyer, received information from a client establishing the innocence of Leo Frank. Frank had been convicted in Atlanta of the murder of a young girl at a trial notoriously marred by anti-Semitism and mob hysteria. Because the client would not consent to disclosure, Powell did not communicate this information to anyone. Frank's sentence was commuted later to life imprisonment, but he was soon afterwards lynched by a mob.[3]

Agribusiness Welfare. The Federal Reclamation Act was enacted in 1906 for the declared purpose of supporting small family farms. The act funds projects that provide water to farmers at heavily subsidized rates. The original act limited eligibility of any farmer for subsidized water to 160 acres or less. Although it is uncontroversial that the intent of this limitation was to preclude large subsidies to wealthy farmers, over the years lawyers for such farmers, including large corporations such as the Southern Pacific Railroad, created a series of devices to qualify their clients for billions of dollars in benefits.

An early approach was to have the client disperse his holdings among various corporations. Although the shares in all the corporations would be owned by the client, together with associates and family members, and the client continued to farm the land as a unit, the lawyers then argued that since each corporation owned only 160 acres, they were collectively entitled to subsidized water for all the land farmed by the client. Another approach was to create a series of trusts for family members and assign 160 acre plots to each. Although a single person might retain control of all as trustee, the lawyers could argue that each trust, as a separate "legal person," was entitled to subsidized water for "its" holdings.[4]

The Recalcitrant S & L. In 1979 the American system of savings and loan banks began to collapse as a result of structural defects aggravated by tight money policy and heavy-handed deregulation. Though the nature and causes of the collapse were well known, Congress and the administration proved unable to act decisively for more than a decade. In the meantime the American public was exposed to an astonishing degree of moral hazard through the deposit insurance system.

Because of deposit insurance, banks could attract deposits without regard to their soundness. The closer they got to insolvency, the more management would be tempted to make exceptionally risky investments. A winning bet would restore the institution to solvency and enrich management, while the costs of a losing bet would be borne by the deposit insurance fund. There was a critical public interest in closing a bank at the point at which this dynamic started to operate. Unfortunately, the resources and powers of the Federal Home Loan Bank Board were pathetically inadequate to protect this interest. The public cost of this systemic failure exceeded $200 billion.

Charles Keating and Lincoln Savings & Loan had pursued a highly aggressive investment strategy that aroused the Board's concern. When the Board expressed doubts about the bank's soundness and the lawfulness of its lending practices, Keating responded by hiring litigators from the New York firm of Kaye, Scholer, Fierman, Hays, and Handler, who represented it in bank examination matters between

1986 and 1989, when Lincoln was finally closed at a cost to the public estimated at more than $3 billion.

With a degree of adversarial contentiousness previously unknown in the bank examination process, the Kaye Scholer litigators spent formidable ingenuity and round-the-clock energy to limit the regulators' investigation of Lincoln's lending practices and forestall intervention in the fiscally hemorrhaging institution. The many examples of obfuscatory conduct alleged by the government (and disputed by Kaye Scholer) include these:

- The firm's study of their client's loan files disclosed a strong pattern of loans made without formal loan applications, with little or no analysis of collateral, and without appraisals or cash flow histories. In an internal memo a firm lawyer said that the files for one group of loans "ran the spectrum from disaster to nonexistent." Yet in seeking to forestall seizure, the firm made such assertions to the Board as, "In making real estate loans, Lincoln has always undertaken very careful and thorough procedures to analyze the collateral and the borrower."
- The bank's staff had altered loan documentation produced for the examiners. They removed information reflecting negatively on loans and added subsequently prepared materials intended to support the loans. These later materials were undated and written in the present tense to give the impression they were contemporaneous with the loans. Without disclosing these circumstances, the Kaye Scholer lawyers repeatedly referred to the doctored files as evidence of the bank's sound underwriting practice.
- To satisfy reserve and capital requirements, Lincoln inflated the book value of Lincoln's assets by a series of "linked transactions." It would sell property to an ally for a price higher than Lincoln had paid for it, recording the increase as a capital gain. In fact, Lincoln or an affiliate sometimes had loaned the ally the money to buy the property, promised to repurchase it, or simultaneously purchased an overvalued property from the ally. The Kaye Scholer lawyers were aware of the transactions and repeatedly expressed concern internally that the examiners would discover them. Without disclosing them, they continued to argue to the Board that the bank was soundly managed and referred to accounting figures

reflecting the "linked transactions" as evidence of the bank's health.[5]

Cases like these illustrate the sources of the moral anxiety associated with the lawyer's role. The conduct of counsel in each of them is at least defensible in terms of prevailing norms of professional responsibility. Powell's silence in the Frank case was and continues to be absolutely mandated by the confidentiality norms.[6] The conduct of the agribusiness lawyers has not been criticized in legal ethics terms and was probably fully within conventional norms. The Kaye Scholer lawyers were sanctioned by the Office of Thrift Supervision (successor to the Bank Board) under a plausible interpretation of the applicable banking rules, but the New York bar's disciplinary authority found no cause for discipline. Although Kaye Scholer disputed some of the factual basis of the government's charges, the firm also suggested that, even if the lawyers had acted as the charges asserted, their conduct would have been appropriate; many prominent lawyers agreed with this defense.

Yet in each of these cases there is at least a suspicion that the lawyers' conduct contributed to substantial injustice. This suspicion persists even after we recognize that our factual knowledge of these cases is limited and that there is often no consensus on the meaning of justice in specific cases. For we know, given the ethical regime under which they operated, that the lawyers involved probably would have behaved as they did even if *they themselves* believed that the likely immediate consequences of their conduct were unjust.

The Dominant View and Alternatives

The prevailing approach to lawyers' ethics as reflected in the bar's disciplinary codes, the case law on lawyer discipline, and the burgeoning commentary on professional responsibility can be crudely but usefully summarized as the Dominant View.

The core principle of the Dominant View is this: the lawyer must—or at least may—pursue any goal of the client through any arguably legal course of action and assert any nonfrivolous legal claim. Thus, if Arthur Powell's client wants him to remain silent, Powell should do so unless some law inarguably requires that he disclose. If the agribusiness clients want subsidized water, their lawyers' manipulations are justified so long as there is a nonfrivolous argument that the law does not prohibit them. The Kaye Scholer lawyers may have engaged in legally prohibited conduct, but many prominent lawyers insisted that they had not, and for them that fact would have been sufficient to establish the propriety of their conduct.

Note that in the Dominant View the only ethical duty distinctive to the lawyer's role is loyalty to the client. Legal ethics impose no responsibilities to third parties or the public different from that of the minimal compliance with law that is required of everyone.

The Dominant View is assumed in the most important provisions of each of the two ethical codes promulgated by the American Bar Association—the *Model Code of Professional Conduct* of 1969 and its successor, the *Model Rules of Professional Conduct* of 1983. One or the other of these codes is in effect in nearly every American jurisdiction.[7] The *Code*'s mandate of "zealous advocacy within the bounds of the law" states the Dominant View in a nutshell. The *Model Rules* are less explicit, but the provisions on advocacy and confidentiality amount to almost precisely the same approach as the *Code*. Both the *Code* and the *Rules* legitimate the lawyer in pursuing any arguably lawful goal of the client through any arguably lawful means. And both contain categorical injunctions to keep information adverse to the client confidential, subject only to narrow exceptions.[8]

Of course, neither the disciplinary codes nor any court or commentator subscribes to the Dominant View *tout court*. The basic precept is nearly always qualified by some norms intended to protect third-party and public interests. But the basic precept remains the governing norm. It influences and structures discussions. It functions as both starting point and presumptive fallback position.

In the writings of some critics of the Dominant view one can discern the outlines of an alternative approach that might be called the Public Interest View. The basic maxim of the Public Interest View is that law should be applied in accordance with its purposes, and litigation should be conducted so as to promote informed resolution on the substantive merits. The Public Interest approach is less defined than the Dominant one, but it tends to mandate the disclosure of relevant information of the sort withheld in the Innocent Convict and S & L case; to reject the manipulation of form in ways that defeat relevant legal purposes, as appears to have happened in the Agribusiness Welfare case; and to forswear the use of procedure in a way that frustrates substantive norms, as may have happened in the S & L case.[9]

The critical fact for our purposes is that both the Dominant and the Public Interest views, for all the differences in their priorities, adopt a common style of decisionmaking that I call categorical. Such decisionmaking severely restricts the range of considerations the decisionmaker may take into account when she confronts a particular problem; a rigid rule dictates a particular response in the presence of a small number of factors. The decisionmaker has no discretion to consider factors that are not specified or to evaluate specified factors in ways other than those prescribed by the rule.

Most broad debate about professional responsibility takes for granted that ethical judgment should be categorical. For example, consider a exchange between Monroe Freedman, an uncompromising exponent of the Dominant View, and Geoffrey Hazard, a drafter of the Model Rules who has flirted with the Public Interest View. Must counsel for the husband in a divorce case insist on disclosure of income that the wife is unaware of? As Freedman tells the story, the "wife is represented by a so-called 'bomber' who has no value in life other than stripping the husband of every penny and piece of property he has, at whatever cost to the personal relation and children, or anything else." Hazard responds that he could retell the story with the wife and children out in the snow while the husband luxuriates in the Caribbean. Expressing the common premise of the categorical approaches, Hazard concludes, "you can't have it both ways . . . You can't make these cases turn on the underlying merits. We are talking about . . . the procedural rule."[10] Freedman would be the last to disagree about the need for a rule, but for him the appropriate rule is "don't disclose" rather than, as for Hazard, "disclose."

In contrast to the Dominant and Public Interest views, I will defend an approach to ethical decisionmaking in which decisions often turn on "the underlying merits." We can call it the Contextual View. Its basic maxim is that the lawyer should take such actions as, considering the relevant circumstances of the particular case, seem likely to promote justice.

Justice, as I use the term, is not an extra-legal concept. I follow the Preambles to the ABA codes in taking justice to represent a basic normative premise of the legal system.[11] Thus an alternative formulation of the basic maxim might exhort the lawyer to act to vindicate "the legal merits" of the matter at hand. Of course, for many lawyers "justice" and "law" or "legal merit" have differing connotations, and the relation of the two is the subject of a classic jurisprudential debate that we will refer to at several points below. How one comes out on this question will affect the way one implements the approach proposed here. But any of the answers that are currently taken seriously is compatible with some variation of my approach.

The essence of this approach is contextual judgment—a judgment that applies relatively abstract norms to a broad range of the particulars of the case at hand. In some moods, especially when talking about the ethics of practice, lawyers speak as if such judgment is necessarily arbitrary. They talk of abstract norms as subjective and of facts as indeterminate. There are two or more sides to every question, they say. One person's justice is another person's oppression. We can never know for certain what happened.

But in other contexts lawyers typically insist strenuously on the plausibility of rational, grounded, discretionary judgment. Indeed, for the past century this has been the central thrust of discussions of the judicial role. The best known modern literature on judicial decision-making has been centrally concerned with defending contextual styles of decisionmaking against more categorical styles. Although this defense has been challenged, it has gained wide acceptance even among lawyers hostile to this style of decision in legal ethics. The preference for categorical norms and decisions in the lawyering context reflects nothing more than a failure to carry through to the lawyering role the critique of formalism, mechanical jurisprudence, and categorical reasoning that has long been applied to the judicial role.

Another pertinent context in which lawyers have been relatively willing to accept the possibility of meaningful discretionary judgment is the arena of the public prosecutor. Indeed, my formulation of the basic maxim of the Discretionary model has been partly inspired by the maxim the *Code* prescribes for the prosecutor: "The responsibility of a public prosecutor . . . is to seek justice, not merely to convict."[12]

Lawyers are so accustomed to associating contextual judgment with judges or with prosecutors and other government lawyers that they sometimes protest that the Contextual View of legal ethics collapses the lawyer's role into that of the judge or prosecutor. But that is a misunderstanding. In appealing to these other roles I mean to invoke only a style of judgment, not the particular decisions judges and prosecutors make. The Contextual View incorporates much of the traditional lawyer role, including the notion that lawyers can serve justice through zealous pursuit of clients' goals. It is fully respectful of the most plausible conceptions of procedural justice and the adversary system. Although it assumes the lawyer's role has a public dimension, that assumption is grounded in the lawyer's age-old claim to be an "officer of the court" and in notions about the most effective integration of the lawyering role with the other roles in the legal system.

The notion of a legal ethics regime of contextual judgment strikes some lawyers as almost inconceivably utopian. Yet in fact we already have a system of lawyer regulation based on contextual norms in place and functioning. This is the system of tort regulation that handles malpractice claims in the courts. The central norm of this system—the negligence concept—is a paradigmatic example of a contextual norm. The process by which the negligence norm has been elaborated in myriad occupational contexts is a familiar illustration of the way an abstract ideal can be concretized and grounded in social practices and expectations through hypotheticals and case-by-case adjudication. The preference for contextual norms in the ethics context does not reflect any practical difference between the spheres of tort and of legal ethics.

For all its differences with the Dominant View, the argument here shares with it a vitally important premise. Both views invoke the aspirational tradition of legal professionalism. They assume that lawyers care about the rightness of their conduct and that they are motivated at least to a limited extent to behave ethically. Lawyers in this view are not simply self-seeking profit maximizers, but people who seek satisfaction and respect in the performance of a socially valuable role. Such beliefs are assumed by nearly all participants in the classic debates about legal ethics. Yet we should acknowledge that they are rejected by some people for whom these debates seem hypocritical posturing. Although I will have a good deal to say about the practical implementation of alternative ethical regimes, I have not sought to engage the extreme skeptic who cannot see any reason to care about the moral appraisal of lawyer conduct.

A Preview

After a discussion of some alternative perspectives on the moral anxiety of the bar and the basic problems of legal ethics, which I believe are at least partly misguided, I go on to criticize the premises of the Dominant View. Chapter 2 focuses on a set of arguments implied in the *Code*'s "zealous advocacy within the bounds of the law" maxim. These arguments suggest that the client generally has a right to the lawyering this maxim prescribes. I assert that these arguments are anachronistic and incoherent.

Chapter 3 focuses on a somewhat different set of arguments for the Dominant View that are more prominent in the *Model Rules* and accompanying commentary. These arguments are instrumental. They contend that, while any one given client may not have a right to the consequences of zealous advocacy, requiring the lawyer to engage in it will generally promote justice in the aggregate. The most important of these arguments concerns confidentiality; another involves the "adversary system." I argue that legitimate interests inherent in confidentiality are best protected by a contextual norm, and that the Contextual approach is consistent with plausible conceptions of the "adversary system."

We then turn in Chapter 4 to the question of whether there is a categorical duty to obey the law. Such a duty represents both the end point of the Dominant model and the beginning point—the first of a series of public-regarding categorical duties—of the Public Interest model. The answer turns out to depend on how we answer the question of the relation of law and justice. If we define law narrowly to exclude important dimensions of justice, then the duty to obey becomes indefensible. If we define it more broadly, we can justify a duty, but the duty is inconsistent with the Dominant View of legal ethics, and perhaps also the Public Interest View.

I relate the jurisprudential critique of the Dominant and Public Interest views to the question of the moral anxiety of the bar in Chapter 5. The argument here is that contextual judgment is an element of the conception of meaningful work entailed by the most powerful moral aspirations of professionalism.

Chapter 6 discusses Contextual View in detail. I give several illustrations of how ethical decisions might be made under that approach and conclude by revisiting the Innocent Convict, Agribusiness Welfare, and Recalcitrant S & L cases.

I consider and reject arguments in Chapter 7 that there is something special about criminal defense that makes the Dominant View more plausible there than in the civil sphere.

Finally, in Chapter 8 I consider what forms of institutionalization and enforcement would be most appropriate for a legal ethics inspired by the Contextual View. I emphasize the curious difference between the categorical style of regulation of lawyering adopted in the legal ethics field and the contextual style adopted in the tort field and argue that the latter is more consistent with the profession's most plausible ethical aspirations. I also consider the pressures that arise from the "market for ethical commitment" and speculate about reforms that might reduce the tension between such pressures and an ethic of contextual judgment.

Except in Chapter 8 and parts of Chapter 3, I do not distinguish between ethical analysis relevant to a regulatory body promulgating rules of professional conduct and analysis relevant to an individual lawyer operating within the limits of promulgated rules. The argument is designed for both contexts. Disciplinary rules should require sound contextual judgment. But any set of rules will leave lawyers a good deal of discretion. For lawyers who take professional responsibility seriously, ethics will never be solely a matter of rule compliance, no matter how the rules are framed. The argument here suggests ways in which lawyers should think about decisions within the range of that discretion.

False Starts

An important premise of my argument is that the key issues of legal ethics are jurisprudential, that is, they implicate questions of the nature and purpose of law and the legal system. Perhaps surprisingly, this claim is not widely accepted. Indeed, it is implicitly denied in much of the most ambitious writing on professional responsibility.

It will be useful to consider four alternative perspectives, three of which locate the most basic issues of lawyers' ethics elsewhere. The first sees professional responsibility as largely a matter of mechanical compliance with positive law. The second and third see it as largely a matter of accommodating professional demands with personal morality or personal relations. The fourth, although it resembles my argument in emphasizing the importance of complex judgment, sees both the possibilities and obstacles to such judgment much differently.

Following the Rules

The contemporary prominence of professional responsibility issues dates from the Watergate scandal. Prior to that time little attention was paid to the subject in the law schools or on bar exams, and there was little doctrine or commentary. Since Watergate, ethics has become a mandatory course in most law schools. An exam devoted to the subject is required of most bar applicants. And there is a burgeoning literature and case law.

What was it about Watergate that inspired such activity? Presumably, it was the spectacle of lawyers participating in a burglary or obstructing justice by making payments to those who were caught so they would not provide information to the authorities about the other participants. This conduct could be attributed either to ignorance of the law or deficient motivation to comply with it. Although the latter seems far more likely, the former is more easily remediable. So there was a tendency within the bar to define the problem as insufficient knowledge among lawyers about the legal requirements applicable them. Hence lawyers need to be taught more about the rules.

Now it did not take an exercise of complex judgment to determine that the most salient lawyer misconduct in Watergate was criminal. The activities involved familiar core instances of conduct prohibited by statutes. Nevertheless, some people drew the lesson that part of the problem of ignorance was that the rules governing lawyering were not simple and straightforward enough for lawyers to readily determine their requirements. So part of the response to Watergate was an effort to simplify the bar's ethical norms.

One casualty of this effort was the "Ethical Considerations" of the *Code*. The *Code* was divided into "Disciplinary Rules" and "Ethical Considerations." The former were relatively specific and mandatory; the latter were broad statements of principle that were characterized as "aspirational"—something lawyers should strive for but would not be disciplined for failing to attain. By contrast, the drafters of the *Model*

Rules sought to create only "black letter rule[s]." They thus dispensed with "aspirational norms" and sought to make the rules as straightforward as possible.[13] These rules (and the Disciplinary Rules of the *Code* in the jurisdictions that still have it) are the common core of required courses in ethics in law schools across the country.

They are also the only subject tested by the Multistate Professional Responsibility Examination, which 42 states require of bar applicants. Since this examination is multiple-choice and machine-graded, it focuses on rules and situations that lend themselves to glib, black-and-white responses. Applicants preparing for the examination are given advice such as this:

> What they are testing is your ability to memorize. If you find yourself engaged in creative reasoning, stop. Remember where you are.
>
> Why we do [something] is not relevant to the bar exam. Whether we can do [it] is.
>
> The key to getting the questions right is to avoid thinking for yourself.[14]

Once the subject of legal ethics or professional responsibility has been reduced in this manner to a set of mechanical disciplinary rules, it is no longer apparent what it has to do with ethics or responsibility. If this is what legal ethics is really about, then the source of the profession's moral anxiety must be the foolishness of its aspirations for moral engagement and public responsibility. Yet at the same time that they reduce ethics to a matter of mindless rule application, the *Model Rules* continue to insist that a lawyer is "an officer of the court and a public citizen having special responsibility for the quality of justice."[15] The bar finds it difficult to give up these aspirations even as it betrays them.

In contrast to the rule-focused approach, the argument here is that the important issues of legal ethics require complex, contextual judgment.

Personal Morality

Many critics of the Dominant View start with the question, "Can a good lawyer be a good person?" They worry that the Dominant View leaves lawyers too little space in which to express their personal values. To them the key problem of lawyers' ethics is the problem of "role morality": the effective performance of the role requires actions that conflict with moral commitments the individual makes outside the role.[16]

In fact, the *Code* and especially the *Model Rules* make substantial concessions to the lawyer's personal moral autonomy. As I have noted, critical norms in these compilations have a categorical and mandatory character. But there are also some norms that delegate broad, unreviewable autonomy to lawyers to consult their personal values. These norms obviate complex judgment in the opposite way from the categorical ones. Instead of rigidly dictating a response to a narrow set of factors, they make no effort to specify how the decisions that fall under them might be made other than in terms of the lawyer's subjective predispositions.

For example, the rule on withdrawal from representation authorizes withdrawal whenever the lawyer "finds the client's objective repugnant." The lawyer has no duty to consider the extent to which withdrawal would cause injustice. I noted above that the confidentiality rule is primarily categorical, but it also incorporates an element of personal morality. The rigid disciplinary prohibitions are accompanied by two types of exception, one permitting disclosure when necessary to some interest of the lawyer herself, and the other permitting it when necessary to save a third person from "death or substantial bodily injury" from a client's criminal act.[17] This second exception, which covers some of the most compelling ethical issues, does not give rise to an obligation to disclose or even to consider doing so. The rules simply give the lawyer permission to disclose; they state that she "may" do so but provide no criteria for such decision and make clear that the decisions are not subject to disciplinary review.

To the extent that the profession's problem is really the need for space for the expression of personal morality, these norms seem responsive. But in fact, this is not an apt characterization of the problem.

If I loathe the Republican party and everything it stands for, and a Republican politician asks me to represent him in asserting a First Amendment claim that, although valid, is likely to further the interests of the party, I may have a conflict between my role and my personal moralities. In that case the dispensation to refuse on the grounds that the case is "repugnant" may accommodate the latter at the expense of the former.

But most of the engaging issues of legal ethics are different. In the cases of the Innocent Convict, Agribusiness Welfare, and the Recalcitrant S & L, the values competing with the clients' interests—reserving punishment for the guilty, distributing public resources in accordance with congressional intent, making available information relevant to the claims involved—are not just personal predispositions of various individuals; they are values solidly grounded in the public culture of the society and the legal system.

The role-morality theorists recognize that the values competing with client interests in the core instances of legal ethics are not just subjective predispositions. Their point is not just that lawyers should be able to respect such values; they think lawyers have a duty to respect such values. At the very least, they believe lawyers should be criticized for failing to respect them.

The role theorists thus tend to portray the conflict between client and third-party or public interests as a conflict between legal values and nonlegal values socially grounded outside the legal system. But why shouldn't we see these conflicts as occurring within the legal domain—as challenges from competing legal values? Why shouldn't we see the critique of the Dominant View as a jurisprudential argument for the improvement of the lawyer's role, rather than a lay moral argument for limiting the intrusion of the role on other commitments? Before we ask whether a good lawyer can be a good person, we should ask whether a person who follows the Dominant View is a good lawyer.

In order to decide between these characterizations of the issues, we need to give more critical consideration than the role theorists have yet done to exactly what the plausible claims of a legal role morality could be. As we will see in Chapters 2 and 4, this issue turns on the meaning and scope of the distinction between legal and nonlegal public values.

The belief that this distinction is an important one and that it cuts off a broad range of public values from the province of the legal is a hallmark of the jurisprudential philosophy of Positivism. In characterizing the values that compete with client loyalty in many core problems as nonlegal, the role-morality theorists implicitly adopt a strong Positivist understanding of legality. Yet on examination, strong versions of Positivism turn out to be implausible, and indeed they are rejected by most lawyers outside the sphere of legal ethics. In most areas of law lawyers typically treat nearly all public values as at least implicitly part of the legal system.

Now it might seem that this question of characterization is just a matter of semantics. In fact, the stakes are important. One concerns the types of discourse available to resolve such issues and the potential for institutional resolution. If the problem involves the reconciliation of competing legal values, lawyers know how to address it. The range of sources and authorities and the modes of analysis and argument that lawyers habitually employ in their everyday work are available and appropriate for the central issues of legal ethics. Moreover, the standards and conclusions that emerge from such efforts might be the basis for professional criticism and discipline of lawyers' conduct.

On the other hand, if the problem arises from the claims of nonlegal values, then lawyers are likely to be uncertain how to deal with these claims collectively and perhaps even individually. They have no common analytical and rhetorical tools for addressing them. The tools offered in popular culture for considering moral problems seem too formless and subjective; those offered by academic philosophy seem too abstract and multifarious.

Role theorists often complain that they have trouble engaging their students in ethical discussions. Discussion often consists of serial streams of consciousness in which each student explains how she "feels" about the matter. When the teachers try to beef things up with philosophical texts, students find them boring or too difficult. The teachers sometimes complain that the students are too "vocational." But even idealistic students who have been drawn to law school by some sense of the ethical possibilities of the lawyering role are not likely to feel that what they are looking for is ways to protect themselves from the role. And all students reasonably expect the subject of legal ethics to engage more directly the craft knowledge that they are learning in their other courses.

If the rule-focused perspective disappoints because its view of legal ethics and professional responsibility seems to have so little to do with ethics or responsibility, the role-morality perspective disappoints because its view seems to have so little to do with law or the profession.

Personal Relations

The tendency to explain issues of legal ethics in terms of extralegal values reaches an extreme in the writings of scholars like Charles Fried and Charles Ogletree, who defend the lawyering role of the Dominant View as an intrinsically valuable personal relation.[18]

They emphasize that the Dominant View encourages loyalty, trust, and empathy on the part of the lawyer toward another person, the client. Such relations have some of the qualities we associate with friendship, they assert, and we should regard the lawyer-client relation of the Dominant View as, like friendship, a good in itself. Raising the lawyer's responsibilities to values and people outside the relation would undermine the worthy qualities within it. The argument is simple and has had an enduring appeal over the past two decades, but it is wrong.

First, the argument has many obvious descriptive problems. Many clients are not persons at all but large organizations. Lawyer relations with individual clients are often brief and impersonal. Most lawyer-client relations are substantially commercial; the lawyer insists that the client pay for her loyalty, trust, and empathy. Unlike friendship, the relation is not reciprocal; the client is not supposed to show loyalty and empathy to the lawyer.

Second, the argument begs the question of why the personal values of the lawyer-client relation are more fundamental than the values—both personal and impersonal—that the relation threatens. However the lawyer regards the relation, the client does not seek legal assistance as an end in itself. He comes in order to get leverage on people or institutions outside the relation. When the client's goal is supported by norms of legal merit and justice, we don't need the personal-relation argument to justify the lawyer's role. When the client's goal threatens such norms, we need an argument as to why these norms should be trumped by those of the lawyer-client relation. Note that the threatened norms—the ones governing the relation of client and third parties affected by the lawyering—might be personal ones as well. For example, the client might be betraying someone else's trust in order to get an undeserved benefit. The proponents have yet to explain why lawyer-client trust and empathy should trump these other values. Honor is an important value too, but it doesn't follow that "honor among thieves" should be exalted or protected.

Third, the personal-relation characterization seems inconsistent with some of the core practical tasks of lawyering. Perhaps the most basic of these tasks is advising clients about their legal rights and powers and helping them enforce and make use of these rights and powers. This task does not imply an intimate personal relation; indeed it is in some tension with such a relation. Consider Charles Ogletree's description of his empathic relation to a man accused of a grotesque rape-murder: "[M]y empathy was based on my ability to relate to him as a person and to develop a relation with him. I viewed Stevens as a man whom the police had surprised in a warrantless arrest; someone from whom the police had seized incriminating evidence without a search warrant. I did not want to know what he had done . . ."[19]

Now this may be a defensible posture for a criminal defense lawyer to take toward a client, but it has little to do with empathy. Empathy would require that the lawyer try to take the client's own view of the situation and identify with the client's feelings. This would almost certainly require knowing "what he had done." Ogletree doesn't view the client as someone whose search-and-seizure rights have been violated because that's the way the client views himself, but because that's the view that emerges from Ogletree's efforts to determine the client's legal rights. Yet Ogletree would make the personal relationship, rather than the client's rights, the core value of legal ethics. Once again we have a conception of legal ethics that seems to have detached lawyering from the law.

Finally, the personal-relations approach ignores some traditionally prominent and ethically plausible elements of the profession's self-conception. In the professional tradition the lawyer mediates between public commitments and the private concerns of the client. The public commitments are expressed in the notion of the lawyer as "officer of the court" and in the idea that the lawyer's relation to the client involves not just loyalty, but also *detachment*. The detachment idea is expressed in a variety of specific prescriptions, such as those that forbid the lawyer to express her "personal belief" in the credibility of the client or the rightness of the client's cause, or the one that limits the lawyer's ability to acquire a personal financial interest in the client's affairs.[20] Such prescriptions underline respects in which the professional tradition requires that the lawyer *not* become the client's friend.

The personal-relations approach jettisons, or at least subordinates, the public and impersonal aspects of the lawyer-client relation in favor of norms of private and personal loyalty. Aside from representing a radical departure from the professional tradition, this moral vision is an unattractive one. It is easy to find portraits of societies in which public values are routinely sacrificed to concerns of personal loyalty. They occur in books with titles like *The Moral Basis of a Backward Society*. This is the world of the Sicilian mafia, or the American ethnic political machine, or the Maoist neotraditionalist bureaucracy, or various Latin American oligarchies. Closer to home, you can find such portraits in books with titles like *The Organization Man* and *The Lonely Crowd*. This is the world of corporate conformism.

In these settings the deepest duties arise from face-to-face relationships. These relationships are described in the rhetoric of family and friendship. Appeals to public values or impersonal norms are seen as betrayals. Conflicts are resolved, not through principle, but through hierarchies of personal deference. The ultimate sins are personal—being disrespectful, or ungrateful, or uncooperative; not a good godson, or collaborator, or team player. Public norms are purely external constraints to be treated as instrumental. Often the personal flavor of the relation is a veneer on a brutal hierarchy.

Many people have found aspects of these settings attractive, but they have one feature that one would expect most lawyers to find unattractive: they are inimical to the rule of law, justice, and democracy. These ideals all require respect for relatively impersonal norms and commitments and for the rights of strangers, all of which the personal-relations approach implicitly denigrates.

I don't mean to deny or dispute the important psychological intuition that inspires the personal-relations argument. The experience of getting to know and helping a particular individual can be enormously satisfying. But for the lawyer to perform the most distinctive and important aspects of his job, this value has to be secondary to that of vindicating relevant norms of legal merit and justice.

Practical Reason

In *The Lost Lawyer* Anthony Kronman explains the contemporary lawyer's moral anxiety in terms of the erosion of capacities and opportunities for practical reason, or as he sometimes calls it, "prudentialism."

Kronman argues that any fulfilling, distinctive moral identity for lawyers must be built around this type of reason, which for him is exemplified by common law decisionmaking. His idea of lawyer's practical reason has two elements. The first is a commitment to contextual judgment. A common law judge tries at once to take account of the particularities of the case before her and to resolve it consistently with past cases. The principles she applies are always embedded in particular factual circumstances. They are never fully articulated and cannot be mechanically applied; rather they are elaborated in the course of the very process of adjudication they govern.

The second quality Kronman associates with practical reasoning is a simultaneous commitment to both sympathy and detachment. The judge has to identify with the parties' various conflicting positions in a series of exercises of empathy and at the same time has to pull back to see these various positions in the perspective of the applicable legal norms. For Kronman the commitments to case-by-case judgment on the one hand and empathy-with-detachment on the other, which have long been associated with the common law judge, also characterize the most fulfilling kinds of lawyering.

In Kronman's account, the capacities and opportunities for practical judgment have been subverted by organizational and theoretical developments. In organization, law practice is now more episodic and more specialized, so that lawyers have fewer occasions to gain broad knowledge of and give broad advice to their clients. The narrow technical matters that now preoccupy them leave little room for the exercise of practical reason.

In theory, the problem is that the common law idea has been challenged by rationalizing, interdisciplinary movements such as Law-and-Economics and Critical Legal Studies, which tend to dismiss case-by-case reasoning in favor of broad generalization and to deny the distinctiveness of legal reasoning by conflating it with social science or politics. Kronman fears that in the absence of a distinctive method, lawyers will be unable to develop a distinctive occupational identity that could sustain a professional ethic. Thus he calls the interdisciplinary move "professional suicide."

Kronman's argument includes several additional features that to my mind detract from the plausibility of his ideal—a claim that practical reason is more a character trait than an intellectual capacity, an insistence that the common law style of reasoning has a logical affinity with conservative politics, and a tendency to see the profession's highest moral qualities exemplified exclusively in wealthy corporate lawyers who occasionally serve in high government posts. But if we ignore these excrescences, we see that Kronman's practical reason is a version of what I call contextual judgment.

It is not the only version. There are others, many of them compatible with Law and Economics and Critical Legal Studies. Nevertheless, Kronman's account and the long tradition of common law jurisprudence it summarizes stand as a compelling illustration of what ethical judgment might involve in an ambitious conception of professional responsibility. But Kronman proceeds from this promising starting point to an argument that misconstrues the profession's current circumstances. First, he misunderstands the practical constraints on the fulfillment of the ideal of practical reason. These constraints long antedate recent changes in the organization of practice, and they have nothing to do with contemporary legal theory, whose hostility to practical reason Kronman exaggerates and which in any event has not influenced practice greatly.

The critical obstacles to the vindication of the ideal of practical reason are far simpler and more direct than those Kronman discusses. The problem is that, for at least the past hundred years, the bar's professional responsibility norms have forbidden this type of judgment across a broad range of the most ethically urgent situations lawyers face. The profession has promulgated an ideology, backed by disciplinary rules and sanctions, that mandates unreflective, mechanical, categorical judgment rather than practical reason. The principal proponents of this ideology have not been highbrow legal theorists but the leaders of the organized bar, including some "lawyer-statesmen" of the sort that Kronman exalts as embodying his ideal.

Second, and perhaps ironically, Kronman underestimates the ethical importance of practical reason or contextual judgment in ordinary law practice. Though he laments the alienation of the legal academy from the world of practice, his book is perhaps the most sustained expression of that alienation yet produced. In 400 pages ostensibly devoted to lawyers' ethics, it does not mention a single instance of lawyering.

The only contemporary lawyers the book mentions are a handful of people famous for traveling back and forth between big corporate firms and high government posts: Lloyd Garrison, John McCloy, William Rogers, Adlai Stevenson, Cyrus Vance.[21] These "lawyer-statesmen" are Kronman's paragons of practical wisdom. To ask why not Clarence Darrow or Thurgood Marshall or Joseph Rauh or Gary Bellow? is not just to suggest that Kronman has a political bias. It is also to emphasize his alienation from lawyering. For one important thing that distinguishes Kronman's list from this one is that his lawyer-statesmen all owe their fame to work in high government jobs, not as practicing lawyers.

It is hard to avoid the inference that Kronman finds the tasks of ordinary lawyering empty of moral and intellectual challenge. Of course, if that were the case, it would hardly be necessary to write a book to explain the demoralization of the practicing bar. Yet many modern theorists of the common law tradition have emphasized that the challenges to complex practical judgment potentially arise in the most mundane tasks of everyday practice. For example, Hart and Sacks's classic, *The Legal Process,* begins with a 100-page exegesis of the legal structure of a shipment of cantaloupes, and then proceeds to a strenuous discussion of ethical issues involved in drafting a small-business lease.[22]

In contrast to Kronman's, my argument assumes that the tasks of ordinary practice are often practically and ethically complex. In doing so I am faithful both to the longstanding premise of the bar—that ordinary lawyering can be intellectually and morally engaging—and to the portrayal of lawyering in the common law jurisprudence that has inspired Kronman in other respects.

The Yale Law School, where Kronman is Dean, has long been home to people for whom law practice is, at best, a means to financial security, and high government posts represent the only truly fulfilling form of work. Thus it is tempting to see Kronman's book as an expression of this peculiar local culture. But *The Lost Lawyer* also resonates with the practitioners' rhetoric of late career lamentation. Its mournful suggestion that law practice does not live up to ambitious moral ideals, unaccompanied by serious consideration of any actual instance of practice, is typical of bar association after-dinner speeches and commission reports. So is the tendency to attribute the problems to broad social and intellectual movements rather than specific practices of the organized bar.

That even highly successful practitioners should express Kronman's alienation from practice might be taken as evidence for the conclusion that ordinary practice is inherently empty. My view is different. I think the abstract, disengaged quality of this rhetoric reflects a reluctance to recognize the role of the bar's ethical ideology and rules in stunting the moral quality of practice. These ideologies and rules protect lawyers from a competing set of pressures and challenges that would be intensified by reforms that defined professional responsibilities in terms practical reason or contextual judgment. Any serious attempt to address and alleviate the moral anxiety of the contemporary lawyer would require a willingness to face these competing pressures and challenges. So far most of the lamenters seem unwilling to do so.

2

A Right to Injustice

The oldest and perhaps still most influential argument for the Dominant View asserts that the client has a right to the type of lawyering it prescribes, even when such lawyering leads to injustice for others. The lawyer should keep the murderer's secret, exploit the agribusiness loophole, and mislead the Bank Board because her client is entitled that she do so, notwithstanding the consequences for the innocent convict, the citizenry generally, and the deposit insurance fund. Of course, since rights are derived from justice, it sounds paradoxical to say that someone has a right to behavior that visits injustice on others. Proponents of the entitlement argument might address this sense of paradox in various ways.

They might suggest that legal rights are a necessarily imperfect approximation of justice, the best we can do given the limitations of our lawmaking abilities. The sense of injustice to nonclients reflects a basically unattainable moral standard that has to yield to more practicable norms. Alternatively, they might assert that the client's right is more important than those of the others, and therefore, in a situation of conflict, the client should prevail. However, the problems with the entitlement argument are more serious and fundamental than such responses recognize.

The entitlement argument has rarely been expounded systematically. It is one of those doctrines which, as Karl Llewellyn said of a related set of ideas, "the profession did not have occasion to study

26

particularly; a lawyer just absorbed it, largely through the fingers and the pores, as he went along."[1] The largely tacit role of the argument has immunized it substantially from critical examination. When the premises of the argument become explicit, it is apparent that they assume a jurisprudence that most lawyers, including those who espouse the entitlement view, regard as discredited outside the field of legal ethics. In particular, the argument depends on core premises of Libertarianism and Positivism that are at once implausible and mutually contradictory.

The argument of this chapter merely applies critiques of Libertarianism and Positivism—and of the distinctive synthesis of these doctrines known as Classical Legal Thought—that are quite familiar in many contexts to an area of the legal culture in which they have been ignored.

The Entitlement Argument

The entitlement argument rests on two basic ideas. One is the Libertarian claim that the unique fundamental goal of the legal system is to safeguard the liberty or autonomy of the citizen.[2] Legal norms create for each individual a zone of autonomy in which she is free to do what she wants without accounting to others or the state. The lawyer's first duty is to the client's liberty; she serves the client by insuring that he can pursue his wants within the full range of his domain. In this perspective liberty is a presumptive background value. Where the "bounds of the law" limit liberty, they must do so unambiguously. Ambiguity should be construed in favor of liberty.

The second idea is the Positivist claim that legal norms are strongly different from nonlegal norms. We can distinguish legal norms procedurally because they are enacted or adopted by recognized lawmaking institutions of the state. We can distinguish them substantively by the fact that they take the form of commands or prohibitions backed by penalties.[3] As a consequence, legal norms have an objectivity and a legitimacy that nonlegal norms lack. They are objective because both the processes of enactment or adoption and the administration of penalties are social facts that can be ascertained through methods on which there is substantial agreement. Legal norms are distinctively legitimate because they partake of the legitimacy of the enacting institution (which owes its own legitimacy to one or more of a variety of values—representative democracy, socially sanctioned expertise, a Hobbesian need for order).

The two ideas are synthesized in the maxim of "zealous advocacy within the bounds of the law." The autonomy idea gives us the "zealous advocacy" norm; the differentiation idea gives us the "bounds of the law" qualification. From the entitlement perspective, the ethically ambitious lawyer—the lawyer who would acknowledge constraints short of the bounds of the law—encounters moral, political, and epistemological objections. Morally, he is accused of betraying the value of liberty. In casual rhetoric, he is often portrayed as "playing God," which can connote both paternalistim and selfishness—sacrificing the client's rights to his own personal desires or interests.

In political terms, the ethically ambitious lawyer is seen as usurping power. How can the lawyer "arrogate to herself" the power to "dictate" to the client how he should behave? critics ask. They see the lawyer as behaving like a self-appointed legislature, imposing new limits on client autonomy rather than enforcing the existing ones. If the lawyer disapproves of the consequences of the client's exercise of autonomy, the appropriate response is to petition the legislature to change the law. But liberty values require that such changes be prospective, so in the interim the right thing to do is to help the client make the most of her autonomy within the existing bounds.

The political danger of the ethically ambitious lawyer is either anarchy or totalitarianism. If the values to which the lawyer appeals are seen as idiosyncratic, then the lawyer's abuse of the client seems anarchic; if the values really are a plausible approximation of some recognizable social interest, then the lawyer seems to sacrifice the client's right to the collectivity in the fashion of totalitarianism. Proponents of the Dominant View take great satisfaction in the fact that their doctrine is anathema to dictatorships of all sorts.

The epistemological objection is that the ethically ambitious lawyer cannot ground her judgments in a way that would be necessary for a plausible professional morality. To the extent that she treats her judgments as anything more than subjective preferences, she deludes herself. She may appeal to justice or public interests, but these terms are not self-defining, and particular applications of them tend to be controversial and hence form an insubstantial basis for a professional ethic. The classic formulation of this point is the exchange between James Boswell and Samuel Johnson:

> BOSWELL: "But what do you think of supporting a cause which you know to be bad?"
> JOHNSON: "Sir, you do not know it to be good or bad till the Judge determines it."[4]

The autonomy and differentiation ideas have each been discredited by modern jurisprudence. The first is undermined by the critique of Libertarianism; the second, by the critique of Positivism. Moreover, the two ideas are inconsistent with each other, so that on examination the entitlement perspective proves incoherent.

In examining the critiques of Libertarianism and Positivism, it will be helpful to refer to two further examples.

The Statute of Limitations Case. A creditor has brought suit for non-payment of money loaned the defendant and now past due. The defendant admits the debt and failure to pay it, and he is able to pay. However, the creditor has delayed bringing suit until after the statute of limitations has run. May his lawyer ethically plead the statute?

The Negligent Railroad. In the mid-nineteenth century railroads were sufficiently new that many aspects of their responsibilities were unsettled. Among these was their liability for goods damaged in transit. In the absence of a relevant contract term, the courts were likely to find the railroads responsible for damage unless they could show that the damage was due to certain causes beyond their control. Whether the courts would enforce a contract term purporting to limit or exclude this responsibility was uncertain. With respect to most of its shippers, the railroad's contract was a standard form it drafted unilaterally without negotiation. The short-term costs to the railroad of adding a term to the form disclaiming liability seemed small. In a famous chapter from their classic, *The Legal Process,* Henry Hart and Albert Sacks ask what advice railroad counsel should have given their clients in these circumstances.[5]

The Libertarian Premise

At its crudest, the Libertarian premise is simply a non sequitur. The value of autonomy cannot by itself legitimate the prescriptions of the Dominant View because that value provides no basis for preferring *the client's* autonomy to the autonomy of the people with whom the client is in conflict.

A basic purpose of law is to resolve conflict, and the situations in which people turn to lawyers are likely to involve actual or anticipated conflict. The resolution of conflict usually involves the limitation of someone's autonomy. Pleading the statute of limitations advances the defendant's autonomy, but only at the expense of the plaintiff's. Limiting liability for damaged freight could enhance the railroads' autonomy only at the expense of the shippers'. But by itself the Libertarian premise gives no reason to think that favoring any of these parties would serve autonomy *in general.* The problem, of course, is that the legal system cannot promise everyone autonomy *tout court;* the most it can promise each is a *just measure* of autonomy. Libertarians who recognize this can make two types of response.

One response is substantive. It views the particular set of rules currently in force as the best available scheme of fairly apportioned liberty, and Dominant View lawyering as the most faithful means of implementing it. For the argument to work as a defense of Dominant View lawyering, it is not enough to say that current rules and the enforcement patterns induced by that view are compatible with *some* plausible ideal of liberty. For even if this were true, it could also be true that other enforcement patterns induced by other lawyering styles would be compatible with plausible ideals of liberty. The substantive defense of the Dominant View is committed to the notion that the current regime of rules coupled with Dominant View lawyering serves liberty better than any available alternative.

To my knowledge, no partisan of the Dominant View argues this today. No one today believes that the substantive legal norms currently in force in America collectively constitute a uniquely defensible scheme of fairly apportioned liberty. Something like this belief was popular among lawyers at the turn of the century—the era of *Lochner v. New York*—in the form of Classical Legal Thought.[6] The classicists thought that an expansive set of common law norms constituted a uniquely defensible scheme of fairly apportioned liberty which the federal Constitution more or less froze in place. But contemporary lawyers see liberty as compatible with many different sets of specific rights. No one would argue, for example, that the ideal of liberty requires any particular statute of limitations or freight liability rule.

Another reason the strong Libertarian claim seems untenable today is that enforcement practices, including lawyering styles, influence legal outcomes in ways that are arbitrary from the point of view of substantive rules and ideals of liberty. The Dominant View permits—indeed requires—the lawyer to leave uncorrected—indeed to exacerbate—the influence of many practical forces independent of the substantive merits of the parties' claims: information, access to evidence, negotiating and advocacy skills, firmness of will, shrewdness, articulateness. Even if the substantive rules were a perfect expression of liberty, outcomes in a system that gives such rein to these influences in the enforcement process could not consistently vindicate liberty.

Recognizing these deficiencies, modern apologists for the Dominant View tend to see its contribution to liberty, not as enforcement of a specific body of rules, but as strengthening some general quality of the legal system that enhances autonomy. The qualities most often suggested are the Rule of Law, equality, or certainty.

The Rule of Law

This argument starts with the assertion that autonomy is served by governance under a system of rules enacted and enforced by officials acting within their publicly prescribed authority.[7] The contrast is to a system of subordination to the unconstrained personal wills of powerful individuals. Under this conception of the Rule of Law, the critical liberty-enhancing property of legal outcomes is that they proceed from relatively general and impersonal rules promulgated and enforced by public institutions, rather than from the wills of individuals. The Dominant View purports to contribute to this goal by precluding the lawyer from imposing her own will on the client.

This argument has some force as a response to the role-morality critiques of the Dominant View. These critiques appeal to nonlegal values, and while they often deny that such values are purely personal or subjective, they have difficulty explaining why a lawyer's nonlegal commitments should trump a client's legal rights. However, the Rule-of-Law argument is not responsive to critiques, such as the Public Interest or Contextual views, which would replace the Dominant View with an ethic of greater responsibility to vindicate legal merits. A lawyer who insists on disclosing information or refusing to cross-examine a witness because of a commitment to legal merit does not impose his personal will any more than does a judge or police officer who acts on the basis of a decision about the relevant legal norms.

The Rule-of-Law argument thus makes the mistake of confusing an exercise of judgment with an exercise of will. Only the latter is inimical to the Rule of Law. Indeed, the former is essential to it. Since legal norms don't apply themselves, a legal outcome can only be true to a governing norm if some role players make plausible judgments about how the norm applies in the particular circumstances of the case. Now it doesn't follow that the lawyer should always be charged with the responsibility to make such judgments, since she will sometimes be in a poor position to do so. But the Statute of Limitations case illustrates that she sometimes will be in a quite good position to do so.

In that case there are two relevant legal norms—the substantive law that says that contracts like this one should be performed, and the statute of limitations that says that, if the suit is not filed until a specified period after the debt is due, and the defendant pleads the statute, the court will dismiss the suit. Respect for the Rule of Law requires some effort to reconcile these norms in the context of the facts.

The statute is a qualification to the substantive rule of contract performance. But the statute does not extinguish all liability after the prescribed period. For example, if the creditor has collateral pledged to secure the performance of the debt, he remains free to liquidate it in accordance with the terms of the security agreement. Presumably, however, our creditor has no such collateral. With respect to his pending lawsuit, the statute says only that after the period the judge will dismiss a case *if* the defendant pleads the statute. The statute is an "affirmative defense," which means that it is waived if not pleaded early in the case. And it says nothing about the question of when lawyers should plead it.

If we want to answer this latter question in terms that respect the statute—which is what the Rule-of-Law idea suggests we should do—then we have to ask what the purpose or principle of the statute is. Consider two possibilities. The statute might be based on the idea of repose—that after the passage of a certain time a debtor should not have to worry about debts incurred in the remote past. Alternatively, the statute might be based on the notion that, because evidence becomes unreliable and disappears over time, courts cannot reliably determine claims after specified periods.

A lawyer who concluded that repose was the underlying principle might decide that pleading the statute was appropriate simply because of the passage of the prescribed period. On the other hand, a lawyer who concluded that the basic principle of the statute was to spare judicial determination of claims on unreliable evidence might infer it inappropriate to plead the statute. For whatever difficulty *the courts* might have in determining this type of claim, there is no difficulty for *the lawyer* in determining the merits of this particular claim once the client has admitted the validity of the debt.[8] Perhaps the statute contemplates that defendants and their counsel will take advantage of its defense only when they dispute the substantive merits of the defense in good faith. Prior to the ascendancy of the Dominant View in the late nineteenth century, this was the espoused practice of some prominent lawyers, including David Hoffman, one of the best known commentators on legal ethics of the day.[9]

For our purposes, the important point is that vindication of the Rule of Law depends on the correspondence between the outcomes of legal disputes and the governing norms. This requires an exercise of judgment on the part of at least some legal actors. The Dominant View gives no reason for thinking that such judgments on the part of lawyers are unnecessary, and we have seen an important reason why they may be: the lawyer often has material information unavailable to the other decisionmakers in the system. By disabling him from acting on it to the detriment of the client, the Dominant model impedes a potential contribution to the vindication of the legal merits and hence undercuts the Rule of Law.

Equality

The second of the more modest Libertarian arguments asserts that the Dominant View contributes to autonomy by assuring equality before the law.[10] The lawyer's commitment to zealous advocacy bounded only by unambiguous legal commands gives everyone an equal opportunity to pursue her rights. This argument is susceptible to at least two constructions, neither of which is persuasive.

The argument might mean that the law is applied to everyone solely in accordance with its terms and does not vary on the basis of irrelevant characteristics of the person such as race, class, religion, or personal connections. Put this way, the argument simply restates the Rule of Law. Equality here means simply that all are equally subject to the terms of the governing norms. In order to know whether people have been equally treated in a particular controversy, we need to know what the terms of the governing norms are and what characteristics of the person are irrelevant. As we have just noted in discussing the Rule-of-Law argument, applying the meaning of the governing norm may require a kind of judgment on the part of the lawyer that the Dominant View forbids.

To return to our debtor example, pleading the statute of limitations results in treating the defendant the same as people who don't owe anything; not pleading it results in treating him like people who owe money. Either move involves equalities and inequalities. We can't say which equalities are relevant until we ask what the purpose or principle of the statute is. If the purpose is repose, then equality with nondebtors seems the relevant one; if the purpose is avoiding hard-to-determine claims, then in a clear-cut case such as this equality with debtors seems the relevant one.

Another variation on the equality argument is the claim that the Dominant View itself treats everyone equally. That is, although it permits withholding information, obfuscating, delaying, and counter-purposively exploiting "loopholes," it permits everyone to do this, so everyone has an equal chance to pursue her interests under these rules. Put this way, the argument sounds very much like the one Roscoe Pound disparaged as "the sporting theory of justice."[11]

To Pound and many others, the argument has seemed both nihilistic and dishonest. Nihilistic, because this kind of equality—an equal opportunity to win without regard to the substantive merits—seemed morally empty, indeed pernicious. Dishonest, because in fact the system doesn't even provide this type of "sporting equality," since access to counsel and other litigation and planning resources usually depends on the wealth of the client.

For our purposes, however, the key point is that most approaches to legal ethics, certainly including the Contextual View, also would provide this type of equality. As long as the rules require lawyers to treat clients consistently, equality is satisfied. A rule that says lawyers should plead the statute only when there is a good-faith dispute about the debt treats clients just as equally as one that says they should always plead it when the prescribed time has elapsed.

Certainty

The third modest argument asserts that Dominant View lawyering contributes to greater certainty in the application of legal rules. Because the norms of the Dominant View are categorical, lawyer decisions under it are more predictable, the argument asserts, and since lawyer decisions are an important part of the legal process, more predictable lawyer decisions yield more predictable legal outcomes. Predictability enhances liberty by enabling people to plan their lives better.

This argument, of course, is unresponsive to the Public Interest View, which imposes greater obligations to third parties and the public than does the Dominant View but is equally categorical. On the other hand, the argument does address a key difference between the Dominant and Contextual models—the commitment of the latter to contextual rather than categorical judgment. In assessing the argument as against the Contextual View, we can concede that lawyer decisions are less predictable under that View than under the Dominant one, though later I will suggest that the difference is exaggerated. The key problem with the argument, however, is its assumption that greater predictability of lawyer decisionmaking tends to produce greater predictability in the social world in which people plan their affairs.

This assumption is wrong. Legal decisions are just one among myriad influences that determine uncertainty in the social world. While legal decisions under contextual norms may be themselves less predictable, they can sometimes, more than decisions under categorical norms, reduce the degree of uncertainty attributable to other factors. A rule that says lawyers will always plead the Statute of Limitations when it is available makes the lawyer's decisions fairly predictable, but it may make business dealings *less* predictable than a rule that says lawyers will only plead the statute when the claim does not appear substantively meritorious. Under the former rule, once the dispute has arisen, we can predict the outcome quite reliably, but before then, the outcome may be affected by the uncertainties of inadvertence, laxness, or generosity on the part of the creditor. By neutralizing these factors in some situations, the contextual norm reduces uncertainties.

The general theme of these responses to the various versions of the Libertarian premise has been that, even if we accept liberty as the preeminent underlying value of law and legal ethics, there is no reason to think that the Dominant View is more compatible with that value than other approaches to legal ethics. But the Libertarian premise is further objectionable because there is no reason we should accept liberty as the preeminent underlying value. Both the legal system and popular morality treat liberty as one among many important values, perhaps preeminent within a narrow sphere, but otherwise to be traded off against and compromised with competing values.[12]

For example, in the Negligent Railroad case, contemporary legal thought treats liberty as largely unimportant. Liberal lawyers insist that the ideal of liberty is not coherent or compelling in connection with large impersonal corporate organizations and that the public interest in an efficient transportation system is likely to require regulatory intervention in the case of organizations with monopoly power. It treats as firmly established the notion that the railroad's autonomy must yield to the public interest in efficiency. Conservative lawyers are more skeptical about the need for regulatory intervention, even in situations involving monopoly, but they too treat efficiency, not liberty, as the critical value in the railroad case.

Hart and Sacks argued that in the railroad case counsel had the responsibility to dissuade their clients from pursuing liability limitation strategies that were patently inefficient, even though they might be in the clients' short-term economic interests. They reasoned that, since the railroads had better control over and more information about the handling of the freight during shipment, it was patently more efficient for them to bear the risk of loss, at least presumptively (that is, subject to the opportunity to prove that the loss had occurred in some way beyond their control). Given the railroad's monopoly power and the absence of genuine bargaining on the part of most shippers, conventional contract processes might not produce this result. But Hart and

Sacks claimed that the railroads should have felt obliged to adopt the efficient approach voluntarily, and their counsel had a responsibility to push them to do so.

Contemporary conservative thought differs from this analysis largely in being more sanguine about the possibility that, even in the presence of monopoly, economic self-interest might motivate the railroads to adopt the efficient solution without any sense of public duties or pressures from counsel.[13] And both liberals and conservatives might question Hart and Sacks's trust in the ability of counsel to make judgments about such questions as what the efficient solution is. But there is little room in mainstream legal thought to argue that Hart and Sacks's proposal threatens any important *liberty* interest.

The Positivist Premise

The Positivist premise is that legal norms are strongly differentiated from nonlegal ones. Its corollary is that legal norms are identified, procedurally, by their lineage to some organ of the state, and substantively, by the fact that they are commands or prohibitions backed by sanctions. The Positivist premise leads us to treat as professionally uncompelling the third-party and public interests in the various cases we have considered.

Many of the best-known efforts of modern jurisprudence have been devoted to showing that any strong distinction between legal and nonlegal norms is untenable. While a few legal philosophers still defend the Positivist premise, nearly all practicing lawyers reject it implicitly in the way they argue cases, advise clients, and draft documents. Legal ethics is the only area in which they continue to cling to it. For our purposes, the two most important problems with Positivism concern interpretation and enforcement.

Interpretation

The issue of interpretation arises from the fact that legal norms cannot be applied to specific cases without some exercise of judgment. The texts of legal norms contain gaps, ambiguities, and contradictions that must be filled, clarified, and reconciled in order to bring them to bear on specific cases.

In our legal culture, literal interpretation—interpretation based only on the words of the enacted text—is generally rejected as either impossible or undesirable. Take the classic example of the statute proclaiming, "No blood shall be spilled in the streets," as applied to the surgeon who spills blood in the course of treating a wounded pedestrian.[14] We all know that the statute should not apply. We know this because we understand its words in the context of a variety of social facts about institutions and values that the statute does not state explicitly.

Or consider the case of *Green v. Bock Laundry Machine Company,* which the Supreme Court decided in 1989.[15] The case interpreted a provision of the *Federal Rules of Evidence* that allows a litigant to attack a witness's credibility by introducing evidence of crimes committed by the witness, "except when the probative value of admitting this evidence outweighs its prejudicial effect *to the defendant.*"

Green, a *plaintiff* in a product liability suit against the Laundry Machine Company, argued that the trial judge misapplied this rule by allowing the company to introduce evidence of Green's prior crimes without considering its prejudicial effect to him. Green argued that, notwithstanding the reference to "the defendant," the protection of the rule should apply also to plaintiffs in civil cases. The Supreme Court agreed with him *unanimously.* Those accepting this conclusion included Justice Scalia, the court's leading textualist, and Justice Rehnquist, whom President Nixon appointed as a "strict constructionist."

The Court supported its conclusion by invoking two principles. The first is that in criminal cases the law should weigh more heavily the danger of prejudice to the defendant than the danger of prejudice to the prosecution. The second is that in civil cases procedural advantages should be allocated evenly between the parties. Although neither of these principles was stated explicitly in the rule, the Court assumed that they applied to the case, and it interpreted the word "defendant" to include a civil plaintiff in order to reconcile the language of the rule with the principles.

Every contemporary lawyer recognizes that values (principles, purposes) such as the one prescribing equal treatment of parties in civil cases are part of the law in the sense that they affect the decisions of cases. Yet such values do not fit the criteria that the Positivist uses to differentiate law from nonlaw. They cannot be traced to any specific enactment of a sovereign agency. Of course, the values are expressed in judicial precedents, but these precedents don't enact the values; they invoke them.

Moreover, these values are different in form from the Positivist notion of law. They are not linked explicitly to sanctions, and they are not commands or prohibitions. In particular they lack the categorical quality of commands of sanctions. A categorical norm is binary; it either applies or it doesn't. But the values we are considering are different; they have a dimension categorical norms lack that Ronald Dworkin calls weight.[16] Where the value applies, it counts as a reason in favor of a particular result, but it doesn't compel that result. The ultimate result may depend as well on other norms and circumstances. (For example, the principle of equal treatment for civil litigants may be outweighed by other concerns in some circumstances. Despite the principle, the plaintiff usually has the burden of proof, and in civil rights cases, a successful plaintiff but not a successful defendant can recover litigation expenses.)

Lawyers use examples like the *Green* case to show that even rules that are categorical in form and potentially susceptible to literal interpretation are and should be interpreted in the light of applicable background values. However, many legal norms take the form of open-ended, unspecified general terms that obviously require resort to implicit background understandings. "Due process," "standard of care," "restraint of trade," "unfair labor practice," "public convenience and necessity," "freedom of speech," "usage of trade," "unconscionable," "reasonable" (as applied to conduct or price), "reckless," "cruel and unusual punishment," "just compensation," and "proper purpose" are merely examples of a vast class of general terms that play central roles in key bodies of law that have no literal interpretations and more or less explicitly compel resort to background principles. Moreover, many of these terms are understood to incorporate the values either of society at large ("cruel and unusual punishment") or of some nonsovereign social group ("usage of trade," "standard of care").

If background values, as well as commands and prohibitions, are part of the law, then the Dominant View's conception of the "bounds of the law" seems unjustifiably narrow. Interpretation erodes the strong distinction between law and nonlaw that the Positivist premise insists on. In all the ethics cases we have considered, the issues arise because the lawyer's conduct appears to conflict with a value that seems relevant under the legal scheme—that substantively valid contracts should be performed (the Statute of Limitations case); that institutions controlling critical economic functions should not exercise monopoly power to impose patently inefficient practices (the Negligent Railroad case); that the Bank Board should have access to information about an S & L's soundness (the Recalcitrant S & L); that wealthy farmers should not get large subsidies (Agribusiness Welfare); and that innocent people should not be punished (the Innocent Convict). The Dominant View ascribes to the lawyer no duty to weigh these principles. If the client wishes to disregard them, it mandates that the lawyer acquiesce. In doing so, it treats them as something other than law. And this, we have seen, is a mistake.

Enforcement

The second broad problem with the Positivist premise concerns enforcement. The practical impact of a legal norm depends not only on the process of interpretation but also on such contingencies as the good faith, abilities, knowledge, and resources of officials and citizens. If officials (judges, administrators, police) are corrupt or incompetent, if they lack relevant factual information, if they have limited resources to investigate and consider claims, then one would expect substantial gaps between prescription and outcome. Moreover, our adversary system, by giving initiative with respect to asserting and adjudicating claims to the parties, puts a premium on party access to information and other litigation resources. If these resources are unevenly distributed, one would expect a further adverse effect on enforcement. No one denies that these adverse conditions apply in the contemporary American legal system, so the enforcement gap is potentially large.

The enforcement gap raises an important question for the Dominant View. Do the "bounds of the law" that define how far the lawyer can go mean the general substantive law as the lawyer believes it applies to the client? Or does this phrase mean the law as applied specifically to the client by state agents? The former interpretation implies considerably stronger obligations to nonclient interests than the Dominant View acknowledges. But the latter amounts to saying that the lawyer can help the client do anything the client can get away with—a conception of legal obligation almost no one espouses.

The problem can be illustrated with several examples. A famous passage from Holmes's explication of Positivism asserts that a person who does not want to perform a contractual obligation has a "right" to breach the contract and pay damages to his contract partner.[17] Economists call such breaches "efficient" because they reason that if the obligated party finds it cheaper to compensate than to perform, it is socially desirable that he do so.

Holmes was adopting a characteristically hard-nosed pose here. He expected tender-minded moralists to be offended by his cavalier treatment of what they would consider an ethical duty to perform one's promises. His main point was that the right to breach followed from his Positivist understanding of law as amounting to the sanction-backed commands of state officials. Yet Holmes himself appears to have been tender-minded in assuming that people who breach legal duties will naturally pay the substantively prescribed consequences. Would Holmes still have said a person had a "right" to breach if he could get away without compensating the other party, say, by fleeing the jurisdiction?

The Uninformed Tenants. State laws typically limit the concessions a residential landlord can demand from tenants. For example, a statute might say that the landlord may not insist on a security deposit of more than one month's rent. Many tenants, however, are unaware of these limits. On occasion, landlords have asked their lawyers to include unlawful terms—for example, a security deposit of two or three months rent—in their lease forms. They say that if the tenant takes them to court or makes a credible threat of doing so, they will concede, return the excess, and pay any penalties. But they think that a sufficient number of tenants will fail to assert their rights to make it profitable to include the term.[18]

The Cash-Heavy Clients. The Tax Reform Act of 1984 requires anyone receiving a cash payment of more than $10,000 to report it to the Internal Revenue Service. The premise of the statute is that people who make large cash payments are disproportionately likely to be engaged in criminal activities. The suspicion seems especially intense with respect to payments to lawyers. Many criminal defense lawyers vociferously protested the application of the statute to them as interfering with the access to counsel of cash-heavy clients. At least one leader of the defense bar and some state bar ethics committees have urged defense counsel not to comply with the reporting requirement until individually ordered to do so by a court.[19]

Here we have a potentially more radical interpretation of the "bounds of the law"'s than Holmes's. Presumably the proponents of resistance are fully aware that many, perhaps most, lawyers who receive the payments will never be specifically ordered to report, if only because prosecutors lack the information and resources to identify them (the whole reason for the reporting requirement in the first place) and to bring suits against them. They do not seem unhappy with the prospect that most of the nonreporting they urge will go undetected and unsanctioned.

Although its proponents may not have intended it so, we can take the resistance proposal as an illustration of a claim about legal obligation in general that might be inferred from a strong Positivist understanding of the "zealous advocacy within the bounds of the law." As a general claim, the proposal effectively says a lawyer can do everything for the client except what she can't get away with.

Generalized in this fashion, the claim is surely unacceptable. For example, no one would argue that a person has a right to commit murder so long as he fails to leave behind proof beyond a reasonable doubt of his act. On the other hand, there are some instances of unsanctioned but substantively illegal conduct that are viewed with more tolerance. An otherwise careful driver who goes five miles over the speed limit, knowing that the police only ticket at 10 miles over, is unlikely to incur much social opprobrium. Between the poles represented by the murderer and the moderate speeder lies a range of cases like the Cash Heavy Clients and the Uninformed Tenants where there is considerable ambivalence and dispute about whether the conduct in question breaches an important obligation.

Such circumstances are an important challenge to the Positivist premise. The Positivist purports to describe the actual contours and operations of the legal system. But in fact the norms to which people attach legal obligation are far broader than those singled out by the Positivist's criteria. Unlike Dr. Johnson, most people do not need to wait for the judge to tell them so in order to know that certain types of conduct are legally wrong. Indeed, social order seems to depend on people's willingness to comply with substantive norms even when they are not faced with immediate or certain sanctions for violation.

Moreover, this broader sense of obligation is not categorical or binary. For the Positivist, legal obligation either exists or doesn't. But like the problem of interpretation, the problem of enforcement shows that legal obligation can be a matter of degree or weight. Legal norms can give us reasons for doing something without conclusively obligating us, and these reasons can have varying strengths. As we will consider in Chapter 4, the lawyers' recalcitrance in the Cash Heavy Clients case, if it is justifiable at all, can only be justified on the ground that the legitimacy of the reporting statute is relatively uncompelling.

Thus, in the Statute of Limitations case, the Positivist is wrong to suggest that the matter is concluded by the fact that the judge will dismiss it if the statute is pleaded. A plausible assessment of legal obligation should consider that the substantive principle of keeping one's promises, even if they will not be enforced through sanctions, might provide a legal reason for paying the debt.

The Dominant View does concede grudgingly that clients are often interested in more than the "law," as the Positivist defines it. No one would deny that a client might wish to voluntarily repay a time-barred debt because of ethical or reputational reasons. Thus the *Model Rules* say, rather gratuitously, that the lawyer, in advising the client, "may refer not only to law but to other considerations such as moral, economic, social and political factors, that may be relevant to the client's situation."[20] But the rule creates only a license, not a duty (and the option here is simply discussion, not active protection). This permissive stance seems a function of the Positivist's mistaken view of legality, which converts many important legal concerns into (mere) "moral, economic, social, and political factors."

Libertarianism versus Positivism

If the Libertarian and Positivist premises are independently implausible, they are also mutually incompatible. At the most general level, the problem is this: the Dominant View depends on Positivism to define the exceptionally narrow vision of legality that underpins its narrow sense of obligation. But Positivism purports to be only descriptive; it has no theory of duty or right. It offers no reason for lawyers to respect even the shrunken "bounds of the law" that it recognizes or to respect client autonomy. Normatively, it cannot distinguish the exercises of state power with which it identifies legality from any other exercise of power, including the lawyer's power to force her own goals on the client. By itself Positivism is useless to a vision of professional ethics.

Hence the Dominant model also needs the Libertarian premise to supply some normative underpinning both to its narrow sense of obligation and its expansive sense of client rights. But while the Libertarian notion of autonomy provides such a normative basis, it also implies a set of principles that do not fit the Positivist's criterion of legality.

For example, the principle that one ought to perform one's contractual undertakings is an important one to most Libertarians. The principles of "repose" and "stale" evidence that underlie the Statute of Limitations are not comparably important in most Libertarian visions. Libertarianism by itself is therefore in tension with the approach of the Dominant View to the Statute of Limitations case. While Libertarian principles supply a normative base, it is not the one that the Dominant View needs, since Libertarianism implies a broader sense of obligation and a narrower sense of client rights than the Dominant View maintains.

The Problem of Retroactivity

Another aspect of the difficulty of combining the two premises is illustrated by the problem of retroactivity. If law were really strongly differentiated from ordinary morality, as the Positivist claims, it would be impossible to justify in Libertarian terms its application to the public.

The Libertarian ideal requires that people have knowledge of their rights and obligations before they act, so they can plan their affairs. Yet most people have neither specialized legal knowledge nor access to professional legal assistance. Much as the profession might wish it were otherwise, most people can consult lawyers only in rare situations of extraordinary desperation or in connection with a small number of routine, bureaucratic transactions. Moreover, even with professional assistance, one cannot know for sure how officials will interpret and apply the law. Explicitly retroactive laws are sometimes unconstitutional and usually suspect. But for most people most law is implicitly retroactive. As John Chipman Gray wrote,

> Practically in its application to actual affairs, for most of the laity, the law . . . is all *ex post facto*. When a man marries, or enters into a partnership, or buys a piece of land, or engages in any other transactions, he has only the vaguest possible idea of the law governing the situation, and with our complicated system of jurisprudence, it is impossible it should be otherwise. If he delayed to make a contract or do an act until he understood exactly all the legal consequences involved, the contract would never be made or the act done.[21]

Yet we hold people accountable for compliance with a vast web of laws that applies to their lives constantly and pervasively. Ignorance of the law is no excuse. When it is acknowledged, this sort of retroactivity is usually accepted as a legitimate feature of the system.

This kind of everyday retroactivity is justified on three grounds. First, to a large extent, the law coincides with ordinary morality with which most people are familiar. (Where law departs from ordinary morality, we sometimes make exceptions to the ignorance-is-no-excuse principle, especially in the criminal sphere.) Second, in a few situations where ordinary morality is out of tune with what judges or legislators feel is an important public principle, the liberty interests protected by the accessibility of the law are outweighed by the principle. Third, ordinary morality may not clearly address the issue, so that there is no way to resolve the controversy that does not involve the application of a norm with which the parties are likely to be unfamiliar.

The first and second points confirm that, contrary to Positivism, legal decisions are grounded in principles that are not explicitly enacted by the state. The second and third points confirm that, contrary to Libertarianism, it is often considered legitimate that liberty interests yield to other concerns. For the Dominant View, the question arises why these same points would not provide justifications for the lawyer's refusal to press the client's interests to the arguable limits of the law.

If there are principles underlying the promulgated law that are binding on the client, then a lawyer's judgment plausibly based on these principles would seem a legitimate basis for declining to press ahead. If liberty interests can be legitimately trumped by other interests, then it would seem appropriate for the lawyer to be concerned with these other interests as well as with the client's autonomy.

The Problem of Private Legislation

Although Positivism and Libertarianism part company in their receptiveness to the idea that informal social norms might be binding, they are united in their insistence that the power to create binding norms through codification or formal enactment is confined to a clearly differentiated sovereign. Both doctrines are hostile to the idea of private legislation.

For Positivism, private legislation is a contradiction in terms. Law is defined by its source in some sovereign action. For Libertarianism, private legislation is a threat to freedom. Legislation involves the exercise of power rather than of right. This power is tolerable only because it is restrained by various substantive (for example, equal protection norms) and procedural (for example, electoral checks) safeguards. Private actors, however, are not subject to these safeguards, so their exercise of power would constitute oppression.

Consider how the image of the lawyer in the Dominant View resonates with this Libertarian/Positivist picture. The lawyer is portrayed as a kind of surveyor/scout whose job is to advance the will of the client up to the edge of "boundaries" that are constituted independently of his efforts. The location of these boundaries cannot itself be affected by the lawyer's efforts. This would constitute legislation and would violate both the Positivist definitional premise and the Libertarian political one.

An obvious but nevertheless often overlooked objection to this picture is that lawyers, rather than taking the output of legislatures and courts as given, sometimes influence it. They lobby and conduct litigation in ways calculated to induce rules favorable to their clients. When the clients are wealthy and well organized, lawyers often assist the clients in translating their wealth and power into a disproportionate influence on the legislative process. For example, it is a familiar tactic of lawyers for organizations with a long-term interest in a particular issue to try to frame a test case raising the issue in a factual context most sympathetic to the client and before the most promising forum. In a classic discussion of the emergence of such practices in the late nineteenth century, James Willard Hurst noted that lawyering here became "an instrument of fixing policy," rather than, as the Dominant View portrayed it, a means "to enforce rights and duties according to an existing body of 'law'."[22]

A more direct form of private legislation occurs when the state incorporates or commits itself to enforce norms adopted by private citizens. Holmes pointed to an important aspect of this phenomenon when he rejected John Austin's version of Positivism as "the theory of a criminalist."[23] Criminal law norms do bear some resemblance to the Positivist image of commands-backed-by-sanctions. But many civil law norms are quite different. They have a character sometimes called facilitative or enabling. This does not simply mean that they allow certain conduct, but that they give the sanction of the state's enforcement powers to private arrangements. Most of the law of contracts and much of every field of civil law has this quality. Facilitative norms are an invitation to private legislation. Once identified, they look like a delegation of legislative power to private parties. To see facilitative norms in their most problematical form, consider the following case.

The Racist Homeowners. In 1917 the Supreme Court held that explicit government efforts to segregate residential areas by race were unconstitutional.[24] Lawyers for private clients trying to achieve segregation responded by deploying the racially restrictive deed covenant. Such a covenant was a term in a deed of real property that purported to preclude the grantee and her successors from retransferring the property to nonwhites. The covenants purported to affect only the particular properties transferred by the deed, but they were often incorporated simultaneously in large numbers of adjacent parcels by land developers or members of neighborhood associations, so that whole neighborhoods were covered by them.

In the 1948 *Shelly v. Kramer*[25] case, the Supreme Court considered a claim that judicial enforcement of these covenants violated the due process and equal protection clauses of the 14th Amendment to the Constitution. The 14th Amendment applies only to the state, and the individuals who sought to enforce them argued that the covenants were private agreements, not state action. The Supreme Court responded that, while the making of the covenants may not have involved the state, their enforcement by the courts would be state action and hence would violate the Equal Protection Clause. It has been widely recognized that the logic of this decision could turn most private law into state action. For all facilitative rules contemplate private initiatives that become enforceable law. (As Mark Tushnet put it, socialism follows from *Shelly v. Kramer*[26].)

The Supreme Court has not followed out this logic in applying the 14th Amendment. But legislatures and courts have applied it in other contexts to justify imposing various regulatory constraints on the exercise of power through facilitative rules. In particular, where businesses unilaterally dictate contract terms to customers who have no opportunity to bargain, courts and legislatures often intervene to preclude terms deemed unfair or inefficient. Liberal legal theorists of Hart and Sacks's generation invented the term "private legislation" to characterize the legal output of this kind of business power, and they justified regulation on the ground that legislative power must be publicly accountable.

For Hart and Sacks this view had strong implications for lawyering. Since counsel in situations like the Railroad case were playing a quasi-legislative role, they should assume quasi-public responsibilities. In the Railroad case, the lawyers should have viewed themselves as "the professional staff of a private legislator, acting within a framework leaving wide leeway for discretion but with power limited to arrangements not plainly unreasonable or contrary to public policy."[27] Although the courts and legislatures eventually corrected the lawyers' excesses, it took time and effort to do so. The fair and efficient result would have been reached more expeditiously if counsel had assumed more responsibility.

The basic idea here—that the pursuit of private interests through facilitative rules often seems to involve a kind of coercion that calls for public control and justification—is not confined to situations of monopoly power or to parties to contractual relations. The restrictive covenant case shows this. Here the coercive exclusion from restricted neighborhoods experienced by nonwhites is the aggregate effect of a series of contracts made by others, each of whom may lack market power. Yet this consequence is tantamount to explicit segregation by a legislature.

The "private legislation" perspective challenges the Positivist premise by emphasizing the role of nonstate actors in lawmaking, and the Libertarian premise by insisting on the potentially coercive nature of the exercise of legal rights. It subverts the distinction between enforcing the client's rights and helping the client exercise power over others.

It may be helpful to consider two distinct stages in the development of a legal practice such as the restrictive covenant or the liability waiver. The first is the period of emergence. Initially, the practice is not part of the practical lawyering repertory for the relevant area. There are no standard forms. Ordinary lawyers don't think of it at all; or if they do, it seems too risky or too difficult to draft. Then a small number of lawyers get the idea to do it. (They might be the first to think of the possibility of using the general practice, or simply the first to think of an effective form in which to implement it.) They make the effort and take the risks of recommending it to clients and concertizing the strategy in a draft. In the second stage, the practice is widely perceived as effective. One or more standard forms become available for doing it. Counsel routinely offer or recommend it to clients, and adoption becomes widespread. At the extreme, not to offer or recommend it is considered malpractice.

Separating out the first stage allows us to emphasize the creativity encouraged by facilitative rules, an aspect of lawyering that both Positivism and Libertarianism encourage us to ignore. It also gives an especially compelling picture of lawyers exercising power on behalf of their clients. Once lawyers have perfected the practice, their clients' capacities for imposing their wills on others have increased. Lawyers have moved back the "bounds of the law."

After the practice becomes standard, it is easier to think of the lawyers routinely implementing it as enforcing some established body of rights, but that is misleading if we understand rights in the Positivist/Libertarian sense of the Dominant View entitlement arguments. The boundaries that the lawyer maintains are not the limits of a legislatively granted zone of autonomy. They were seized through an act of creative aggression. The client's claim of entitlement to the practice simply because it is established seems no better than a warring army's claim to disputed territory it has occupied for some limited period.

Of course, as a practical matter, it is far easier for the lawyer who believes the practice is irresponsible to forego it in the first stage than in the second. In appraising the lawyer's conduct in the second stage, we should take the pressures to conform into account, but they enter by way of excuse rather than justification. They are reasons why the lawyer should be forgiven, not why his conduct should be approved.

Conclusion

It should now be clear why the moral, political, and epistemological objections to the lawyer stopping short of the "bounds of the law" are mistaken.

The moral basis for the lawyer's decisions are the same principles that underlie and legitimate legal judgments generally. A lawyer who limits the distance she will go for a client on the basis of norms of legal merit or justice does not deprive the client of anything he is entitled to; on the contrary, she simply insists on respecting the entitlements of others.

The suggestion that the lawyer who disapproves of an arguably legal plan of the client should focus her reformist energies on future legislative change, rather than thwart the client in his current activities, is unfounded when the ground of the lawyer's disapproval is legal merit. Of course, where the relevant legislature or court has acted deliberately to allow activities such as the client proposes, he has a strong claim of entitlement to act. But in situations like the Statute of Limitations and Railroad cases, the state had not spoken clearly on the matter, and while the action in question was arguably legal, it may have been contrary to the most plausible assessment of its legal merit.

If it were possible to induce a court or legislature to make a judgment on the matter before many people were affected by the conduct, then it might be a good idea for the lawyer to encourage the client to wait and petition for such a judgment. But more often than not, this is impractical. It may be beyond the capacity of lawyer or client to induce the legislature to act. It will certainly take time. (John Maynard Keynes conceded that economic depressions might be self-correcting in the long run, but argued for his proposed interventions on the ground that, "In the long run, we are all dead.") And legislative and judicial action is invariably costly in both private and social terms. Hart and Sacks report that in the Railroad case courts and ultimately the Congress did intervene effectively to curb the railroad's unreasonable liability limitations, but they emphasize both the harm done pending this resolution and its procedural costs.[28]

Moreover, even if a court or legislature were willing and able without cost to address the matter, it may be less well situated to do so than is private counsel. In the Railroad case, Hart and Sacks suggest that private contract, if responsibly deployed, would have provided a more flexible array of solutions than did the eventual statute, which necessarily involved more uniformity and rigidity. They also suggest that experienced railroad counsel might have been better informed about the industry than legislators and their staffs.[29] In the Statute of Limitations case, the role for counsel arises from the fact that she has the best access to relevant information in the particular case.

Far from being politically totalitarian, a commitment to norms of legal merit and justice resonates with democratic values. In a democratic society the norms of justice and legal merit will express democratic aspirations, and fidelity to them will thus reinforce democracy. After all, the commitment is to the principles accepted in the legal system, not to the state officials who run the system. Indeed, commitment to these principles will sometimes provide a strong basis for opposition to officials. Note also that a system in which individual lawyers are given responsibility for the vindication of legal merit decentralizes law enforcement in a way that, if successful, reduces the need for more bureaucratic modes of enforcement.

The answer to the epistemological objection is that the lawyer has access to principles of legal merit and justice through both his membership in the society and his training as a lawyer. His ethical decisions are grounded in the same principles judges—whose training is the same as that of practicing lawyers—apply in deciding cases. Without some access to such principles he would not be able to perform his job of advising clients on the law and advocating for clients before judges.

A lawyer who conditions her service to clients on respect for these principles does not impose her own values except to the extent these values coincide with these principles. (The same would be true of a judge deciding cases.) Of course, not all lawyers would agree in any given situation on how the applicable principles apply. Individual lawyers will make mistakes. But as we readily recognize in the case of judges, the fact that a practice of judgment sometimes produces some controversial or even mistaken decisions does not make the practice an illegitimate one.

It may be that the lawyer is often poorly positioned to make certain decisions. If there are others better able, the lawyer should defer to them. This is consistent with fidelity to legal merit if, as we should, we understand legal merit to include procedural as well as substantive considerations. But there is surely a substantial class of situations within which lawyers are relatively well positioned to make decisions that contribute to the vindication of merit. The Statute of Limitation and Negligent Railroad cases seem appropriate examples. In these situations, the discouraging arguments of the Dominant View are unpersuasive.

3

Justice in the Long Run

A second set of arguments for the Dominant View concedes that clients often do not have a right to the style of advocacy it recommends and that this advocacy occasionally leads to injustice. Defenders of the Dominant style of advocacy assert that it produces a higher level of justice in the aggregate and the long run. They portray the injustices of aggressive advocacy as sacrifices that have to be made in order to avoid greater injustices. They see the beneficiaries of injustice as private attorneys general who, by taking advantage of rules that give them things they are not entitled to, improve the overall performance of the legal system.

The change from the *Code* to the *Model Rules* as the organized bar's official normative paradigm involves a change in emphasis from entitlement toward such instrumental arguments. The *Model Rules* abandon "zealous advocacy within the bounds of the law" and the Libertarian rhetoric associated with it. Instead, they emphasize the instrumental function of various elements of aggressive advocacy in promoting justice in the long run. These instrumental rationales in favor of the Dominant View include, as we shall see, arguments for strong versions of confidentiality, arguments concerning litigation preparation (which often suggest that the "adversary system" entails aspects of the Dominant View), an argument that appeals to the psychological phenomenon of "cognitive dissonance" to support a strong ethic of client loyalty, and finally, an argument that categorical norms tend to be more efficient than contextual ones.

In each case the argument turns out to depend on unsubstantiated and perhaps indeterminable behavioral assumptions. Uncertainty about these matters is a problem for any view of legal ethics. But since the Public Interest and Contextual views are more consistent with both ordinary morality and legal principles applied in analogous contexts, it seems appropriate to charge the Dominant View with the burden of proof. Moreover, as we will see in Chapter 5, the most important arguments for the Dominant View do not depend on behavioral assumptions at all.

Confidentiality

The Dominant View prescribes close-to-absolute confidentiality norms for client information. Under the *Model Rules,* concerns about injustice or the public interest warrant the lawyer to disclose information without the client's consent only when the client is about to commit a "criminal act that is likely to result in imminent death or severe bodily injury."[1]

Under this rule, a lawyer may not disclose a client's intention to commit a criminal act that will violate someone's property rights, no matter how great the injury. Nor may she disclose the client's intention to commit any noncriminal illegality, no matter how great the likely injury. She may not disclose information about past criminal acts of the client, even if they have current consequences of great magnitude. (For example, the client has committed a crime for which someone has been wrongly sentenced—the Innocent Convict case—or she has killed someone and hidden the body while family is searching desperately for the missing person.) The lawyer may not disclose information from the client about *someone else*'s criminal activity, no matter how grievous. (The client knows, for example, that another person has committed a crime for which there has been a wrongful conviction or has killed or kidnapped someone and hidden him.)

The purpose of confidentiality safeguards, of course, is to induce clients to make disclosures to lawyers. If clients thought lawyers might repeat their statements to their disadvantage, they would make fewer disclosures, and that would be bad because lawyers would give them less effective advice. To its strongest proponents confidentiality is more than a duty of silence. It is a duty to insure the client against suffering disadvantage from disclosure to the lawyer. This conception entails a willingness to undertake deceptive practices where the lawyer knows that the practices are deceptive only because of something the client has told her. At the point where this line of thought involves the lawyer actively in fraud or perjury, it is unacceptable even within the Dominant View. It is generally not permissible for the lawyer to present perjury even if he knows it is perjury because of a client disclosure.[2] But less direct forms of deception—for example, impeaching a witness the client has admitted is truthful—are often defended as entailments of confidentiality.

The key question about confidentiality is: granting that full client disclosure is conducive to good legal advice, why do we value the improvement in legal advice to the client that confidentiality facilitates above the prevention of injustices to others that confidentiality inhibits? The profession's answer is that it promotes justice in the long run.

One argument is that confidentiality helps deter wrongful *future acts* by the client. By renouncing disclosure to outsiders the lawyer gives up some deterrent leverage, but she remains free to try to dissuade the client from illegal conduct. Without the disclosure threat she will succeed less often, but the confidentiality assurance will give her more opportunities, since it will induce clients to reveal antisocial plans that they wouldn't reveal if they feared disclosure. The bar apparently has concluded that the lower success rate will be more than compensated by the higher base.[3] In the aggregate, its position implies, more injustice will be deterred with the close-to-absolute rule.

The second way confidentiality promotes long-run justice concerns past conduct. Here the concern is that, without confidentiality, the client may fail to disclose information relevant to *valid claims* she might have.[4] It is in her interest to tell the lawyer such information, but since she is not legally sophisticated, she may misunderstand her interest, withhold helpful information, and suffer injustice from failure to assert her claims. There is always an initial temptation to respond to this argument, as Jeremy Bentham did, that such injustice is an appropriate price for the client's dishonesty.[5] But there is no guarantee that the price will be proportionate to the offense. And for some clients—criminal defendants, for example—the stakes can be very high.

In assessing these arguments, one ought to be clear about the alternatives against which the close-to-absolute confidentiality rule is being assessed. Defenders of such a rule sometimes speak as if the relevant alternative was a regime with no confidentiality safeguard whatsoever. But this is far from the most plausible alternative. A better candidate would be the precept of the *Restatement of Agency*, which says that agents must not disclose confidential information obtained from their principals *"except in the superior interests of another."*[6] This rule is proposed by the drafters as the presumptive norm for professional and business relations. A similar alternative that employs the rhetoric of the Contextual View would be, "The lawyer should hold client information in confidence except where disclosure is necessary to avoid substantial injustice."[7]

My view is that the agency rule and the "substantial injustice" rule are better than the bar's current rule. The most important argument in favor of the former rules is the general claim I make in chapters 5 and 6 for the Contextual approach to legal ethics—that it minimizes the lawyer's participation in injustice. For the moment, I propose to consider some reasons to be skeptical of the major claims made for the bar's rule—the points about future conduct and valid claims.

Although *ad hominem* arguments are frowned on these days, the indications of bad faith in the bar's claims for confidentiality are too salient to pass over. The bar has always defended confidentiality in sloppy, cavalier, and dogmatic ways. The arguments are rarely articulated in any systematic manner (and then, usually, by their critics). These arguments depend on assumptions about behavioral trends, but the bar has never adduced any evidence for them and never shown any interest in investigating them. Although the American Bar Association supports an excellent research institution—the American Bar Foundation—to the tune of several million dollars a year, this institution has never done any work on the factual premises of the bar's most important normative pronouncement.

In the *Model Rules* the rationale offered for the confidentiality rule is ludicrously inconsistent with its substance. The drafter's comments press the "future acts" argument as the basis for the rule. At the same time, the rule's single public-regarding exception is for a category that includes the most harmful future acts—those that are likely to cause death and serious bodily injury. If the drafters really believed that confidentiality deterred crimes, would they have withdrawn it for the most harmful crimes and left it inviolable for relatively minor ones? Is the bar less interested in deterring murder and battery than, say, passing bad checks and littering?

The future-crimes rationale is also inconsistent with the *Model Rules'* treatment of organizational clients, which applies to the bulk of business practice.[8] Under this rule, when an agent of the organizational client—say a corporate manager—tells the organization's lawyer about a continuing or contemplated criminal activity likely to injure the organization, the lawyer may inform the organization's senior managers or board of directors. If the future-acts logic were correct, this would not be in the organization's interest, since it would mean fewer harmful crimes would be disclosed and deterred. The most likely reason for exempting physical injury and organizational crimes is that lawyers regard acts inflicting bodily injury and acts inflicting any kind of injury on their clients as especially grievous. But to cut back confidentiality for the worst acts implies a belief that confidentiality impedes, rather than advances, deterrence.[9]

A second objection to the future-acts rationale arises when we consider that in other notable instances in which public institutions have weighed the deterrent value of professional confidentiality safeguards against that of professional disclosure duties, they have concluded that disclosure duties provide greater deterrence. I have already mentioned the *Restatement's* agency rule that withdraws confidentiality in the face of "superior" third-party interests. Another important example is the recent panoply of laws requiring professionals such as teachers, social workers, and therapists to report evidence of child abuse to public authorities.[10] If the bar's future-conduct rationale had any merit, it would be strongly applicable in this context. Without confidentiality, people will be more reluctant to confide their harmful intentions to these professionals and the professionals will have less opportunity to persuade them to desist. Yet in adopting the child abuse rule, the legislatures appear to have concluded that this loss is outweighed by the increased deterrent effect of professional disclosure.

There are some instances in which institutions have resolved the issue in favor of confidentiality, as has the bar. Most of them, however, are professional associations proposing or promulgating norms for their own members. They are thus subject to the suspicion that they are oversensitive to the parochial interests of their members, who have material and psychological stakes in relations with clients and who often regard responsibilities to nonclients as uncompensated burdens. On the other hand, whatever their defects, legislatures do not suffer from any comparable bias against confidentiality or the interests of professionals. Perhaps, then, their determinations on the deterrence issue have more credibility.

A third objection is that the effective protection of the confidentiality rule is far narrower and more idiosyncratic than its text suggests. Given the limited scope and unpredictability of its incidence, it is implausible that it could have much reassuring effect on client disclosure. Although the bar's confidentiality rule is subject only to two narrow explicit exceptions (for future crimes involving severe physical injury and protection of the lawyer's own interest), it is subject to a cavernous expanse of implicit exceptions for situations where some independent legal duty requires disclosure. These exceptions have been forced on the bar by other institutions and are typically unmentioned in the rules, but they play a powerful role in practice. For example, if the lawyer were asked pursuant to a valid subpoena to disclose client information, he would have a duty to do so unless the information were protected by the attorney-client privilege of the law of evidence. The evidentiary privilege is much narrower than the bar's confidentiality rule. Among other things, the evidentiary privilege doesn't cover communications in which the client seeks help in committing a crime.[11] Here is yet another example in which lawmakers have rejected the bar's dogma that confidentiality is better for deterrence than disclosure.

By far the most important source of independent disclosure duties is the civil discovery system. There has been a steady trend since the mid-nineteenth century to afford civil litigants easy pretrial access to facts known to their adversaries. A critical step was the adoption in 1938 of the *Federal Rules of Civil Procedure,* which have since been emulated in most of the states. Under this system, "either party [to a lawsuit] may compel the other to disgorge whatever facts he has in his possession."[12] Amendments in 1993 extended the trend by requiring that a variety of information be volunteered even in the absence of demand.[13]

Lawyers representing clients in the discovery process have substantial responsibility for the accuracy of the client's responses. They may not knowingly make untrue statements or transmit untrue statements from their clients. This responsibility applies despite the bar's confidentiality rule and the attorney-client evidentiary rule. The law distinguishes between the client's communication and the factual content of the communication. The confidentiality rules preclude disclosure of the communication, but they don't affect legal duties to report facts the lawyer knows because of those communications. Thus, if the client tells the lawyer she ran over the plaintiff's husband before certain witnesses, the lawyer should not repeat that the client told him that, but if the client is asked whether she ran over the victim, she, or the lawyer if he answers for the client, must respond truthfully, and under the recent federal amendments, they must volunteer the names of the witnesses even if they aren't asked.[14]

The bar's confidentiality rule is thus subject to the implicit exception that if information the lawyer learns from the client becomes relevant to civil litigation, it will have to be disclosed on demand and perhaps even without demand. The point is not that confidentiality norms are inconsequential. There are many situations outside the litigation sphere where they have significant effects. And even in litigation, the opposing side sometimes fails to make an adequate demand for relevant information that doesn't have to be volunteered, and in such situations confidentiality is important.

From the perspective of the typical lawyer-client interview, however, these effects are unpredictable. Most transactional work is done in contemplation of potential civil litigation, and most criminal conduct is civilly actionable. Thus a client fully informed about the relevant confidentiality norms—and this is the kind of client the bar's norms assume—would typically recognize a vague but substantial risk that information she discloses to the lawyer might later have adverse effects. (Some of these effects may be avoidable by switching lawyers and withholding the adverse information from the new lawyer, but switching lawyers is often costly and sometimes impracticable.[15]) Since neither the magnitude nor the incidence of this risk can be known, the bar's residual confidentiality assurance is vague and incomplete, and hence unlikely to be reassuring.

It is also worth noting that lawyers have not asserted, much less demonstrated, that the steady enlargement of discovery over the century has substantially inhibited client candor with counsel, though that is what the bar's confidentiality rationales would predict. The increase in disclosure that would be required from a shift to the Contextual View in legal ethics is probably much smaller than the increase that occurred with the change to modern discovery systems. Yet the latter has been relatively uncontroversial.[16] As the privilege exception for criminal assistance seems particularly harmful to the future-acts argument for confidentiality, the discovery duties seem particularly harmful to the valid-claims argument. Most of the information on which this argument focuses would be relevant to litigation claims, and in the litigation context, the confidentiality protections are thoroughly truncated by the discovery system.

A fourth objection to the bar's claims for confidentiality is that they are not supported by psychological intuition. Consider first the client presupposed by the "future acts" argument. Why won't she disclose her plans to the lawyer without the assurance of confidentiality? Presumably because she thinks that she may want to proceed even if her plans turn out to be illegal. Thus she apparently is not a person with a strong disposition to obey the law. (Judge Frank Easterbrook might object that "even an honest [client] may fear that [the lawyer] would misunderstand the situation and ring the tocsin needlessly, with great loss."[17] This point doesn't seem strong with respect to ongoing or future conduct. The lawyer will ring the tocsin only if the client persists after being advised that the conduct is unlawful. And if the client doubts the advice in good faith, one would expect the lawyer to wait while the client gets another opinion. It is questionable whether a client unsure enough to seek advice in the first place, and who decided to proceed with conduct in the face of advice that it was illegal, could plausibly be called "honest," if by that we mean law-abiding.)

At the same time, the argument assumes that she is susceptible to dissuasion. What can the lawyer say to convince her? The lawyer can talk about the penalty. This information will tend to discourage the client if the penalty is higher than she expected, but it will have the opposite tendency if the penalty is lower than she expected, and there is no reason to expect the former to be the case more often than the latter. Thus the net effect of penalty advice is indeterminate. The lawyer can talk about possible unofficial costs, such as loss of reputation or good will. However, the effect of this information is similarly indeterminate. Moreover, there is no reason to think that the lawyer is more knowledgeable about unofficial costs than the client. If talking about the penalty and other costs fails, then the lawyer is left to appeal to considerations of duty. Given the client's presumed predisposition to illegality, however, there is no reason to think the client will be susceptible to such arguments.

What about the "valid claims" argument? For this argument to work, the client has to be so poorly informed that she cannot identify the information that would be helpful to her, but well enough informed to understand the confidentiality rules that define what she can tell her lawyer safely. This state of affairs isn't inconceivable. It might be that the helpfulness of the key information depended on rules far more complicated than the confidentiality ones. However, it is far from being obviously true, and two points supported by casual empiricism suggest that it is wrong.

The first is that a common and perhaps predominant style of interviewing among white-collar criminal defense lawyers is to probe the client for information the lawyer thinks might be helpful without asking the client for a full account of the facts.[18] Apparently the lawyers do this to avoid learning facts that would limit their ability to make helpful claims or defenses. At least for these lawyers and their clients, even the current levels of confidentiality protections are insufficient for full client disclosure. (Because, for example, they forbid the lawyer to make statements she knows to be false and to present perjury knowingly.) The practice is ethically unattractive, but the accounts of it do not suggest that lawyers miss important information. On the contrary, lawyers often seem able to extract the relevant information by indicating to the client what would be helpful and not pressing in areas likely to be unhelpful. This challenges the notion that confidentiality is necessary to or effective in inducing disclosure of facts relevant to "valid claims."

The second fact is that many clients do not understand the confidentiality rules and do not trust their lawyers to abide by the rules.[19] Misunderstanding is rife. A large fraction of the population both overestimates and underestimates significantly the scope of protection of the confidentiality rules. Moreover, many clients, especially poor ones, mistrust their lawyers. Given misinformation and mistrust, clients may be inclined to withhold information *regardless of what the rules on confidentiality are*.

Although both these facts may not be true generally across the population of clients, one or the other is likely to be true of most clients. If a client is sophisticated and has long-standing relations or intuitive rapport with his lawyer, the lawyer will usually be able to make him understand the type of information that would be helpful without requiring that he disclose damaging information. On the other hand, if the client is unsophisticated, he is likely to misunderstand the confidentiality protections or mistrust the lawyer. In that case he may withhold helpful information, but not because of the scope of protection in the confidentiality rules.

Recall that the alternative confidentiality standard suggested by the Contextual View would have the lawyer disclose client information only where necessary to avoid "substantial injustice." This is far from abrogation of confidentiality. However, some people fear that the indeterminacy of the "substantial injustice" term will leave clients so bewildered and insecure about what they can safely disclose that it will severely inhibit candor.

As a claim for the comparative merit of the status quo, the objection ignores the extent to which the present standard is riven with exceptions that turn on technical matters—for example, the distinction between the ethical duty and the evidentiary privilege, the scope and effect of civil discovery duties, the crime-fraud exceptions—that are not readily comprehensible to lay people. Most people have some sense of the meaning of justice, and most clients will have some intuition of what their lawyers mean by it. It is not obvious that they would have a better understanding of the more technical parameters of the current standard even if their lawyers tried to explain these matters to them.[20]

Note also that the problem of client bewilderment and insecurity under the Contextual standard seems most palpable in circumstances where clients don't trust or share values with their lawyers. But in such situations the prospect that lawyers will be able to dissuade clients from wrongful conduct by appealing to client values—the main rationale of strict confidentiality with respect to "future acts"—seems practically nil. While adoption of the Contextual standard would probably bring some inhibition of disclosure, there is no reason to think that it would be extensive or that any inhibition that did occur would entail the sort of costs the bar purports to fear.

The Adversary System and Trial Preparation

Proposals that increase lawyers' responsibilities to nonclients are often attacked as inconsistent with the adversary system. Sometimes this argument is traditionalist: it justifies the adversary system as a historically ingrained social commitment or a defining element of American legal identity. Sometimes the argument is instrumental in the sense we have been considering in this chapter: it justifies the adversary system as productive in the aggregate of socially desirable outcomes.

In either mode, the argument often suffers from failure to specify what "adversary system" means. Sometimes the term is conflated with the Dominant View of legal ethics, but on that view, the claim that the adversary system is deeply ingrained in American culture would be contestable. The adversary system in America has always been considered compatible with some duties to nonclients. The lawyer in the American legal tradition has always been both a partisan of the client and an "officer of the court." There has never been any consensus on where to draw the line between these two aspects of the lawyer's role, and the two have always been in tension within the professional culture.

The Dominant View has never been unchallenged within the profession, and it seems not have become dominant until the late nineteenth century. The most prominent view in the late eighteenth and early nineteenth centuries emphasized public responsibility and complex normative judgment in a manner resembling the view I argue for in Chapter 6. The compilations of ethical precepts by David Hoffman in 1817 and George Sharswood in 1854, which are often regarded as the foundations of American legal professional discourse, prescribe contextual judgments under general norms of justice. For example, Hoffman wrote: "In civil cases, if I am satisfied from the evidence that the fact is against my client, he must excuse me if I do not see as he does, and do not press it: and should the principle also be wholly at variance with sound law, it would be dishonorable folly in me to endeavor to incorporate it into the jurisprudence of the country, when, if successful it would be a gangrene that might bring death to my cause of the succeeding day." Sharswood insisted that "[c]ounsel have an undoubted right, and are duty bound, to refuse to be concerned for a plaintiff in the pursuit of a demand, which offends his sense of what is just and right."[21]

Comparisons of the adjudicatory systems of America and Britain on the one hand—the paradigmatic instances of the adversary system—with the "inquisitorial" systems of continental Europe on the other tend to see the defining feature of the former as the principle of party autonomy. The adversary system gives the major responsibility for preparing and presenting the case to the parties and their counsel at the expense of much of the control over these matters given to judges on the Continent.[22]

Party control is necessarily partisan control. Each side can be expected to be influenced by its own interests. But as Hoffman and Sharswood knew, it doesn't follow from the idea of partisan control that lawyers will do anything arguably legal to advance their clients' interests. There are always limits to partisanship, and nothing in the idea of partisanship requires that the limits be those of the arguably legal. A requirement that lawyers pursue their clients' claims in a manner likely to contribute to just resolution, common to Sharswood and Hoffman and the approach I argue for in Chapter 6, is compatible with a broad range of partisanship.

If the Dominant View is not logically entailed by the principle of party control, perhaps it is functionally necessary to it. That in any event is another important instrumental claim of its proponents. Like the confidentiality arguments considered above, this one focuses on the information and incentive effects of duties to volunteer information to third parties. While the previous arguments were concerned with incentives for client disclosure to counsel, these are concerned with incentives for lawyer preparation.

The main point is that information is less valuable to a party if she must make it available to the other party, so she will develop less of it if she is subject to such an obligation. Of course, a party will always be willing to publicize information helpful to her case, but she would prefer to do so at a time and in a manner of her own choosing. Disclosure requirements reduce her ability to maximize the strategic effect of such information, for example, by giving the other side an opportunity to plan to challenge its credibility or to develop contradictory information in advance of trial. A person has no incentive to disclose information harmful to her claims. Yet often she cannot know whether investigation will turn up helpful or harmful information. So if she has to turn over relevant information, the danger that her preparation will make it easier for the other party to obtain information harmful to her will discourage her from investigating.

Sometimes the case against disclosure duties is put moralistically: "forcing counsel to do the other lawyer's job for him" or "to make the other side's case." This, however, is conclusory; the matter in issue is precisely how counsel's job should be defined.[23] The real concern is that there will be less investigation. This is bad, the argument asserts, because more investigation makes for better outcomes. Moreover, higher outcome quality benefits society as well as the parties. The social ordering function of legal norms depends on people's belief that the norms will be enforced in accordance with their terms. Nonenforcement or misenforcement can lead to insecurity and lawlessness.

Although the argument is widely made, it has obvious problems. For one thing, withheld information will often be independently discovered by the other party, and the duplication of expenses imposes costs that would be avoided in a mandatory disclosure regime. For another, to the extent that the additional information resulting from enhanced incentives is suppressed (because unfavorable), it contributes nothing to the quality of the process.

Thus the proponent of the Dominant View must argue that the fact that a party cannot benefit from the other party's investigation will cause the first party to investigate more than she otherwise would, and that the value of the resulting additional information will outweigh the costs of duplicative efforts, additional efforts that lead only to suppressed information, and the loss of suppressed information that would have been discovered and turned over under a regime of mandatory disclosure. Of course, this position depends on factual assumptions that the bar has barely articulated, much less researched, and in any event, it is probably not susceptible to confirmation or disconfirmation.

Once again, the argument is in tension with the discovery system. That system in fact mandates disclosure of much of the information that the argument suggests should be confidential. The incentive effects of the remaining confidentiality guarantees are too haphazard and speculative to play a major role in encouraging investigation. Again we have a rule enacted by institutions other than professional associations that seem squarely to reject the premises of the bar's argument.

As we have noted, the preeminent model—the *Federal Rules of Civil Procedure*—mandates disclosure either on a party's own initiative or on demand by the opposing party of a broad range of information. Some of this information, such as facts about the client's insurance status, would be available without investigation and thus disclosure would not affect incentives under the bar's theory, but some of it, such as the identity of witnesses to the relevant events, could depend on investigation. The *Rules* do recognize a "work product" privilege that exempts from discovery some materials prepared by counsel. But the exemption is narrow: it applies only to documents. Relevant facts discovered through investigation have to be disclosed whether or not contained in documents subject to the exemption. Moreover, even the exemption for documents can be overcome by a showing that the party seeking discovery "is unable without undue hardship to obtain the substantial equivalent of the materials by other means."

If the incentives argument were correct, this rule would make no sense. It is precisely a party's fear that she will *not* be able to obtain information available to the other side that is supposed to motivate her to exert herself in investigation. If a party can always obtain from the other side information she can't readily get elsewhere, then the laxness the incentives argument anticipates would ensue. (If the information had *never* been accessible to the requesting party, then incentives could play no role, and it would be consistent with the bar's argument to allow discovery. But the unavailability provision applies where the information is *currently* unavailable, whether or not it was previously accessible.[24] Thus, it does not square with the incentive argument.)

Many people, including most lay people, will of course find ludicrous the idea that a substantial reduction in the amount of litigation preparation would be inefficient. The United States judicial system is the most expensive large-scale system of dispute resolution known to humankind. Since few cases are actually tried, most of this expense takes the form of preparation, and a lot of it involves the kind of preparation that, under the bar's interpretation, adversary norms are supposed to increase. No one who has looked into the matter believes that the quality of justice (at least in private law cases) in countries like Germany, where lawyers do far less preparation on average, is lower than here.[25]

Turning from casual empiricism to social theory, we find further support for the notion that private incentives tend to encourage socially inefficient overpreparation. This is so *even* if we make the heroic assumption that the bar is right in asserting that adversary norms produce a net gain in relevant information.

One reason for this tendency is that litigation involves coordination problems akin to those of an arms race or a "Prisoner's Dilemma," in which each party feels compelled to be aggressive solely in anticipation of the other's aggression. The parties thus do things they don't expect to advance the presentation of their claims simply in order to counter similar expected moves of their opponents. Hiring an expert to testify on an issue that only marginally requires expert testimony might seem a waste of money if viewed in isolation, but if each party expects that the other will do so if he doesn't, and thereby gain a comparative advantage, each will feel compelled to do it. An aggressive cross-examination of an able, truthful witness can be neutralized by additional witness preparation. Everyone would be better off without the aggressive cross or the defensive preparation, but if the offering party anticipates the cross, she has to do the extra preparation, and if each party anticipates that her witnesses will be aggressively crossed, they will feel compelled to cross aggressively the other's witnesses. Litigation is thus a paradigmatic situation of the sort in which economic theory emphasizes the potential efficiency of rules that limit aggression. Rules that mandate disclosure and preclude obfuscation seem consistent with the implications of this analysis.

A second reason for the discrepancy between private and social value of preparation is that the two values depend on different factors.[26] From an instrumental perspective, the social value of an outcome depends on its contribution to either increasing compliance with, or reducing uncertainty about, the law. On the other hand, private value depends most on the potential recovery in the case. Potential recovery does not strongly correlate with contribution to compliance or clarification. The contribution to compliance comes from the credibility that imposition of sanctions in a particular case gives to the state's threat to impose sanctions in future cases involving similar conduct. The contribution to clarification comes from the fact that the court's declaration that the conduct in a particular case is lawful or unlawful provides guidance for those contemplating similar conduct in the future. However, many cases with large recoveries involve unusual conduct. Since there will not be many similar future instances (actual or contemplated) of such conduct, the compliance and clarification effect in such cases is necessarily limited. There may even be a tendency for preparation expenses to be especially high in just such cases, since cases with unusual facts are more likely to be "close" on the merits, and "close" cases will induce especially large preparation expense.

Moreover, by definition, either the facts or the law or both must be in doubt in a close case, and if there is no resolution on the merits, the case cannot contribute to compliance or clarification. Yet most cases, even most cases involving elaborate preparation, are not resolved on the merits; they are settled in ways that leaves their factual and legal ambiguity largely unaffected.

Any potential social benefit from elaborate preparation in high-stakes, close cases is thus limited. On the other hand, the private incentives for litigants to incur expenditures are powerful. The litigants measure the value of additional preparation by multiplying the increased probability of victory it promises by the potential recovery. The larger the claim, the lower the probability needed to induce the expenditure. In high-stakes cases, the calculation will have a powerful tendency to induce a socially inefficient level of expenditure. Rules mandating disclosure and limiting aggression have the potential to enhance efficiency by curbing this tendency.

Identification with Clients and Cognitive Dissonance

Another prominent rationale for the Dominant View focuses on the effect that responsibilities to nonclients have on the lawyer's capacities for effective analysis and advocacy on behalf of the client. The argument is based on what the psychologists call cognitive dissonance—the tendency of preconceptions to validate themselves by obscuring inconsistent data. It begins with the claim that adjudication is most reliable when the judge decides the case after a proceeding in which each side develops as effectively as possible the arguments favorable to its claims—the core idea of the adversary system.

The cognitive dissonance argument then asserts that the lawyer contributes best to such a proceeding by developing her presentation with a strong psychological commitment to her client's claims. Responsibilities to nonclients or public ideals would interfere with such a commitment. They would require her to entertain hypotheses about the ultimate merits of the client's claims early in the proceeding, potentially blinding her to considerations favorable to her client that she might otherwise have perceived.[27]

This argument, even on its own terms, provides only limited support for the Dominant View. It supports the lawyer in adopting a strong cognitive bias in favor of the client's claims, but it does not warrant the lawyer in pressing the client's arguably legal claims where she has concluded, despite her bias, that they ought not to prevail. Moreover, the argument seems mistaken in two respects.

First, the proponents of the theory have been unable to explain why a procedure substantially controlled by willfully biased partisans is the one best calculated to produce good decisions. Evidently they believe that opposing biases neutralize each other rather than simply creating confusion, but this is doubtful. In other areas where accurate decision among a variety of contested positions is important, such as business and science, decisionmakers rarely adopt the method of adversary presentation by biased advocates. The most common procedure is to ask the participants to approach the question with an open mind and in good faith, not to tell them to commit themselves arbitrarily to a position and make the most of it.[28]

Second, the theory does not even accurately depict the methodology of partisan advocates. It ignores that effective advocacy depends on sympathetic understanding not only of the client's position, but also of the people the lawyer is trying to persuade. Without understanding the decisionmaker's perspective, the advocate would have no way of determining which facts or arguments are likely to be effective.

The advice of successful advocates often turns the cognitive dissonance theory on its head. Thus, in a classic article, John W. Davis declares the "cardinal rule" of advocacy to be, "Change places (in your imagination of course) with the Court."[29] Robert Keeton's text on trial practice cautions that identification with the client may blind the lawyer to conflicting considerations that will be important to the judge, leaving her unprepared to meet these concerns at trial.[30] New lawyers often adopt the cognitive dissonance theory instinctively, sometimes with disastrous consequences, when they find that they have focused so intently on developing their own cases that they have failed to think through, and thus have nothing to say in response to, opposing counsel's points.

The Efficiency of Categorical Norms

Categorical norms—like the all-but-absolute confidentiality guarantee and the Dominant View's general "arguably legal" norm—require simpler judgments based on a narrower range of factual considerations than do contextual norms. Some believe that these features make categorical norms more efficient.

Consider three charges of inefficiency that Stephen Bundy and Einer Elhauge make against contextual legal ethics norms:

- Contextual norms are more costly because they "make . . . a broader range of information potentially relevant" and hence require "more extensive investigation."[31]

Even if contextual norms did entail more investigation, that wouldn't necessarily mean inefficiency. More investigation might well improve decision quality, which would compensate for the added costs.[32]

In fact, however, contextual norms do not entail more investigation. True, under a contextual norm more facts are "potentially" relevant, but there is no requirement that all relevant facts be investigated if it would be inefficient to do so. A contextual norm tends to require the decisionmaker to make wider use of the information *she has;* it doesn't necessarily say anything about what level of investigation she should do. If the level of investigation under the Dominant View regime were considered optimal, we could elaborate a contextual norm that required only that the lawyer take account of the information she acquired in pursuing her client's interests.

To assume that enhanced responsibility to nonclient interests requires more factual development is to overlook a central fact about the ethical circumstances of lawyering. All of the cases we have considered so far, from the Innocent Convict through the Negligent Railroad, resonate precisely because the lawyers involved—operating under Dominant categorical norms—had acquired information that the Dominant View precluded them from acting on in a way that would further a just resolution.

- Contextual norms tend to be "nebulous" and "uncertain"; under such a regime lawyers and clients would have to "guess" as to how they applied in specific cases.[33] It is a lot easier to determine whether a course of action in the client's interest is "arguably legal" than whether it would "promote justice."

While there is some truth to the claim that decisions under contextual norms tend to be harder to predict, the claim is often exaggerated. The law is full of general standards like reasonableness, good faith, usage of trade, customary practice, and public convenience and necessity. They are often quite determinate when they correspond to well-developed, though tacit, social understandings. In a variety of businesses you can find consensus across a broad range of options as to whether a buyer's disposition of properly rejected goods was "commercially reasonable" within the meaning of the Uniform Commercial Code. This contextual standard is supported by a tacit social gloss of shared understanding and practice.

Moreover, as we noted in considering the Libertarian variation of the certainty argument in Chapter 2, the argument focuses arbitrarily on a single kind of uncertainty—uncertainty surrounding the decisions one's own attorney will make (or those someone reviewing that attorney's decision will make). Even where a contextual norm does increase this kind of uncertainty, it may reduce other kinds—for example, the kind that arises from the opportunity of debtors to stiff their creditors by pleading the statute of limitations. A norm that says lawyers will never voluntarily disclose information damaging to the client increases the client's certainty about the attorney's loyalty; arguably, however, it decreases the opposing party's certainty that her substantive rights will be enforced.

- Decisionmakers under contextual norms tend to "reach sharply different conclusions" and make decisions that are "often inaccurate."[34]

If we put aside the issue of certainty just discussed, it is hard to see why inconsistency should mean inefficiency. Without knowing anything about the substantive quality of the decisions, we cannot say whether a group of consistent decisions is better than a group of inconsistent ones. (Inconsistent decisions are better than consistently bad decisions.)[35] If the claim that contextual decisions are more often "inaccurate" has any plausibility, it merely means that categorical decisions are less often perceived as misapplying their governing norms than are contextual ones. But the efficiency of a decision depends not on its compliance with the governing norm, but on its fit with the norm's underlying goal. If the underlying goal of the rule in Article II of the Constitution that the President be at least 35 years old is to insure maturity in the executive, then many "accurate" decisions under this rule will be inconsistent with the goal, since many people under 35 are in fact sufficiently mature. Since the greater "accuracy" (ease) of decisionmaking under categorical norms tends to come at the cost of a looser fit with the underlying goal, greater "accuracy" does not neccessarily mean efficiency.

All three anticontextualist arguments could as readily be made against much of common law. The common law of accidents, for example, does much of its work through the elaboration of a single contextual norm of reasonableness. It doesn't proliferate a series of categorical norms specifying the permissible dimensions of every dangerous activity. The latter approach is more characteristic of the Occupational Health and Safety Act (OSHA). The coexistence of both approaches reflects the premise that each is potentially efficient under some circumstances. You cannot say *a priori* or generally that either is more efficient than the other.

In general, the choice between categorical and contextual norms turns most importantly on, first, the costs of discrepancy between a norm's prescriptions and its goals (high costs cut in favor of contextual norms), and second, confidence in the capacities for judgment of the people applying the norms (high confidence cuts in favor of contextual norms). In matters involving substantial fairness issues, the legal culture tends to treat the discrepancy costs of categorical regulation as unacceptable. Matters of legal ethics of the sort we are considering always involve substantial fairness stakes. As for capacity for judgment, Bundy and Elhauge do not disparage the abilities of lawyers to make contextual judgments, and as we will shortly elaborate, it would be difficult to do so within the context of a discussion of professional ethics.

Bundy and Elhauge embellish their efficiency points with the claim that the costs of a contextualist standard will fall disproportionately on poor and middle-class clients. They point out that the increased requirements of factual investigation and the need to insure against uncertain liability will raise the cost of legal services, which will most affect nonwealthy clients. Further, a contextualist regime, by increasing lawyers' duties of candor and fairness to nonclients, makes lawyers more dependent on their clients' credibility. This in turn will mean that clients who aren't well known to the lawyer will seem to pose more risk of liability than clients with whom the lawyer has long-term relations, and they will tend to be the wealthier ones. Thus, Bundy and Elhauge argue, lawyers will respond by refusing cases from economically marginal people and giving excessively cautious advice to nonwealthy clients.[36]

This argument is helpful in suggesting that, if contextualist norms impose too high a burden on the lawyer to verify the client's statements, then one-shot and short-term clients, who may tend to be nonwealthy, could be disproportionately hurt. This would be especially likely if the norms ignored the scope and length of the lawyer's relation with the client. It is also true that if contextualist norms define or enforce duties to third parties more strongly than duties to clients, lawyers will give excessively cautious advice.

But neither of these possibilities depends on any inherent tendency of contextual norms. Both depend on the assumption that the Contextual regime will be misimplemented. This is an odd assumption for Bundy and Elhauge to make, because their argument, which measures efficiency by the degree of conformity to substantive law, is premised explicitly on the idea that substantive legal norms are "optimal."[37] It seems strange that a society capable to designing its substantive law to meet this demanding standard should make such a botch of its legal ethics regime.

Bundy and Elhauge also make the common mistake of measuring the costs of a Contextual ethical regime solely in terms of its costs *to clients*. Their solicitude for the nonwealthy is limited to poor and middle-class people as consumers of legal services. But since most nonroutine private legal services are rendered to business organizations, it seems likely that the most important impact lawyers have on ordinary people does not arise from legal services *to them* but rather from services to business organizations whose conduct affects them in their capacities as customers, employees, neighbors, and bystanders. If a Contextual standard increases the efforts of business lawyers to restrain their clients from fraud, pollution, marketing hazardous products, and union busting, these effects might provide major benefits to middle-class and poor people. Such benefits have to be counted in assessing the standard.

Aptitude for Complex Judgment

Because categorical norms require less demanding interpretive efforts than contextual ones, distrust of the judgment of the people subject to the rules or charged with enforcing them often weighs in favor of specifying them categorically.

If one thought that lawyers tended to be inept at complex judgment, one might argue instrumentally for categorical approaches to legal ethics on the ground that they are better suited to the capacities of lawyers. Lawyers as a class are not stupid, and they are highly educated. But maybe they have a disposition to literalistic or mechanical rule interpretation or a tendency to strong identification with their clients that inhibits complex judgment. Such notions may be implicit in the demands one sometimes hears from lawyers that their ethical obligations be spelled out in black letters so as to obviate difficult judgment. If fact, however, lawyers rarely press this point explicitly, because it has unwelcome implications outside the realm of legal ethics.

As we have noted, a strong disposition to literal rule interpretation or overidentification with the client would impair the lawyer's ability to protect client interests almost as much as her ability to respect nonclient interests. If judges, administrative officials, and private parties with power over the client interpret legal norms purposefully, then lawyers would not be able to help the client anticipate the judgments of such people or persuade them if they were inept at such interpretation themselves.

Moreover, doubt about lawyers' capacities for complex judgment would raise questions about the professional project of self-regulation. The Dominant View contemplates individual lawyer regulation under categorical norms *legislated by lawyers collectively.* Regardless of the form the norms take, the process of legislation always involves complex judgment. It is not inconceivable that lawyers might be better at collective than individual judgment, but it seems doubtful that a group of individuals proclaiming their ineptitude at the latter should be trusted with the former.

Conclusion

> And the varieties of circumstance which influence these reciprocal interests are so endless that all endeavor to deduce rules of action from the balance of expediency is in vain . . . No man ever knew, or can know, what will be the result to himself or to others of a given line of conduct. But every man may know, and most of us do know, what is a just and unjust act.[38]
>
> —John Ruskin, UNTO THIS LAST

The instrumental arguments tend to be frustrating and exhausting. Often they start out with conceptual mistakes—misidentifying or ignoring the jurisprudentially relevant costs and benefits or attributing some *a priori* efficiency properties to confidentiality or categorical judgment. At some point, however, they recognize, at least tacitly, that their conclusions depend on socially contingent assumptions about the way people behave. Then they fall back on a kind of speculative empiricism, spinning out hypotheses that might, if they were true, rationalize the existing norms, but that are neither supported by evidence nor susceptible to empirical confirmation.

It would be pointless to try to refute these hypotheses systematically, even if one had the resources. It is too easy to produce such rationales. As soon as I had shown one to be false, a horde of new ones would show up like ants at a picnic. I have tried in this chapter to respond in kind by matching each of the major nuggets of empirical speculation adduced by Dominant View proponents with an opposing nugget that, at the fanciful armchair level to which the discussion is likely to be confined, seems at least as plausible. However, I can't be confident that you will find my nuggets consistently more plausible than those of the proponents, and even if you did, tomorrow the proponents will have a new bunch ready.

It is tempting to respond with John Ruskin that people—for our purposes, lawyers (both as rule-makers and individual practitioners)—are likely to have better judgment about justice than about the aggregate behavioral effects of different rules. But this assertion would be widely controversial today. A substantial contingent of the most articulate contemporary lawyers doubt their own and others' capacities to make plausible judgments about justice, while asserting (at least on their own behalf) powerful insight into the empirical dynamics and utilitarian valuation of aggregate behavior.

I think it an important job to try to convince these people that they underestimate the possibilities of decentralized judgments about justice and overestimate the possibilities of technocratic social engineering, but this is a long effort. For the moment, the key point is that the instrumental perspective is insufficiently responsive to the most basic concern motivating debates over legal ethics: the belief that the practices prescribed by the Dominant View frequently implicate the lawyer in injustice.

This degradation typically does not appear in the instrumentalist's cost/benefit calculus. If it were included, its weight would depend less on the behavioral speculation to which the instrumentalists are prone and more on normative intuition. In Chapter 5 I will give some reasons to think the weight very great.

There is a further sense in which the instrumental arguments are unresponsive. If these arguments were correct, they might provide a justification for the Dominant View's conception of the lawyer's role, but they would not alleviate the widespread sense of disappointment and anxiety about that role. If the arguments were correct, the lawyer's role would be a little like the executioner's, necessary but degraded. If capital punishment were really necessary to public order, the executioner's job would be justified. But even reflective people might still feel there was something shameful about the job, and they wouldn't want its practitioners' to feel good about their work. (A common practice of military execution by firing squad is interesting in this respect. One of the guns is loaded with a blank, and the members of the squad are not told which one, so each can entertain the possibility that his gun may not have done any harm. By presupposing that the job becomes easier to perform when you can imagine you have no effect, the practice concedes that it is degrading, even if socially valuable.)

If you cannot refute the instrumentalists' arguments, you can at least accuse them of moral frivolousness for their cavalier willingness to sacrifice the deepest aspirations of professionalism to the technocratic fancies of the armchair empiricist.

4

Should Lawyers Obey the Law?

At the same time that it denies authority to nonlegal norms, the Dominant View insists on deference to legal ones. "Zealous advocacy" stops at the "bounds of the law." By and large, critics of the Dominant View have not challenged this categorical duty of obedience to law. They typically want to add further public-regarding duties, but they are as insistent on this one as the Dominant View.

Now the idea that lawyers should obey the law seems so obvious that it is rarely examined within the profession. In fact, however, once you start to think about it, the argument for a categorical duty of legal obedience encounters difficulties, and these difficulties have revealing implications for legal ethics generally.

The basic difficulty is this: the plausibility of a duty of obedience to law depends on how we define law.[1] If we define law in narrow Positivist terms, then we cannot provide plausible reasons why someone should obey a norm just because it is "law." In order to give substance to the idea that law entails respect and obligation, we have to resort to broader, more substantive notions of law. However, these broader notions of law are hostile to both the narrowness and the categorical quality of the Dominant View's idea of legal obligation. We saw in Chapter 2 that these broader notions often require advocacy to stop short of the limits prescribed by the Dominant View. Now we consider that they sometimes may warrant the lawyer to go beyond them.

Lawyer Obligation in the Dominant View

The Divorce Perjury Case. Suppose we are in a jurisdiction with an old-fashioned divorce statute that conditions divorce upon proof of a small number of specified grounds, such as adultery and abuse. A childless couple has agreed on divorce and on reasonable arrangements for separating their financial affairs. The lawyer believes that the proposed divorce and financial arrangements are in the interests of both husband and wife. However, they cannot honestly prove any of the grounds the statute requires.

Suppose further, as was true in some of the jurisdictions that used to have statutes of this sort, that it is possible, at virtually no risk to either lawyer or clients, for the lawyer to help the couple get a divorce by coaching and presenting perjured testimony about, say, adultery.[2] The risk is small because judges, although aware of the practice, accept all such testimony passively, and prosecutors and the police devote no resources to uncovering these practices. (Perhaps the authorities would initiate charges of some sort if they were confronted with a flagrant case, though even this is not clear. In any event only the most careless or unlucky lawyer would create a flagrant case.)

The Dominant View forbids the lawyer to help clients in this way, no matter how strongly she believes that the couple is entitled to a divorce. If the lawyer believes the divorce statute is unjust, it says, she should work to induce the legislature to change it. But it condemns coaching and presenting perjury as a transgression of the "bounds of the law."[3] The Dominant View is less clear, however, about lawyer activities that encourage or facilitate illegality less directly. Some legal advice—for example, information about the express terms of a statute—is clearly both a right of the client and a core function of lawyering. Other forms of advice—say, about where to hide from the police or how to build a bomb—clearly represent improper participation in illegal conduct.

However, at least one form of advice that clients often seek is harder to classify, namely, advice about the enforcement practices of officials. Suppose I tell a tax client that while the aggressive position he wants to take is unlikely to survive an audit, less than one percent of returns in his class are in fact audited. Or suppose, knowing my client's expenses are far lower than 70 percent of revenues, I tell her that the

IRS's practice is not to question returns for businesses like hers unless they show expenses above 70 percent. Such advice is probably not unlawful,[4] but since its main effect is to impede the enforcement process, it is troubling.

The Dominant View has yet to produce a clear answer to the question of whether such advice is improper. It hesitates between, on the one hand, defining it as legal advice and thus categorically appropriate, and on the other hand, defining it as assisting illegal conduct and thus categorically improper. In fact, neither answer is plausible. The only satisfactory answer to the problem calls for contextual judgment. Most lawyers will concede this in the case of enforcement advice, for this is one area where the commitment of the Dominant View to categorical judgment is out of step with mainstream views and practices. The conclusion may be harder to accept in the case of direct participation, such as the Divorce Perjury story, but the same considerations that support contextual judgment in the indirect cases apply here as well.

Positivist versus Substantive Conceptions of Law

Recall that Positivism is committed to differentiating legal from non-legal norms by virtue of a norm's "pedigree" rather than its intrinsic content. A pedigree links a legal norm to a sovereign institution through jurisdictional criteria that specify institutional formalities. An example of such a jurisdictional criterion is section seven of Article I of the United States Constitution, which says that when each house of Congress overrides the President's veto of a bill by a two-thirds vote, the bill "shall become a Law."

When legal norms conflict, the Positivist resolves them in terms of jurisdictional criteria that specify which of the institutions to which the norms are traced should prevail. If the conflicting norms emanate from the same institution, then the Positivist applies further jurisdictional criteria—for example, later over earlier or specific over general—to decide which should have priority.

Positivism has a strong affinity with the commitment of the Dominant View to categorical judgment. The Positivist perspective facilitates categorical judgment by banishing a broad range of potentially relevant factors (the putatively moral ones) and by providing for the rigid priority of jurisdictional over substantive norms. The Dominant View of legal ethics conjoins the Positivist notion of law with a commitment to obedience to law (and only law).[5] But the narrow way in which law is defined makes it hard to explain why law should be regarded as binding. Positivist legal philosophers are not much help here. Their concerns are more analytical and descriptive than normative. They are prone simply to take it for granted that people should obey the law or to start out with the observation that, for whatever reasons, people simply do regard the law as binding. The Positivism of the Dominant View thus differs from its jurisprudential analogues in being a *Moralistic Positivism*.

Moralistic Positivism makes three arguments for a categorical duty of legal obedience: First, obedience to law promotes social order; without it we would have anarchy. Second, obedience promotes fairness; we get the benefits of other people's obedience, so in return we ought to give them the benefits of our obedience. Third, obedience promotes democracy; the laws are made pursuant to procedures of popular representation and accountability that entitle them to respect.

These arguments might be persuasive against a position asserting that one ought categorically to disobey the law, but hardly anyone has ever asserted such a position. Against the various positions of selective disobedience, such as those we shall shortly consider, they are entirely unpersuasive. The problem with the arguments is that each rests on an appeal to a value that does not consistently track the Positivist's jurisdictional criteria of legality. However the Positivist specifies her criteria, there will always be particular situations in which social order, fairness, or democracy will not be served by obedience to what the Positivist's criteria identify as law.

How often such situations arise will depend on how the Positivist defines her jurisdictional criteria. For example, some Positivists are literalists who insist on narrowly construing the norms they identify as laws. Others, however, prescribe that the norms be interpreted in the light of their underlying purposes or principles (perhaps on the theory that the sovereign intends this or has implicitly enacted such values into law). Of course, the more the Positivist's criteria permit resort to such background norms, the less likely will her interpretations be in tension with them. But to insist on some distinction between law and other types of norms is what it means to be a Positivist. So all Positivists will sometimes find themselves in situations of tension between the norms they identify as legal and other norms.

Consider an example. Several years ago Raoul Berger decided on the basis of extensive historical research that the Reconstruction Congress did not expect the 14th Amendment to ban racial segregation.[6] Under his criteria, the expectations of the Congress determined the correct interpretation of the Amendment, so it did not forbid segregation, and *Brown v. Board of Education* was thus incorrectly decided. Berger became quite exercised about the Warren Court's 14th Amendment cases and condemned them as betrayals of the rule of law.

Berger's argument was controversial. Some people insisted he was wrong about what the expectations of Congress were. Some people thought that the congressional expectations were not the critical criterion; they argued either that some other set of expectations—say those of the members of the ratifying conventions—or something beside expectations—say, the current conventional meaning of the Amendment's language—was the critical criterion. But the most vulnerable part of Berger's argument was the assumption that, if he had been right about what the 14th Amendment provided as law, that law would have been entitled to any respect. Why should we not simply admire the Warren Court for flouting this unappealing law and lending its efforts to the fight against segregation?

The arguments from social order, fairness, and democracy do not seem powerful here. The Warren Court's decisions may have contributed to social disorder, but anarchy did not ensue, and arguably what Berger thought the legally correct decisions would have caused more disorder. Few people today would regard a ruling against the *Brown* plaintiffs as a contribution to fairness. The balance of burden and benefit in the legal order of the day was not fairly struck for African-Americans; the Warren Court's arguably lawless decision inarguably pushed the balance toward greater fairness. And although the United States was in some relative sense a democracy, it was a highly deficient democracy, and the Warren Court result was plausibly calculated to mitigate those deficiencies.

The Dominant arguments for obedience demand that we look at the legal system as a whole, ask if on balance it serves some good, and if the answer is yes, obey its commands categorically. But unless we have some reason to think our selective disobedience will trigger some independent and unjustified lawlessness, we should not consider it a threat to the desirable aspects of the legal order. The fact that other people are obeying the law is often a fairness reason why we should, but if the law itself is unfair, the fairness concerns supporting disobedience will usually outweigh those supporting obedience. And the fact that the law has emerged from a generally democratic political process is a reason for obedience, but not one that should prevail if the process has not been democratic in this particular case.

Now turn to a conception of law radically opposed to Positivism. We can call this conception Substantive, though there are many variations of and names for it. Some people prefer the term "natural law," though that term has connotations too exotic and metaphysical for what, I hope to show, is a familiar, mainstream notion. Libertarianism, which we discussed in Chapter 2, is an example of a Substantive doctrine, though there are many more plausible ones, such as utilitarianism, wealth maximization, social rights theories such as that of John Rawls, neo-Aristotelian theories of personal virtue, or coherence theories such as that of Ronald Dworkin. Lawyers are not by nature systematic moral philosophers, but their working theories include intuitions from all these doctrines.

The Substantive conception rejects Positivism's core premises—that law is strongly separated from nonlaw and that law is distinguished by jurisdictional criteria. It interprets specific legal norms as expressions of more general principles that are indissolubly legal and moral. It acknowledges the jurisdictional rules that Positivism regards as preeminent, but it regards them differently. First, it does not regard them as independent or ultimate social facts, but as expressions of underlying values, such as order, fairness, and democracy, and it insists on interpreting the rules in the light of these values. Second, it denies that jurisdictional principles that prescribe the allocation of authority for dispute resolution are more fundamental than substantive principles that prescribe the just ordering of the social world.[7]

Consider the case of *Walker v. Birmingham*.[8] At the high tide of civil rights activism in the South, Martin Luther King and the Southern Christian Leadership Conference planned a march in Birmingham to protest racial practices they believed unconstitutional. At the behest of the city's white leadership, a state court issued an injunction forbidding the march. Believing the injunction unconstitutional, the protesters marched in defiance of it. The court held the organizers of the march guilty of contempt and jailed them.

When the Supreme Court reviewed the lower court's contempt judgment, it held that it made no difference whether the protesters were correct in their belief that the injunction was unconstitutional. The Court decided that, since the lower court had jurisdiction and the protesters had ignored available procedures for appealing the injunction to higher tribunals, respect for law required affirming the punishment. The *Walker* conclusion is plausible only on a Positivist conception of legality. On a Substantive conception, a "citizen's obligation is to the law, not to any particular person's view of what the law is."[9] From this perspective, an officially promulgated norm merits respect only by virtue of its substantive validity, and the *Walker* injunction, as the Supreme Court eventually conceded,[10] had none. Respect for law required vindication of the protester's conduct.

If the nightmare slippery slope of Positivism leads to compliance with jurisdictionally adequate but morally evil laws, like the Nazi enactments requiring reporting Jews and dissidents or the antebellum Fugitive Slave Laws, the nightmare slippery slope of Substantivism leads to anarchy. We ought to be clear, however, about what anarchy can mean. For the Positivist, anarchy is tantamount to lawlessness, but for the Substantivist (and for most anarchists) anarchy is simply the most decentralized legal system imaginable. In such a system every citizen is a common law judge of what the law requires. This is not to say that the citizen has no rights or obligations. On the contrary, she may be subject to an elaborate set of rights and obligations. It is just to say that enforcement takes place through spontaneous citizen action—by "the People Out of Doors" to use the phrase current at the time of the Boston Tea Party, a notable instance of popular law enforcement[11]—rather than formally constituted authority. The tendency to see all conduct in defiance of constituted authority as normless or unprincipled is a Positivist prejudice. The examples of the Boston Tea Party and the Birmingham march remind us that disobedient conduct can be intensely normative and intensely structured. They also remind us that some of the most radical manifestations of Substantivism have achieved legitimacy in our culture.

In contemporary legal culture, the broadest acknowledgment of the more radical manifestations of Substantivism occurs in discussions of nullification. Nullification is a term most readily associated with the power of the jury to disregard the judge's instructions and acquit even in the face of conclusive proof of what the judge has defined as an offense. This power was secured and legitimated in many nineteenth-century state constitutions. These provisions have disappeared over the years in all but two states—Indiana and Maryland—and the practice has been explicitly disapproved in many others.[12]

Nevertheless, it has strong defenders, and it continues to lead a "subterranean life" in jury practice.[13] Today, as before, nullification occurs with significant frequency where the jury finds prescribed punishments excessively harsh, especially in cases of victimless crimes. The history of nullification in the North in Fugitive Slave Law cases and in the South in trials of white killers of blacks and civil rights activists serve as reminders of the noble and ignoble aspects of the dramatic history of the practice.

Nullification also describes two other important and less controversial practices—the judge's power to declare unconstitutional legislation invalid and the prosecutor's power to decline to enforce legislation when enforcement would not serve the public interest. Prosecutorial nullification is widely considered legitimate in circumstances where the application of a statute produces an especially harsh or anomalous result or where an entire statute, usually an old one, seems out of tune with contemporary sentiment—for example, the laws against fornication.

These nullification practices are never defended as forms of lawlessness, but rather as decentralizations of law application. The power to nullify is not a license to impose one's own views, but a duty to interpret what the law requires.[14] When it was given explicitly, the jury's nullification power was expressed in language making the jurors "judges of the law as well as the facts."[15] The nullifying judgment is a judicial—that is, law-interpreting—one. The notion of law assumed is Substantive, that is, a broad one that refuses to privilege jurisdictional norms and makes no rigid distinction between legal and nonlegal norms.

Hence the jury may interpret the applicable statutes and precedents for itself. It may also decide these statutes are unconstitutional. And it may consider that the statutes and precedents are out of harmony with background social norms; for example, that as applied they are unduly harsh or reflect values that have become outmoded. Though a Positivist might consider these background norms as nonlegal, a Substantivist would disagree. On a Substantive view these norms are implicitly incorporated in the criminal law in a way analogous to that by which the negligence norms incorporate the background standards of social practice associated with various activities. To the extent we see the jury as revising the law, that power is analogous to the power of a common law judge to revise governing norms in the light of new circumstances.

To a radical Substantivist there is no distinction between legal and nonlegal norms. For him it is always the case that, as Justice Cardozo said in the course of interpreting a tax statute, "Life in all its fullness must supply the answer."[16]

Unlike the Positivist, once the Substantivist has defined the law, she does not need to struggle for a further argument as to why it should be obeyed. The duty to obey follows more or less straightforwardly from the definition. Any argument for disobedience against a particular command would also be an argument that the command was an incorrect interpretation of the law. The Substantivist may well experience conflict between different values—say, between the values of majoritarian democracy that support deference to the legislature, and the values of fairness that cut against enforcement of statutes unfairly disadvantaging minority groups. But she understands such conflicts as occurring between competing legal values, not between law and nonlaw.

At best, however, explicit legitimate nullification occupies a marginal and generally uneasy place in the legal culture. Strong Substantivism threatens anarchy, and lawyers are dispositionally repelled by the prospect of anarchy. No doubt this is a partly a matter of occupational self-interest; there's not much work for lawyers in anarchy. But it also reflects a plausible belief that anything approaching full-blown anarchy is unlikely to accommodate a high level of justice or welfare.

Thus neither Positivism nor Substantivism, in the uncompromising, full-strength versions of each, is plausible. Positivism seems incompatible with any sense of legal obligation. It either disavows normative intentions, or it defends them clumsily and over-inclusively. Substantivism, by incorporating the reasons for obedience directly into its description of law, makes a clear and compelling case for obedience, but it tends to erode commitments to a stable institutional structure and calls up the threat of anarchy.

The Pervasiveness of Implicit Nullification

The mainstream of American legal culture incorporates both Positivist and Substantive perspectives, giving emphasis to one or the other in some areas, trying awkwardly to synthesize them in others. The working philosophies of individual lawyers vary in the relative emphases they give to the two perspectives, but, outside the realm of legal ethics, rarely embrace either fully. I don't propose to reconcile the two perspectives here. The contextual approach to lawyer's ethics I argue for is compatible with most variations of the two perspectives, except for the stronger versions of Positivism. However, as we have seen, the Dominant View presupposes a strong version of Positivism. A strong Positivist notion of legality underlies the Dominant View's categorical injunction of legal obedience (as well as its denial of authority to nonlegal norms).

I am going to offer a series of examples illustrating the pervasiveness of even the more radical Substantive themes—those associated with nullification—in mainstream legal culture. These themes are often implicit and under-acknowledged, but they recur in conventional practices and understandings. My purpose is not to deny the presence or partial validity of Positivist themes, but merely to suggest how inadequate the strong Positivist notion of legality is as a basis for a general lawyer's ethic. More specifically, the discussion shows how radically incompatible the idea of a categorical duty of obedience is with the broader legal culture.

Constitutional Revolution

Bruce Ackerman has recently emphasized that the major alterations of constitutional arrangements in America have been accomplished in ways that appear to have violated the laws that governed such alterations.[17]

The original Constitution was enacted in defiance of the prescriptions of the Articles of Confederation that amendments be initiated by the Congress (rather than a Constitutional Convention); that they be accepted unanimously by the states (rather than by nine of the 13 states); and that the states act through their legislatures (rather than through conventions). In adopting the Constitution at the Convention, delegates from several states exceeded the authority granted in their commissions. Although ratification of the federal Constitution entailed amendment of the state constitutions, most state conventions proceeded in defiance of the provisions governing amendments to their constitutions.

The 14th Amendment was initially rejected by nine legislatures of the defeated Southern states, more than enough to defeat it under Article V. These states accepted the Amendment only after Congress and the Army forcibly reconstructed their political processes and then conditioned their further representation in Congress on ratification.

During the New Deal, the President, Congress, and the Supreme Court dramatically restructured the constitution by adopting a new set of understandings of basic structural issues without any resort to the amendment process.

Ackerman does not believe that the many failures to "play by the old rules" he documents challenge the legitimacy of these constitutional revisions. To the contrary, he argues that the old rules were "deeply defective" expressions of democratic values, and that the actual practices used in the revisions vindicated these underlying values better than rule compliance would have.[18] In each case of revision, the process involved mass deliberation and mobilization in which large majorities of the electorate expressed their support for the new arrangements. In the classic tradition of radical Substantivism, Ackerman shows how conduct that departs from all but the most unconstrained readings of the positive law can nevertheless be intensely normative and structured.

Interpretation as Nullification

We earlier noted the basic tension in the legal culture between strict, literalistic interpretation on the one hand, and broad, purposive interpretation on the other. To sustain its commitment to segregating law from nonlegal norms, Positivism has to support relatively literal modes of interpretation. But there is ample warrant for broad interpretation in the culture. As interpretation becomes broader, it becomes harder to distinguish from nullification.

Consider this example. Article I, section 6 of the Constitution—the "Emoluments Clause"—provides, "No Senator or Representative shall be appointed to any office the emoluments of which shall have been increased during his term [in Congress]." In 1992 President Clinton nominated Senator Lloyd Bentsen Secretary of the Treasury. The salary of the Secretary of the Treasury had been increased several times during Bentsen's term as Senator. Congress responded to this concern by decreasing the Secretary's salary to its level at the beginning of Bentsen's Senate term and then confirmed his nomination.

One might characterize Congress's action as a broad, purposive interpretation of the Emoluments Clause. That is what then Acting Attorney General Robert Bork did in connection with an earlier and similar nomination about which he wrote, "The purpose of the constitutional provision is clearly met if the salary of an office is lowered after having been raised during the Senator's or Representative's term in office. . . ."[19] (The purpose is to insure that legislators will not set executive salaries with an eye toward their own benefit in the event they should themselves be appointed to executive office.)

The objection to Bork's argument is that the prohibition of the Emoluments Clause is specific and categorical. Thus, Professor Michael Paulsen has written an article deploring Bentsen's confirmation as a flagrant violation of the Constitution. Moreover, he gives several other examples of violations of Constitutional provisions concerning governmental structure. In each of these instances, Paulsen concedes, the applicable provision is a "nuisance" whose enforcement would serve no purpose. Nevertheless, Paulsen shows great distress at what he regards as a betrayal of the rule of law.

Paulsen gives no specific reasons for his disapproval. He does not suggest that society's tolerance of this sort of nullification has in any way weakened its ability to enforce constitutional provisions in situations where there are substantial stakes. He just regards it as self-evidently wrong to fail to comply with a legal rule. At the same time, however, he takes note of an interesting fact that seems to both puzzle and infuriate him: "[N]obody seems to care."[20] For present purposes, we can take Paulsen's frustrated observation as evidence that there is broad tolerance (and some active support) for the type of broad, purposive constitutional interpretation that shades into nullification.

It is not difficult to find analogous instances concerning the interpretation of statutes. In 1982 Guido Calabresi published a book arguing that judges should nullify statutes which, although constitutional, had been made obsolescent by social changes following their enactment.[21] Calabresi claimed that he was simply proposing for judges to do openly what sophisticated lawyers knew they routinely did as a matter of "subterfuge" under the guise of constitutional adjudication or broad construction of the statute's language. Judges should not be so bashful about statutory nullification, he said, because it is not very different from judicial revision of common law rules. As with a common law rule, a decision nullifying an obsolescent statute can be reversed by legislative enactment of a fresh statute. And the fact that, unlike a common law rule, a statute was once supported by a legislative majority should have little weight against the practice. A *long-ago* legislative majority is scant evidence of current support.

Ian Ayres has reinterpreted a series of close corporation cases in the light of Calabresi's proposal.[22] These cases consider whether close corporation control agreements that allocate board representation and management responsibility conflict with statutory provisions conferring managerial power and duty on a board of directors chosen by election. Earlier cases sometimes struck down the agreements as inconsistent with the statutes. The clear trend of the modern cases is to enforce the agreements. Modern lawyers consider it desirable that small-business participants be able to contract for the control arrangements they want. The older doctrine that inhibits their ability to do so is simply a "nuisance." Thus cases eroding the doctrine have been applauded.

To my knowledge Ayres was the first to discuss these cases as a form of nullification. He suggested that the older doctrine was strongly supported by statutory language. On the other hand, since the statutes, so interpreted, were out of tune with contemporary policies, they were good candidates for Calabresian nullification. Moreover, Ayres pointed to specific defects in the state legislative process that made it an unreliable safeguard of small-business interests. While states compete with each other to attract public corporations and the fees that come with incorporation, they have a captive market among small businesses for whom out-of-state incorporation is rarely feasible. He argued that reduced deference to the legislature is thus appropriate where small-business interests are concerned.

Now for our purposes the interesting feature of these arguments is that no commentator ever treated these cases as instances of nullification until one of the most prestigious mainstream legal scholars made a case for the legitimacy of nonconstitutional statutory nullification. Before then, to have treated the cases in terms of nullification would have made them hard to defend. Yet people approved of them on policy grounds. Thus they treated them as instances of broad, purposive construction.

It is a familiar trope of legal rhetoric—often found in dissenting opinions—to accuse someone whose decision you disagree with of changing—nullifying—rather than interpreting the law. The accusation is usually taken as simply a conclusory assertion of disagreement. The idea that a nonconstitutional statutory decision could be both nullification *and right* was generally banished from polite conversation before Calabresi (and it is still a minority view). But in fact once we acknowledge the creative aspects of interpretation and the principled aspects of nullification, it is often hard to distinguish them. Although the charge of nullification still raises a red flag, the practices associated with it are secure in the mainstream of the culture.

Casual Nullification

Many laws are unenforced or underenforced because people disobey them and officials are unable or unwilling to sanction them. With some laws this fact is a tragedy that reflects the inadequate socialization of the actors and practical difficulties of enforcement. With others, however, it seems a largely desirable mode of accommodating formal law to practical circumstances. In these situations citizens often violate the laws without any sense of wrongdoing, and their actions are ratified by officials who decline to sanction them even when they have the ability to do so. This sort of nullification sometimes takes a quasi-Calabresian form involving the disregard of laws that have grown out of touch with mainstream social values. The underenforcement of the laws against fornication and adultery or against marijuana possession are examples.

Another variation is motivated by a desire to avoid the inefficiencies of purposeless formality. In some areas, scrupulous compliance with the law is so burdensome and even disruptive that it occurs only as a form of protest. A familiar example is the practice of "working to rule"—or as the French call it, the "strike of zeal"—in which workers bring an enterprise to a halt by refusing to cut the corners necessary for things to function smoothly. Air traffic controllers and airline pilots, for example, are able to disrupt air traffic to the point of collapse by insisting on literal compliance with the rules.

Still another type of casual nullification occurs because of the cost of ascertaining the law. I recall from my childhood in the 1950s an episode of a TV game show called "People Are Funny" in which a contestant was challenged to go through the week between the current show and the next one without breaking any laws. A detective was to accompany him throughout the week, and there was a big prize for a week of law compliance. Even with these laboratory-like incentives, the contestant was unable to do it. The detective observed him breaking a federal law of which he was unaware: prohibiting the opening of a package of cigarettes without breaking the tax stamp.

An especially interesting realm of casual nullification is highway speed limits. During the era of the 55-mile-per-hour limit, nearly everyone violated the limit a lot. Many people believe that they are allowed an extra 10 miles above the posted limit by customary enforcement practices. Some experts believe that, within a broad range, the posted limit has no effect on the behavior of most drivers. "Repeatedly traffic studies confirm that 85 percent [of drivers] run at what is called a 'comfortable speed' regardless of the posted limit."[23]

Here is a situation of anarchy in the sense of decentralized norm application, but not in the sense of chaos. There is no indication that the widespread nullification of the 55 mile-per-hour limit has jeopardized safety. Many experts think that the dominant practices are optimal, and several jurisdictions have adjusted their rules to bring them more into line with practice.

Ronald Dworkin, in other respects one of the most Substantivist of legal theorists, repeatedly invokes the proposition that "the speed limit in California is 55" as an example of an easy case of uncontroversial legal judgment.[24] In fact, it is an easy case only if our goal is to describe the explicit terms of the legislature's enactment. It is a hard case from the point of view of obligation. (Or if it is an easy case, the answer is the opposite of the one Dworkin assumes. As a native informant, I can report that virtually no Californian feels obliged to go 55—as opposed to 56 or 57—miles per hour. The case becomes hard when we try to draw the line between acceptable and unacceptable speeding.)

Conscientious Nullification

We have already noted examples of the glorious American tradition of principled disobedience to law in the area of civil rights. Some of these instances are discussed under the rubric of civil disobedience. The difference between nullification and civil disobedience concerns only the degree of success of the activity in question. Nullification refers to a largely successful effort to alter or erase enacted law; civil disobedience refers to an effort of limited or no success. If *Walker v. Birmingham* had been decided in favor of the protesters, the march would have been an instance of nullification; given the way the Supreme Court ruled, it was an act of civil disobedience.

A striking fact about the American civil rights tradition is how much of it has been animated by Substantivist ideals of legality. The marchers in Birmingham and elsewhere who ignored injunctions and parade ordinances, the boycotters in Montgomery and elsewhere whose conduct was often prohibited by state law against trade conspiracies, and the sit-in demonstrators whose conduct was a form of trespass did not see themselves as defying the established legal order. They were inspired in part by their understanding of the values of equality and solidarity codified in the Constitution and other federal laws. In their view, they were not disobeying the law but merely the lawless commands of local officials and property owners. Moreover, their substantive claims have been largely vindicated within the legal order. The story of 1950s and 1960s civil rights activism in the South is vivid testimony to the benign possibilities of the kind of anarchy associated with radical Substantivism, just as the longer history of racist lynching and vigilante terrorism testifies to the malign possibilities.

There is a contested but strong tradition of tolerance for civil disobedience in the legal culture. The most strongly supported instances are those like the Birmingham march, in which the ultimate tribunal comes to share the defendant's substantive views. But there is also support for the view that open disobedience based on good faith but wrong interpretation of the law ought to be tolerated if the interpretation is not too unreasonable, and the conduct does not impose large tangible costs. The argument is that such conduct is a potentially valuable form of citizen participation in the process of legal elaboration. Even when ultimately held wrongful, the conduct may have been useful in putting issues on the public agenda and framing them as a specific case in a way that facilitates productive deliberation. A more radical view would protect some range of mistaken good-faith *private* disobedience. Such conduct makes no intentional contribution to public deliberation, but it involves a kind of individual moral deliberation that society might want to encourage.[25]

Lawyer Vigilantism in Popular Culture

Although we are primarily interested in the internal professional culture of lawyers, that culture is influenced by the surrounding popular culture. So it is worth noting that the treatment of lawyers in popular culture has been overwhelmingly Substantivist. Popular culture finds lawyers unattractive when they behave as the Dominant View prescribes, when they sacrifice broader notions of justice to narrow Positivist notions of legality.

Radical Substantivism is especially salient in the theme of lawyer vigilantism that recurs in Hollywood's approving portrayals of lawyers. Robert Post summarizes this theme in terms of the maxim, "the lawyer must be lawless in order to uphold the law."[26] For example: in *The Talk of the Town* (1942), Ronald Coleman portrays a Harvard Law professor who has been nominated to the Supreme Court. In order to save an innocent man who has been framed for arson and is about to be lynched, he kidnaps the person he believes to be the real culprit and then confronts the lynch mob with a pistol (we're not told whether it's licensed), lecturing it on the importance of respect for legality.

In *The Man Who Shot Liberty Valance* (1962), James Stewart portrays a tenderfoot lawyer who comes to a rugged Western town to hang out his shingle. When the town is terrorized by a gang of thugs, he challenges its leader to a duel (which is of course a crime). When he amazes everyone by appearing to kill his opponent, the town elects him to office, and he ambivalently rides his reputation as "the man who shot Liberty Valance" to a career in the United States Senate. It turns out that he didn't kill Liberty Valance. John Wayne secretly shot Valance from a nearby hiding place. When he tells Stewart the truth, Wayne concludes, "It was cold-blooded murder, but I can live with it." Presumably, under the felony murder rule, Stewart shares Wayne's guilt, but Stewart too decides he can live with it.

In *The Verdict* (1982), Paul Newman portrays a struggling lone practitioner litigating a wrongful death case against scions of the Boston medical establishment and an army of lawyers from a big corporate firm. The defendants have driven the principal witness to their negligence out of town, and threaten to destroy her career if she cooperates with the plaintiff. Newman can't locate the witness because the defendants deny they know where she is (probably perjuriously) and have threatened to ruin anyone who cooperates with the plaintiff. With the trial about to begin and no witness, Newman breaks into the mailbox of the witness's best friend on the day after the phone bills are mailed out and steals her bill. He checks the most frequent out-of-town number on the bill, finds the witness, and turns the case around.

In all these instances the lawyer's criminal behavior is portrayed as admirable, and objections to it as priggish and naive. *The Verdict* is a cynical work that sees corruption as ubiquitous and inevitable; it makes the ideal of legal obligation seem hypocritical and fatuous. But *The Talk of the Town* and *Liberty Valance* are idealistic works that show great respect for law as they insist on its complexity.

The themes of these two films are strikingly similar. At the beginning, the Coleman and Stewart characters each exemplify rigidity associated with limited experience of the world. Each has been formed in the sheltered environment of the Eastern city and the university. Their rigidity takes two forms that the movies treat as analogous. One is sexual: they are awkward with women. The other is intellectual: they are disposed to the kind of categorical normative judgment entailed by Moralistic Positivism. Their reverence for law is sanctimonious and naive. Each is transformed, first, through love of an extraordinary woman (Jean Arthur, Vera Miles), and second, through participation in a crisis in which his commitment to the broader ideals of justice and legality requires him to violate the Positive law. At the end of each film, the hero has acquired the worldliness of capacities for both love and complex normative judgment.

These films strikingly contradict a traditional dogma of the bar that popular respect for law requires lawyers to abide rigidly by the letter of the law. As the *Code of Professional Responsibility* puts it, "Because of his position in society, even minor violations of law by a lawyer may tend to lessen public confidence in the legal profession."[27] The implication seems to be that, while lawyers may be capable of more sophisticated understandings of legality, Moralistic Positivism is all that can be expected of the lay public. Of course, this is yet another of those empirical assertions that the bar has never investigated, much less supported with evidence. The evidence from Hollywood suggests that the bar has things backward. Popular respect for law may *require* lawyers to violate the positive law.

Moreover, the understanding of law reflected in these films is a thoughtful one. In effect, the films offer a critique of Moralistic Positivism, which they personify in the early Coleman and Stewart characters. The critique is a psychological one similar to Jerome Frank's critique of classical legalism.[28] Both Frank and the movies see the disposition toward categorical judgment as a form of emotional and intellectual immaturity. In this condition, people deny or shield themselves from the real world because they are afraid of its complexities and contradictions. Maturity involves acknowledging these complexities and contradictions by abandoning categorical normative judgment without becoming cynical.

On the rare occasions when lawyers acknowledge nullification as legitimate, they tend to do so diffidently, focusing on a single type and treating it as distinctive. Thus Bruce Ackerman in his defense of constitutional revolution, Guido Calabresi in his defense of nonconstitutional judicial nullification, and Ronald Dworkin in his defense of civil disobedience ignore the other types of nullification and take pains to assert the limited and exceptional nature of the practice each defends. But when we line up these practices along with the other forms of nullification that are solidly, if tacitly, grounded in mainstream legal culture, we recognize that they constitute a strong general theme of radical Substantivism.

Some Clarification about Nullification

My purpose here is less to defend Substantivism than to show that, even in its more radical forms, it pervades the mainstream of the legal culture, albeit sometimes in a low-profile way. Because some people tend to misinterpret the doctrine in a way that makes it seem more bizarre than it is, I want to clarify some misconceptions about it.

One misconception is that Substantivism is indifferent to values of effective decisionmaking that sometimes support over- or under-inclusive rules. When the traffic light turns red as I reach the intersection and there are no other cars in the area, I am tempted to say that the purpose of the law requiring that I stop would not be served by my doing so. But this would be to construe the purpose too narrowly. The principal purpose is to reduce accidents. While I may think that my proceeding through the red light would not risk an accident, I may not be a good judge of that. Moreover, even if my judgment is excellent, a police officer observing me going through the light has no way of assessing the quality of my judgment. Thus, all things considered, the best rule may be an over-broad one requiring me to stop even if I see no one in the intersection.

Nothing should prevent even the most radical Substantivist from taking into account the social interests that support an over-inclusive rule in deciding about compliance in this case. The need to constrain people from acting on potentially impaired judgments that pose risk to others and the need for effective enforcement systems are aspects of the social interest in accident reduction.

Yet to see what difference a Substantive commitment might make, let us modify the story to add that at the time I approach the intersection I am rushing a desperately wounded person to the hospital, and I plausibly believe that any delay would pose serious risk for him. My judgment is still fallible and the crisis may have made it more so, but since the new circumstances have greatly increased the costs of stopping without affecting the benefits, the calculation is now much simpler. The red light rule may have an explicit exception for emergencies of this sort, or it and the surrounding law may leave open the possibility of implying such an exception. If it denies such an exception, however, I might as a Substantivist conclude that the denial is simply wrong, perhaps unconstitutional or out of harmony with the surrounding law. In doing so, I wouldn't be denying the social interests that support the general rule, just deciding that they were outweighed by the competing social interest in saving a life.

Similarly, it is incorrect to accuse Substantivism of ignoring the values of relatively centralized and institutionalized legal decisionmaking. Legislative and judicial decisionmaking, as opposed to the kind of popular decisionmaking involved in nullification, potentially allows better notice of the law, since it occurs in public and takes the form of promulgated rules. It is potentially more democratic, since the decisionmakers are subject to mechanisms of political accountability. And the decisions are potentially richer, since they proceed from deliberation and debate.

A Substantivist doesn't ignore any of these factors. However, she does differ from the Positivist in the ways she takes account of them. First, she is open to considering that the general association between legislative and judicial processes and the values of notice, democracy, and decisional quality may not hold in the particular case. For example, in the emergency-red-light scenario, nullification might be more compatible with people's reasonable expectations and hence with the values of notice than the literal terms of the statute (which the typical actor would be unable to consult at the relevant time). Second, the Substantivist is open to considering that these institutional values, even where present, might be outweighed by competing values in the circumstances of the particular case.

Nullification versus Reform

It is occasionally argued against nullification that it reduces the pressure for the reform of bad laws. The social pain caused by enforcement of bad laws feeds back into the legislative system to hasten efforts at reform. Nullification, by reducing the pain, slows the feedback and hence the process of self-correction. Since nullification is rarely uniform, a lingering bad law continues to have some bad effects, and activity that retards self-correction contributes to perpetuating these effects.

If the factual premise of this argument were true, there is no reason why the Substantivist couldn't consider it as a reason weighing against nullification in her decision. But the factual premise is not true in any uniform or linear fashion. Sometimes nonenforcement, especially as it becomes more widespread and visible, increases pressures to reform the law to bring it into line with practice. One reason may be that a visibly unenforced law is an embarrassment to the government. The reform of highway speed limits discussed above is an example.

Moreover, even where nullification does reduce pressure for reform, one still has to consider whether it is fair to the individual involved to force her to submit to an illegitimate command simply to make a marginal contribution to some broad social interest. In cases where the law imposes a serious unfair burden or infringes an important liberty, the individual's interest should trump or outweigh the social interest.

A hypothesis relevant to both points is that enforcement against relatively disadvantaged or marginal people is least likely to generate pressures for reform and most likely to be unfair. In a case that involves such an individual, that circumstance might weigh toward nullification.

Tax versus Prohibition

In the nullification situation we have been discussing, an official or institution has one interpretation of what the law requires, while some other actor declines to comply with it on the basis of a better interpretation. In these situations, disobedience or nonenforcement of the inferior interpretation is desirable. A different type of situation arises in circumstances where some level of enforcement is considered a good thing, but we nevertheless excuse or even justify some disobedience. We sometimes speak of the actor in this situation as regarding the law as imposing a tax on his activity rather than prohibiting it.

The core example here is breach of contract. People generally feel entitled to breach contracts and pay damages when it is cheaper to do so than to perform. Although Holmes explained this in Positivist terms as following from the fact that damages are the only sanction the law provides, the action is equally plausible on Substantive terms. Doctrines such as the preclusion of penalties in contract remedies, the duty to mitigate, the bankruptcy discharge, and the prohibition of involuntary servitude all support the idea that fairness and efficiency are best served by a duty to perform that is not absolute. On the other hand, as I argued in Chapter 2, the fact that we do not regard most criminal and tortious conduct causing serious injury this way can be explained only on Substantive terms. It would not be fair or efficient to treat the prohibition of battery or rape as a tax on an acceptable activity, and no lawyer would counsel a client in this manner. Between the realm typified by contract, where duty and penalty seem coextensive, and the realm of serious criminal activity, where duty is broader than penalty, there is a large area of ambiguity and disagreement. This area includes many regulatory and tax laws.

In such areas we confront the further question whether, if it is appropriate for the citizen to treat the law as a tax, the relevant tax is the full prescribed penalty (which implies a duty to pay it voluntarily), or the penalty discounted by the likelihood of enforcement (which might be quite low and might be lowered further by things the citizen could do).

In many towns it is illegal for me to park my car at a metered space, pay for the maximum time, and then return when the time expires to put more coins in the meter. If on occasion I violate this rule—say because my meeting takes longer than I anticipated—and I get caught and ticketed, hardly anyone would think I had been treated unjustly or had any ground for resistance. On the other hand, if I get away with avoiding a ticket, few people would condemn me either. There are many situations in which insistence on obedience to law seems sanctimonious or fetishistic.

The Dominant View is unable to deal with issues of this sort. For the Positivist criteria of legality it subsumes do not distinguish between laws that we appropriately treat as prices (or risks) and those we should treat as commands. These distinctions depend on the sorts of principles that Positivism does not recognize as law and on the sort of complex judgment the Dominant View disclaims.

Determination versus Obligation

For the Positivist, determining what the law demands is relatively easy. That is the point of separating of law and morals. On the other hand, figuring out whether the law merits obedience is relatively difficult. At least, Positivism provides no guidance on this subject other than the conclusory exhortations of its Moralistic variation.

There is thus a strong affinity between Positivism and those legal ethicists who portray the core dilemmas of practice as matters of role morality or conflicts of law and morals.[29] In assuming pervasive tensions between legal commands and individual commitments, these ethicists presuppose—often apparently inadvertently—a Positivist conception of legality.

Such conflicts are less salient for the Substantivist. Indeed, they never arise for the radical Substantivist, because all the grounds for commitment have been subsumed into law. For the Substantivist, the hard question is not whether the law is binding, but what it prescribes. Conflicts the Positivist defines as law-versus-morality take the form, for the Substantivist, of legal norms in tension with each other. Few lawyers are either radical Positivists or radical Substantivists; most combine both perspectives in their working philosophies. Thus it is often unclear when an ethical struggle ceases to be an effort to determine what the law prescribes and becomes an effort to decide if the law is morally binding.

Consider the Paul Newman character in *The Verdict* (with the modification that he is ethically reflective). Let's assume that he has exhausted all the conventional possibilities for locating the key witness. He has deposed the witness's friend, but she denies knowledge of her whereabouts. He has good reason to believe she is lying for fear of retaliation by the defendants. He gets the phone bill idea. He knows there is a federal statute that makes it a crime to intercept mail addressed to someone else, and state statutes that make it criminal trespass to enter on someone's property for the purpose of larceny, and larceny to take someone's mail from her mailbox (even if you return it). Does he think of the matter as a conflict between legal and moral duty?

That would be a crude judgment. First, the "moral" side of the issue—his client's interest in discovering the identity of the witness—is also freighted with legal considerations. For one thing, the lawyer and his client are legally entitled to this information under the discovery laws, and it is necessary to the proof they have to make for a damage award, to which he also believes them legally entitled. Moreover, on the "law" side of the balance, further analysis is called for. Perhaps the relevant jurisdictions have a "necessity" defense to criminal charges, such as the *Model Penal Code* provision that justifies otherwise criminal conduct "necessary to avoid a harm of evil" when the "harm or evil sought to be avoided . . . is greater than that sought to be prevented by the law defining the offense charged."[30] Even if they don't have such a statute, there might be a reasonable possibility that the courts would imply one. Even if the courts have rejected such a defense or held it inapplicable in circumstances like these (say, where a key fact, such as that the friend is testifying falsely, isn't known with certainty), there may be a possibility that the court would change its mind if the issue were presented in a new case. A statute might preclude the defense specifically, but even if the statute is completely unambiguous, there might be a chance that a court would find it unconstitutional or a prosecutor or jury would nullify its application in this case.

Finally, we reach the point where the lawyer is certain that the Positive law forbids taking the phone bill: there's no doubt that the prosecutor will prosecute on these facts, that the trial judge will instruct the jury that the facts constitute a crime, that the jury will convict, and that the highest court will affirm. Even at this point, the lawyer may view the matter not as a conflict of law and morality, but as a misinterpretation of the law on the part of constituted authority. The lawyer might simply believe that these actors would be wrong in their judgments that taking the phone bill under these circumstances would be criminal. Of course, believing this, he could still acknowledge reasons why he should defer to them, such as those on which the Supreme Court relied in sustaining the punishment of the petitioners in *Walker v. Birmingham.* But he would continue to think of the conflict as intralegal. The point in the chain at which the lawyer stops thinking of the conflict as intralegal depends on the balance of Positivist and Substantive commitments in his working philosophy.

Frederick Douglass, the antislavery activist, emphasized the psychological importance of the difference between the legal determination and the law-versus-morality perspectives:

> Brought directly when I escaped from slavery, into contact with abolitionists who regarded the Constitution as a slaveholding instrument, and finding their views supported by the united and entire history of every department of the government, it is not strange that I assumed the Constitution to be just what these friends made it seem to be. . . . But [I later had occasion] to re-think the whole subject, and to study with some care not only the just and proper rules of legal interpretation, but the origin, design, nature, rights, powers, and duties of civil governments, and also the relations which human beings sustain to it. By such a course of thought and reading I was conducted to the conclusion that the Constitution of the United States—inaugurated to "form a more perfect union, establish justice, insure domestic tranquility, provide for the common defense, promote the general welfare, secure the blessings of liberty"—could not well have been designed at the same time to maintain and perpetuate

a system of rapine and murder like slavery, especially as not one word can be found in the Constitution to authorized such a belief.[31]

Douglass began by seeing the antislavery crusade as fight against the constitutional order; when he joined the radical constitutionalists, he saw it as a struggle to redeem it. The consequences of such a change can dramatically affect a person's orientation to his commitments as well as the rhetoric, strategies, and alliances he pursues. For Douglass, the change was connected to a determination to join the antislavery cause to the cause of preserving the union.

The stakes involved in such competing characterizations vary with the context. In contemporary American legal culture, the issue has two significant implications. First, the law/law characterization suggests that the matter is susceptible to resolution in terms of the analytical methods and sources of legal argument. While these methods and sources are loose, they are typically thought to be more structured and grounded than popular moral discourse. Second, the law/law characterization suggests that the legal profession or some subgroup of it might have some collective responsibility for its resolution that might call for disciplinary review or simply critical assessment. Moral considerations, on the other hand, are presumed to be a matter for the individual decisionmaker to resolve privately. The resolution of law-law issues is considered relevant to one's professional reputation, while the resolution of moral ones is a matter of one's "personal reputation" in the larger community, which, to most lawyers, has considerably less social substance and importance.

The Dominant View's tacit Positivism privileges the law/morals characterization, and particularly the choices associated with "law." The psychological effect of this privileging is to reinforce lawyers' commitment to conventional responses—client loyalty in all cases where the client's projects are not prohibited by the positive law, obedience to the positive law in other cases. Typically, the conventional response is portrayed as the "legal" one, and competing ones as "moral" alternatives. The rhetoric connotes that the "legal" option is objective and integral to the professional role, while the moral option is subjective and peripheral. Even when the rhetoric expresses respect for the "moral" alternative, it implies that the lawyer who adopts it is on his or her own and vulnerable both intellectually and practically.

The usual effect is to make it psychologically harder for lawyers and law students to argue for the "moral" alternative. The effect of showing that in fact both alternatives could be understood as "legal" is thus sometimes to make the alternative positions seem more grounded and less subjective.

A Prima Facie Obligation?

Theorists who appreciate the implausibility of a categorical duty of obedience sometimes retreat to a "prima facie" or rebuttable duty.[32] You can't say this idea is wrong, but it is not especially useful, and it can be misleading. Abstractly stated, it still begs the question of what we mean by law. If the phrase refers to a Substantivist conception, then it is tautological. If it refers to a Positivist conception, then it is misleading.

Law is prima facie binding if it is prima facie just (subsuming such values as order, fairness, and democracy under this heading). On a Substantive view, law is prima facie just *by definition*. The Substantivist insists that at least some dimensions of justice be incorporated into law (and does so precisely in order to make law binding).[33] So the claim of a prima facie duty adds nothing to the Substantivist definition of the legal enterprise.[34]

On a Positivist view, a prima facie duty might have two different meanings. It might mean that the jurisdictional principles that define the law constitute a process that is intrinsically just—for example, democratic—and therefore entitled to presumptive respect. Or it might mean that the laws that emerge from this process are usually just, and there is thus a strong empirical likelihood that any particular norm it has generated is just.

Now as long as one remembers to perform the moral and empirical analyses required to sustain such conclusions, there is nothing improper about expressing them as a "prima facie duty to obey the law." Nevertheless the phrase is objectionable to the extent that it suggests that the relevant analyses are more abstract than they should be. Lawyers practice law in discrete localities with discrete institutions (even though they may be dispersed around the country or the world). Thus presumptions derived from global or national characterizations of law are not helpful. Even a novice lawyer knows too much about the locales where she practices for a global or national presumption to be of use. The important question for her is whether there is a prima facie obligation to obey the local municipal court or the state Appellate Tax Board or the Ministry of Trade and Industry of some foreign country. Perhaps the answer is usually yes, but it won't always be so. It is unlikely that the petitioners in *Walker v. Birmingham* had reason to assume they had a prima facie obligation to obey the local state courts.

It is a mistake to think that any general sense of obligation, prima facie or otherwise, is critical to the enforcement of either important coordination schemes, such as automobile driving rules, or rules that protect basic human interests, such as the rule against murder.[35] For one thing, habit and sanctions secure a substantial measure of compliance with such rules without any sense of normative compulsion. More importantly, precisely because the values that underpin these rules are so clear and compelling, the rules don't depend on any categorical obligation to obey law. Responsible people will obey the traffic laws and the law against murder because they respect the values that underlie them, even if they are completely unmoved by the fact that these rules constitute "the law."

A categorical norm of obligation becomes important only when the actor confronts a norm that does not appear grounded in any compelling substantive value (and for which habit and sanctions do not induce compliance). There is no categorical answer to the question of whether a categorical obligation is warranted in such cases. Everything depends on our relative confidence in the particular law-making authority on the one hand and the particular citizens on the other. Conventional discourse thus seems much too eager to embrace such a duty, even when it is qualified as prima facie.

The Positivist's strongest argument for separating law and morals is that by thus forcing us to confront the issue of legal determination separately from the question of legal obligation, he encourages us to face the latter more squarely.[36] But the moralist who seeks to add to Positivism's constricted notion of law an abstract presumption of obligation, even a rebuttable one, seems to deprive us of this intended benefit. At worst, his rhetoric discourages us from taking full account of the local characteristics of our practices. At best, it merely makes us complacent.

Divorce Perjury and Enforcement Advice Revisited

We return now to the problems of divorce perjury and enforcement advice discussed above as illustrations of the treatment in the Dominant View of direct and indirect participation in illegality.

Let us begin with the problem of advice, since the inadequacy of categorical approaches is most obvious here. In at least some cases, enforcement advice would be unacceptable to nearly everyone. For example: the client is a serial rapist who wants information about the schedules and routes of police patrols in the area where he plans to strike next. Giving such information might constitute unlawful assistance under the criminal law, but that is far from clear. If it is not itself illegal, then it is not unethical under the Dominant View, and that surely is an objection to the Dominant View.

On the other hand, hardly anyone is going to support a categorical ban on such information either. Many feel strongly that clients are entitled to know the extent to which the laws against fornication, sodomy, misprision of felony (failing to report someone else's criminal activity), small-stakes gambling, marijuana possession, and nonpayment of employment taxes for part-time domestic workers are not enforced or under-enforced.

Health and safety regulations and environmental regulatory enforcement also resist categorical treatment. Where evasive behavior threatens serious harm the regulatory scheme is designed to protect against, advice that facilitates evasion seems wrong. But sometimes evasion seems to be not only far from threatening major harm, but indeed acceptable to the enforcement authorities and perhaps even the legislature. Maybe the agency under-enforces because it thinks the statutory standards are too strict. Maybe it under-enforces because the legislature, divided on the efficacy of the statute, has cut the agency's enforcement budget, intending to limit enforcement. To be sure, this type of administrative and legislative behavior is objectionable because it impairs political accountability. However, there is no doubt that it occurs, and given that it occurs, it seems both unfair and inefficient to preclude lawyers from providing relevant information about enforcement practices.

Any plausible assessment of the propriety of enforcement advice requires a willingness to distinguish the relative weights of different substantive norms. This requires an at least moderately Substantive approach and contextual judgment. Some cases are easy. (Although not everyone will have the same list of easy cases, each person will have some list of cases she finds easy, and some cases will appear on most people's lists.) Advice that facilitates violence and large-scale property crime will usually seem clearly inappropriate. Advice that facilitates moderate speeding, misprision of felony, and consensual fornication will usually seem proper, or at least tolerable.

Other cases are harder. For example, there is playing the "tax lottery"—submitting a weakly grounded tax claim, knowing it is unlikely to be audited. The case is potentially hard because of the possibility that, while the claim may be weak in terms of the narrow positive law, it may be stronger when viewed more broadly and substantively. Playing the "tax lottery" might then be viewed as an appropriate form of nullification of a normatively weak positive law. This may seem un-likely—it does to me—but the point is that a plausible defense of advice that has little function other than to facilitate evasion requires the type of principled Substantive justification associated with nullification.[37]

Although it may seem more radical in the context of direct lawyer illegality, the same analysis applies there. We have already noted the broad variety of circumstances in which the culture accepts, and occasionally exalts, direct violation of the positive law. However, most of these examples involve ordinary citizens rather than lawyers, and some lawyers believe that they have a stronger obligation to the law than do lay people (because they publicly profess commitment to it, have a strong exemplary influence on the lay public, or acquire special privileges through participation in a regulated monopoly). Thus, it is said, a categorical prohibition of direct participation in illegality makes more sense for lawyers than for lay people.[38]

This argument is yet another variation on the jurisprudential mistake we have noted repeatedly. It doesn't follow from the fact that lawyers have a stronger obligation to the "law" that the type of conduct we are considering is less appropriate for them. For the conceptions of law most compatible with strong obligations are Substantive, and on a Substantive conception, obligation to "law" may require violation of some legal norms in order to vindicate more basic ones.

The argument comes close to making explicit the effect I noted above of the Dominant View's jurisprudential commitments. By adopting a Positivist notion of law, it characterizes the considerations favoring compliance as legal and those weighing against it as nonlegal, perhaps "moral." If we accept this characterization, unless we are prepared to reject the appealing proposition that lawyers have an exceptionally strong obligation to law, we will find it very hard to support lawyer noncompliance in situations like the Divorce Perjury case.

But there is no reason why we should accept the characterization. Many of the most important reasons weighing toward noncompliance can be aptly expressed in legal—especially nullification—terms. For example, perhaps the strongest case for lawyer participation in the divorce perjury would portray it as an instance of Calabresian nullification. For one thing, the statute is an old one. It is also out of harmony with more recent legal developments that imply that for childless couples the social interest in preserving marriage is much weaker, and the individual interest in structuring one's own intimate relations is much stronger, than the statute presupposes. In addition, there are apparent institutional dysfunctions that provide more likely explanations for the failure to repeal the statute than current popular support. Perhaps the statute is supported by only a small minority. This group would not be able to secure the enactment of the statute today, but it can block repeal because it is well organized; because most of the statute's opponents feel less intensely; and because those who are tangibly harmed by the statute, such as the clients in question here, are not able to organize (because their status is hard to anticipate and episodic) and are relatively poor (because affluent people can avoid its effects by taking advantage of the more accommodating laws of other states).

Of course, we should consider why, if there is a strong case for nullification, it has to be accomplished by the lawyer rather than, as Calabresi proposed, the court. Why not have the lawyer bring an action on the true facts urging the court to nullify and grant the divorce? One answer is that most states reject judicial nullification except on constitutional grounds, which might not be available. But even if judges could nullify, they might refuse to do so because they are, for example, unwilling to take the heat from a small but passionate minority that supports the statute. Or perhaps the judges would think that the existence of such a minority would make nullification illegitimate. It might be, however, that the statute is of largely symbolic importance to this group, and it has no stake in low visibility enforcement decisions. While public judicial nullification would thus not be feasible, low visibility ad hoc lawyer nullification would be.

Conclusion

Whether lawyers should obey the law turns out to depend on what we mean by law. If we define law in Positivist terms, then we should acknowledge that the practice of principled disobedience has strong support in our legal culture. If we define law Substantively, then we should recognize that the duty of obedience to law requires more complex judgments than legal ethics discussions often suppose. The notion of nullification, which fits with either of these rhetorics, expresses what should be an important theme of any plausible legal ethic.

The Dominant View tends to deal with issues of legal obligation by distinguishing between advice likely to impede enforcement, which it permits indiscriminately, and more active participation in illegality, which it categorically forbids. This approach is implausible. The more aggressive forms of enforcement advice are not justifiable without a principled rationale of the sort associated with nullification. And a strong rationale of this sort could provide plausible support for more active participation in conduct that disregards the positive law. If we define law in terms of the Positivist's jurisdictional criteria, then lawyers have no strong reason to obey it. If we define law Substantively, we make transparent the obligation that attaches to it, but we also erase the line between law and morals.

5

Legal Professionalism as Meaningful Work

The basic objection to the Dominant View is that it excessively attenuates the lawyer's responsibility for her conduct and requires her to participate in injustice. Most of my argument takes the form of a critique of the conventional arguments that defend these effects as necessary to some higher, but also more remote, justice. I haven't said very much about why, if the conventional arguments are wrong, reduced responsibility for justice and participation in injustice would be bad.

To some extent I simply take for granted that these conditions are bad, and assume that the reader will agree that they are. This assumption seems consistent with the premises of popular culture, which portrays the lawyer as personally unattractive when he disclaims responsibility for his acts and participates in injustice, even where his conduct is warranted by the Dominant View. It is also consistent with the unstated premise of the Dominant View that its distinctive ethos requires justification. Most of the rhetoric of the Dominant View is framed as a reply to an often unstated starting point that lawyers should seek justice. The rhetoric seems to concede that the duty to seek justice is the default position that would govern if its own more sophisticated arguments were incorrect.

It is tempting to rest the case for the Contextual approach on this implicit concession. It is much easier to show the inconsistencies and nonsequiturs in someone else's argument than to construct an affirmative vision of the good. Nevertheless, though this type of claim can never be conclusive, there are some worthwhile arguments that more directly support the Contextual approach.

One type of affirmative argument is the indirect kind we find in literature and dramatic art. It defends a moral ideal by trying to show how appealing a life or career that incarnates it can be, and conversely, how repellent a life or career that repudiates it can be. Lacking the talent to exploit this approach, I refer the reader to the favorable portrayals of lawyers in the better Hollywood productions and the unfavorable portrayals in the novels of Dickens and Dostoyevsky, and indeed most of the great nineteenth-century European novelists. I do, however, want to make more direct use of two great novels that are not focused on lawyers but strikingly portray the stakes involved in our understanding of work—George Eliot's *Middlemarch* and Franz Kafka's *The Trial*.

Another type of affirmative argument defends an ideal by trying to show that it is entailed by, or responds to, some commitment or need acknowledged by the group to which the argument is directed. Thus I see support for the Contextual approach in the bar's broad rhetorical commitments to justice and in the widespread expressions of alienation among prominent practitioners.

In this chapter I will use both types of argument to give substance to the intuition that the Dominant View promotes a dispiriting, personally costly alienation of the lawyer from her work. I begin by invoking a notion of alienation from work that literature and social theory pervasively identify as a core problem of modernity. I then recall how certain core features of professionalism, and especially American legal professionalism, have been embraced and defended as remedies to this problem of alienation and as supports of meaningful work. These are occupational self-regulation and contextual judgment. Conventional accounts of American legal professionalism tend to emphasize only the first. I argue that the second is more important to the experience of meaningful work and has been and continues to be more important to the professional self-conception of American lawyers. My goal is to show how the dominance of an ethical regime that repudiates contextual judgment is both an anomaly and an obstacle to the deepest ambitions that animate legal professionalism.

The Problem of Alienation

Alienation is a diagnosis in most critical portrayals of modernity. The symptoms are a sense of personal weightlessness and ineffectuality and of the strangeness and impermeability of the social world. In modern social theory, alienation appears as a problem in the transition from organically integrated societies to looser, more individualistic ones. For some, the history of the West over the past five centuries or so is simply one long transition of this kind. Others see more partial and intense versions of the transition occurring in specific periods. For example, Robert Wiebe has portrayed the period of emergence of the institutions of modern professionalism in late nineteenth-century America as such a transition:

> An age never lent itself more readily to sweeping, uniform description: nationalization, industrialization, mechanization, urbanization.
>
> Yet to almost all the people who created them, these themes meant only dislocation and bewilderment. America in the nineteenth century was a society without a core. It lacked the national centers of authority and information which might have given order to such swift changes. American institutions were still oriented toward a community life where family and church, education and press, professions and government, all found their meaning by the way they fit one another in a town or a detached portion of a city. As men ranged farther and farther from their communities, they tried desperately to understand their larger world in terms of their small, familiar environment. They tried, in other words, to impose the known upon the unknown, to master an impersonal world through the customs of a personal society.[1]

This picture stands in opposition to the classical liberal portrayal of modernity as the happy triumph of invididualism. In that portrayal, the erosion of relatively fixed roles and institutions and relatively self-contained communities is a boon that makes possible both prosperity and individual self-realization. The theorists of alienation find this view naive. From the point of view of social welfare, the decline of traditional social institutions creates a host of problems that cannot be solved through independent individual action but require the collective creation of a new set of stable institutions. From the point of view of the individual, the new society leaves the social dimension of self unsatisfied; it fails to provide the feelings of place and connection that are essential to self-realization.

It is the latter point of view that most concerns us. Its premise is that people need a sense of both relation to the larger society and solidarity with concrete others, not just family and friends, but a wider circle of potential collaborators in material and political projects. At the same time, this view often concedes, people have a need to express their individuality and impress their wills on their surroundings.

For many, the satisfaction of these potentially conflicting needs for connection and self-assertion lay in the idea of meaningful work. Work is "meaningful" when the worker experiences it as both a form of a self-assertion and a point of connection and solidarity with the larger society. The most common reference point for the theorists of alienation has been the artisan, especially under the regime of the guild. The artisan then had a sense of place in society as the producer of an important product. His skills and a variety of cooperative practices in the production process provided the basis for a shared occupational community among members of the craft. At the same time, craft production involves individual self-expression. The artisan working alone, or with a small number of collaborators, controls the work process, deciding when, what, how much, and how to produce. Furthermore, the products are not standardized but varied, and they are often customized for a particular purchaser. The artisan's techniques take the form of general principles and general-purpose tools that can be adapted to a variety of specialized uses. Thus the artisan's work leaves room for, and often demands, creativity.

Although nostalgia for the guild regime is common among alienation theorists, many acknowledge that even at its best the opportunities for self-expression the regime provided were highly limited, and they were often accompanied by heavy social costs in terms of monopolistic practices and technological stagnation. For most theorists, traditional craft production is not an institutional ideal so much as a set of clues about the possibilities of meaningful work. They do not prescribe a return to the guilds but seek the adoption of some of their animating principles.

In their paradigmatic, unreformed state, the core institutions of modernity—the market and the bureaucracy—appear as threats to meaningful work. The alienation theorists emphasize the similarities of these two institutions: both are premised on specialization of function, involve potentially large-scale coordination, and above all, typically regulate through impersonal rule. The two most influential alienation theories—the Marxist/Romantic critique of the market and the Weberian/Romantic critique of bureaucracy—both emphasize the role of impersonal rule in defining the institutions on which they focus.

The Marxist perspective portrays the worker in the capitalist labor market as "a mechanical part incorporated in a mechanical system. He finds it already pre-existing and self-sufficient, it functions independently of him and he has to conform to its laws whether he likes it or not. . . . [Under these laws] all issues are subjected to an increasingly formal and standardised treatment and in which there is an increasing remoteness from the qualitative and material essence of the 'things' [that are the subjects of decision]."[2]

According to Weber, the "specific nature" of bureaucracy "develops the more perfectly the more the bureaucracy is 'dehumanized,' the more completely it succeeds in eliminating from official business love, hatred, and all purely personal, irrational, and emotional elements which escape calculation." The paradigmatic way in which bureacracy accomplishes this is by mandating "'rational' interpretation of the law on the basis of strictly formal conceptions."[3]

The psychological consequence is that the worker (or official) does not experience work as personal expression or as meaningful social participation. The Weberian perspective emphasizes the first loss; the web of rules becomes an "iron cage" that restrains the exercise of will. The Marxist perspective emphasizes the second; the rules obscure the social meaning of the worker's activity. They blind him to the ways in which the particular acts she and his fellows engage in contribute to the larger social ordering. The functions of social ordering take place "behind the backs" of the workers, so that they seem to operate independently of human action. Such a process of coordination resembles the "invisible hand" that earlier political economists had described in benign terms. Later theorists saw its overwhelming psychological costs.

One consequence is isolation. By subordinating individuals directly to the norms and rigidly specifying their conduct, the regime of impersonal rule eliminates the need and opportunities for collaboration. Another cost is ineffectuality. The new system induces a stultifyingly passive, "contemplative" posture toward the larger patterns of social life. It denies to the worker the Promethean satisfaction of leaving some lasting impression of himself on the world; the new worker has no opportunity for creativity. The craftsman had the experience of directly producing some useful product. The worker of the industrial era has only the most limited sense of how her regimented, specialized activity contributes to some final product, and little sense perhaps even of the usefulness of the final product.

Finally and most importantly for our purposes, there is the loss of moral agency. The new worker lacks the autonomy or the understanding—or both—required for ethical responsibility. Whatever moral understanding the worker has must be subordinated to the unbending commands of the rules. And perhaps most distressingly, the worker may not develop moral understanding because she lacks motivation or ability to understand how her conduct relates to larger goods and evils.

This loss of moral agency is the most salient quality in literary portrayals of lawyers. One memorable symbol of it is the habit of Jaggers in *Great Expectations* of constantly washing his hands, so that one of the first things we notice about him is the smell of scented soap. It is easy to see why the lawyer is such a fascinating figure in considerations of the moral dimension of alienation. On the one hand, the lawyer seems distinctively powerful in a system of impersonal rules; rule mastery is his specialty. On the other hand, he is at the same time distinctively vehement in disclaiming responsibility for the consequences of his actions. This disparity between power and responsibility drives Mr. Gridley in *Bleak House* into a frenzied harangue that concludes,

> I mustn't go to Mr. Tulkinghorn, the solicitor in Lincoln's Inn Fields, and say to him when he makes me furious by being so cool and satisfied—as they all do, for I know they gain by it while I lose, don't I—I mustn't say to him, "I will have something out of some one for my ruin, by fair means or foul." *He* is not responsible. It's the system. But, if I do no violence to any of them, here—I may! I don't know what will happen if I am carried beyond myself at last. I will

accuse the individual workers of that system against me, face to face, before the great eternal bar![4]

Another dimension of the loss of agency is the lawyer's insensitivity to the underlying moral stakes of his work. Dostoyevsky's lawyers, who are usually government officials, exercise considerably more agency than Dickens's, but they are blind to the values implicit in the rules they enforce. Dmitri Karamazov and Raskolnikov each has exactly the same complaint about the magistrate who interrogates him: he will not go to the heart of the matter. Both magistrates are preoccupied with procedural formalities or circumstantial evidentiary matters and seem indifferent to the protagonists' first-person testimony about the core issues.[5] Dickens portrayed this tendency comically in his portrait of the bureaucrats of the Circumlocution Office in *Little Dorritt*.

Perhaps the most powerful portrayal of moral alienation under regime of categorical rule is Kafka's *The Trial*, especially in the Parable of the Doorkeeper, which Joseph K. hears in the cathedral. This occurs toward the conclusion of his nightmarish experiences while trying to clear his name of the unspecified charges that have triggered an official proceeding against him. Although we sometimes think of the novel as a portrayal of totalitarianism or bureaucracy, it is quite explicitly an account of life under a certain type of law. Kafka tells us at the beginning that "K. lived in a society with a legal constitution, there was universal peace, all laws were in force."[6]

When the warders come to arrest K., they tell him they don't know why they are required to do this but suggest that their boss, the inspector, whom they portray as a formidable person, will explain things. But the inspector turns out to be as ignorant as they. This sequence, in which people we expect to be powerful and intimidating turn out to be confused and silly, recurs. The sense of menace that we start to associate with individual characters recedes repeatedly into a social background that no one seems to have any control over.

In the book people constantly refer to the governing rules either as "law," "duty," or "authority," the latter typically defining the boundaries of official roles. We are repeatedly told that people exceed their authority or that they try to circumvent the rules by using personal influence to get favors. But the author and the characters also often explain behavior as complying with the rules, and this behavior is invariably meaningless to both K. and the actors themselves, except as a requirement of a rule. The recurring discovery that the behavior is as meaningless to the actors as to K. intensifies the sense of shallowness and silliness of the characters and the sense of menace of the social background.

These themes are crystallized in the "Doorkeeper" chapter. K. hears the Parable from a priest whom he encounters in the cathedral. K. has gone to the cathedral for the purpose of showing it to a client of the bank, but the client never arrives. He notices a priest mounting the pulpit and, deeming it "absurd" for the priest to preach a sermon to an all but empty church, wonders "if it were the priest's duty to preach at a certain hour regardless of circumstances."[7] It turns out, however, that the priest's appearance has a point; he has come to talk to K. to offer him a parable that will illuminate his experience with the Law.

In crude summary, the Parable of the Doorkeeper tells the story of a man seeking "the Law" who arrives at an open door apparently leading to "the Law" and finds it guarded by the Doorkeeper, who tells him that he cannot admit the man "at the moment." We soon learn that the Doorkeeper is the lowliest of a series of many guards before many doors that must be opened before reaching the Law. The man waits before the initial door for years, cajoling, importuning, and trying to bribe the Doorkeeper, to no avail. Eventually the man grows sick and weak, and, on the verge of death, he puts a final question to the Doorkeeper: why during all these years has no one else come here seeking admittance to the Law? The Doorkeeper replies, "No one but you could have gained admittance through this door, since this door was intended for you. I am now going to shut it."[8]

There follows a parody of legal and religious textual exegesis in which K. and the priest discuss the meaning of the Parable. The discussion focuses on the character of the Doorkeeper. K. begins by condemning him for contributing to an injustice. But the priest replies that it is possible the Doorkeeper was simply following the rules, or as he puts it, "doing his duty." Perhaps, he implies, the man could only be admitted at a particular time. Perhaps when the time came, he failed to take the required actions to perfect his rights to enter. This may have been because the man was unaware of the requirements, but it may not have been the Doorkeeper's duty to inform him.

The priest than suggests different ways of appraising the Door-keeper's performance. One, which might be called Romantic/We-berian, suggests that the Doorkeeper sympathized with the man and his quest for the Law but was constrained by the rules from doing more than he did to help him. Another, which might be called Roman-tic/Marxist, suggests that the Doorkeeper had no understanding of his circumstances, that he was in fact "more deluded" than the man. He is, after all, the lowliest of the many Doorkeepers. It is unlikely he himself has seen the Law. While the man can at least see the light shining out the door, the Doorkeeper has his back to it. Moreover, the priest reminds Joseph K. that whatever we may think of his service to the man after his arrival, "for many years, for as long as it takes a man to grow to the prime of life, his service was an empty formality, since he had to wait for the man to come."

Toward the end of the discussion, the priest advances a new inter-pretation that sees the Doorkeeper as not at all "deluded," but rather exalted by virtue of his attachment to the "Law": "It is the Law that has placed him at his post; to doubt his dignity is to doubt the Law itself." The discussion then concludes: "'I don't agree with that point of view,' said K. shaking his head, 'for if one accepts it, one must accept as true everything the Doorkeeper says. But you yourself have sufficiently proved how impossible it is to do that.' 'No,' said the priest, 'it is not necessary to accept everything as true, one must only accept it as necessary.' 'A melancholy conclusion,' said K. 'It turns lying into a universal principle.'"

This seems to satirize Positivism, but perhaps also, more generally, all arguments asserting that alienating (or unjust) conduct in the here-and-now is necessary to effect some more remote, abstract end (order, efficiency, justice) in the long run. We might generalize the priest's remark that it is not necessary to accept everything as true to suggest that the immediate values of truth and justice must yield to the more abstract imperatives of order. And we might interpret K.'s re-sponse that the priest's appeal to necessity requires embracing dishon-esty (which on a literal reading is a nonsequitur, since the priest has just disclaimed belief in truth) as a claim that the necessitarian justifica-tions for the Doorkeeper's conduct are either unconvincing or in-sufficient to alleviate the sense of strangeness and terror the novel associates with governance by categorical rule.

The Trial is usually discussed from the point of view of the oppressed citizen represented by Joseph K. However, most of the characters in the novel are identified and described in terms of their work as insiders of various kinds in the system (and part of the novel portrays K. himself as a worker in a bank). More often than not, we see them as grotesque and pathetic. This impression is in part due to the opacity of their practices, their disconnection from larger social purposes, which the novel links in turn to the categorical nature of the norms that govern them.

This indictment of role is different from complaints about the specialization and conformity roles require. Some critics object that roles narrow the range of capacities an individual can express and develop and presuppose a large measure of acceptance of the surrounding society. But the version of the alienation critique that invokes the artisanal ideal does not press such objections; it accepts both the finitude of human potential and the claims of social acquiescence, both saliently embodied in the artisanal role. Its complaint focuses instead on the individual's experience of alienation from the very values that undergird her own role. And this experience arises from the denial to the worker of the discretion to shape her work in accordance with these values.

The Trial evokes this alienation when, for example, it imagines the priest as obliged to preach a sermon even if the cathedral is empty or the Doorkeeper obliged to guard the door even if no one is likely to come. It evokes it most stunningly in the Doorkeeper's next-to-last words—"This door was intended for you." The effect of this declaration is to make the Doorkeeper's practices, which already seem grotesque, appear even more so by suggesting that they are inconsistent with their very purposes.

It is worth contrasting this critique with the more familiar critique of role morality in works such as Herman Melville's *Billy Budd* and Jean Anouilh's *Antigone*. Each of these works involves a character—Captain Vere, Creon—who occupies a political role that commits him to the defense of order. Each depicts a situation in which order appears to require the sacrifice of a morally admirable person—Billy Budd, Antigone—for actions that are justifiable or at least excusable but that, if left unpunished, will incite disorder.

Each work begins with a sympathetic portrayal of the subversive hero and his or her crime. Each then shifts perspective to that of the political officeholder. After that they proceed to surprise and discomfort us by inducing at least provisional sympathy with Captain Vere and Creon. Each man does an apparently necessary job, and the authors, with great artistry, make us sense how, from within the perspective of their roles, the sacrifice of Billy Budd and Antigone seems necessary.

Then a second shift of perspective occurs. We pull back from the identification with the political role and begin to doubt its necessity and moral attractiveness. The doubt applies less to the assumption that the sacrifice of the innocent hero is necessary to the preservation of the political order than to the belief that the preservation of the political order is worthwhile. Neither work resolves these doubts explicitly. Anouilh's play, which was written and first performed during the Nazi occupation of Paris, is usually interpreted to suggest that preoccupation with the internal morality of role can blind us to the evil of the larger structure that the role serves. Creon thus exemplifies Hannah Arendt's "banality of evil."

Melville's work is more ambiguous. It flirts with—and never rejects—acceptance of both Vere's understanding of the demands of his role and the necessity of the larger order it serves. From this perspective, there is a tragic dignity to Vere's (and Creon's) position. All political decisions involve moral costs; thus one who assumes political responsibility must be willing to sacrifice some of the innocent for the sake of order. The job is psychologically difficult, but we should be sympathetic and grateful to those who can do it effectively.

Notice that both the "banality of evil" and the "tragic choice" interpretations are quite different from the alienation critique exemplified by the Parable of the Doorkeeper. *Billy Budd* and *Antigone* assume a decisionmaker who acts in harmony with the logic of his role and decisions that directly incarnate the role's fundamental purpose. To put it somewhat differently: in both cases, if the legislator who enacted the rules under which the official operates were himself making the decision, he would have done exactly what Captain Vere or Creon did. In both cases the reservations about the decision arise from values outside the role, and the question we are pressed to consider is whether the system the role helps constitute is legitimate.

But the Doorkeeper story and the Marxian and Weberian critiques of alienation present a different image. While Vere and Creon have intuitive access to the norms that govern their roles, the Doorkeeper cannot see the Law. His stunning final line emphasizes that he has not acted in harmony with any role logic. Either the purposes of the role escape his understanding, or he is not trusted to implement them directly. The surprise and irony of the last line arises from the suggestion that, if the legislator were there to make the decision directly, he would decide differently. There is no hint of dignity, nor even of banality in the Doorkeeper. The Doorkeeper is, on any of the interpretations Kafka evokes, simply grotesque. Kafka has wrought an image of the distinctive degradation associated, not with role in general, but with role defined by categorical norms, and he suggests that this degradation is an exceptionally corrosive one.

Of course, I don't suggest that the Dominant View is refuted simply because Kafka rejected it. (There may be novels that portray conformity to categorically defined role as fulfilling, though I can't think of any great ones.)[9] But if correct, my interpretation usefully links one of the most resonant and compelling portrayals of contemporary alienation with an important premise of the Dominant View. In this manner it offers a clue to what might lie behind the vaguer expressions of alienation in recent anguished literature on lawyering, and it makes available a vivid image to support the intuition that there is something stultifying about the role prescribed by the Dominant View.

The Professional Solution

One response to the alienation critique was to deny the need for meaningful work. Sinclair Lewis produced a memorable image of this approach in Dr. Roscoe Geake, a character in *Arrowsmith* who finds his calling on leaving a medical professorship for the presidency of the New Idea Medical Instrument and Furniture Company. His farewell advice to his students emphasizes the importance of attractive office furniture on the doctor's ability to inspire the confidence necessary for "putting over and collecting an adequate fee." He concludes, "For don't forget, gentlemen, and this is my last message to you, the man worthwhile . . . instead of day-dreaming and spending all his time talking about 'ethics,' splendid though they are, and 'charity,' glorious virtue though that be, yet he never forgets that unfortunately the world judges a man by the amount of good hard cash he can lay away."[10]

Another approach was to make a virtue of what the Marxists disparaged as the disengaged, "contemplative" aspect of alienated work. No parody could develop this position to a greater extreme than Oliver Wendell Holmes did on two occasions when he spoke to law students. He conceded the stultifying character of law practice, asking, "How can the laborious study of a dry and technical system, the greedy watch for clients and practice of shopkeepers' arts, the mannerless conflicts over often sordid interests, make out a life?" His recommendation was that they cultivate the "secret isolated joy of the thinker" by burying themselves (presumably in their spare time) in study of the "remoter and more general aspects of the law." "The law is the calling of thinkers," he continued. Though practice mires them in particularity, leisure time study permits them to express their disposition to "make plainer the way from something to the whole of things."[11]

Others, however, produced more ambitious responses to the alienation critique. They conceded the horrors of alienated work engendered by the market and the bureaucracy. Yet they suggested that the conditions of modern society permitted, indeed required, a different form of productive organization more hospitable to meaningful work. This was the profession. The designers and theorists of the modern profession, often in self-conscious reaction to the alienation theorists, suggested that professionalism might produce the sort of work that could be experienced as both self-expression and compliance with social norms. They argued that professionalism could and should be institutionalized in ways that differed from paradigmatic markets and bureaucracies, especially in their repudiation of governance by categorical rule.

One of the earliest expressions of this view, and still one of the most powerful, is George Eliot's *Middlemarch,* published in 1871 and 1872. *Middlemarch* has been aptly called a "novel of vocation," as most of its many characters are portrayed in relation to their work. The gallery also includes a few characters who seek nothing from work but material self advancement, notably the grocer Mawmsey, who replies to a candidate's suggestion that he exercise his newly won vote in a "public spirit,": "When I give a vote . . . I must look to what will be the effects on my till and ledger."[12] As Lewis did with Dr. Geake, Eliot portrays Mawmsey as shallow and foolish.

However, she reserves her most intense scorn for those who follow Holmes's advice and seek the isolated glory of contemplative abstraction. There is, for example, the preacher, Mr. Tyke, who is preoccupied with doctrinal niceties and indifferent to the concrete problems of the parishioners; he is compared unfavorably to Mr. Farebrother, "a parson among parishioners whose lives he has to try to make better."[13] And above all, there is the grotesque Casaubon who, at the expense of everyone around him, has devoted his life to researching a monumental study synthesizing all mythological thought—a work Eliot portrays as arid and vacuous, a project of vanity and self-delusion.

Eliot shows sympathy for two different vocational paths. One is that of Caleb Garth, the only happy male character in the book. Garth is a self-employed builder and part-time manager who has the skills and values of the artisan. "[B]y business, Caleb never meant money transactions, but the skillful application of labor."[14] Work for him is a source of pride and fellowship. But the novel entertains diffidently the prediction made so vehemently by Marx that the opportunities for the artisanal career are shrinking. Larger-scale and more impersonal forms of economic organization, represented in the novel by the coming railroad and the banker Bulstrode, appear as potential threats to the skills and autonomy of the craft worker.

The vocational aspiration that most fascinates Eliot is that of Dr. Lydgate, who wants to apply new scientific developments in medicine to the care of patients. From the point of view of the novel's sociological themes, Lydgate is an exciting figure because he is simultaneously at the vanguard of modernizing social developments and yet, like Garth and Farebrother, committed to personal service to concrete individuals. Again and again Eliot emphasizes the distinctive combination of the general and abstract on the one hand, and the particular and personal on the other, in Lydgate's vocation.

> [H]e carried to his studies . . . the conviction that the medical profession as it might be was the finest in the world; presenting the most perfect interchange between science and art; offering the most direct alliance between intellectual conquest and social good. Lydgate's nature demanded this combination; he was an emotional creature, with a flesh-and-blood sense of fellowship which withstood all abstractions of special study. He cared not only for 'cases,' but for John and Elizabeth . . .[15]

Lydgate's youthful efforts depicted in the novel are tragically unsuccessful, and the book is ambiguous about the moral quality of his success after he moves to London. Yet the doctor seems to represent some of the author's deepest aspirations.

In the years since *Middlemarch* appeared, these aspirations have been expressed over and over by prominent professionals and academics out to refute the alienation theorists. In America they were at the core of the views of the Progressive movement in politics and the Functionalist movement in academic sociology. Perhaps their best known proponents were the Progressive lawyer Louis Brandeis and the Functionalist sociologist Talcott Parsons. In strikingly convergent terms, Brandeis and Parsons (and following them, myriad allies and disciples) elaborated a view of modernization that put professions at the center.[16] In crude summary, the theory was this. Marx and Weber had based their visions of inexorable marketization and bureaucratization on industrial production and military and welfare state organizations. The premise of governance under categorical rule may have been plausible in these instances because such organizations tend to produce standardized products and routinized services. (Later writers would severely question this concession.) But a central and growing sector of modern economies is concerned with the provision of services that are at once technical and particular. These are the professions, as typified by law, medicine, and engineering; soon to be augmented by a host of newer service groups such as nursing and social work; and augmented further—so both Brandeis and Parsons argued—by the transformation of business management into a professional activity. Because such services depend on technical knowledge and resist standardization, they are not readily compatible with market or bureaucratic organization. The market is not viable because consumers lack the expertise to evaluate the quality of such services. Bureaucracy fails because professional performance cannot be specified categorically.

So this type of work has to be organized differently. At the level of practice, workers have to be given autonomy and responsibility. At the level of occupational regulation, collective self-governance is needed. The system can function in the absence of the material incentives of the market and the bureaucracy because professional work organized in this manner provides its practitioners with satisfactions that motivate responsibility. These are precisely the psychological satisfactions that the alienation theorists had despaired of achieving in the emerging social order.

Told in this manner, the story explained professionalism as a solution to a technical problem of organizing a certain kind of work. But while they didn't put the moral point in the forefront, the advocates of the Progressive-Functionalist view at least implicitly shared Eliot's aspiration that professionalism would be the answer to the problem of meaningful work. Although they often spoke of this feature of professionalism as a by-product of a technological development, they exulted in it. Here, for example, is historian Robert Wiebe again on turn-of-the-century America:

> As this society [of small towns and urban neighborhoods] crumbled, the specialized needs of an urban-industrial system came as a godsend to a middle stratum in the cities. Identification by way of their skills gave them the deference of their neighbors while opening natural avenues into the nation at large. Increasingly formal entry requirements into their occupations protected their prestige through exclusiveness. The shared mysteries of a specialty allowed intimate communion even at long range, as letters among the scattered champions of public health demonstrated. Finally, the ability to see how their talents meshed with others in a national scheme encouraged them to look outward confidently instead of furtively.[17]

Here are precisely the elements of meaningful work. "Identification by way of skills" and "shared mysteries" provide a basis for cooperative relationships that overcome isolation. "Specialized needs" requiring individualized service means that the practitioner will have a sense of control over her work and of creativity in adapting her general knowledge to the particular circumstances of the client. And the ability to place one's skills in a transparent "national scheme" means that the practitioner will have a sense of how her acts relate to larger social purposes.

The professional's moral agency is secured at two levels. On the level of the profession as a whole, the members participate in defining the broader social needs it serves and the occupational norms that implement these needs. On the level of individual practice, the essence of the professional's work is the adaption of these general norms to the particular circumstances of the client. To be sure, these arrangements would vindicate the ideal of meaningful work only to the extent the professionals' own values converged with broader social norms. The Progressives and Functionalists were confident that this would happen, in part because they found professional norms, as they were actually evolving, both appealing and well adapted to the surrounding institutions of modern society. But they supplemented this belief with further ideas.

One such notion, amply illustrated in *Middlemarch,* was that criticism and "reform" were integral elements of professional work. Professional work is a continuous process of self-reconstitution, and this creates legitimate and productive roles for dissidence, such as Lydgate's. In addition, members of a profession might undergo a "secondary socialization" through processes of professional initiation, such as prolonged schooling or apprenticeship, during which they would be induced unconsciously to accept the governing norms as if they were their own. This notion sits less comfortably with the ideal of meaningful work, but it was occasionally useful in explaining how the professional project might be viable in a society characterized by extensive normative conflict.

American lawyers pursued the Progressive-Functionalist project in two broad respects. First, they developed an institutional model of self-governance. The model provides for collective control by incumbent practitioners over the admission of newcomers and over a disciplinary process that enforces norms of good practice. The norms are primarily concerned with the adequacy of service to clients, and secondarily with fairness to third parties. For many years lawyers also attempted to structure the market for legal services to give themselves some insulation from competitive pressures by inhibiting price cutting, advertising, and solicitation. (This effort would have been of interest to Eliot, who doubted that the professional project was compatible with the funding of services through the market. Lydgate comes to grief in part because of such competitive pressures.)

The project of self-regulation has suffered substantial setbacks in recent years. The effort at market control has been largely abandoned. The admissions process has been streamlined and loosened. Although disciplinary activity has increased, its relative importance has declined with the growth of extra-professional lawyer regulation through the malpractice system, court and legislature-imposed litigation rules, and the activity of specialized agencies such as the Securities and Exchange

Commmission and the Office of Thrift Supervision. My own view is that the relative decline of these particular self-regulatory institutions is desirable and does not threaten the important aspects of the professional project. I return to the institutional aspects of the professional project in Chapter 8.

The second and more important expression of the Progressive-Functionalist vision was the elaboration of a conception of legal judgment that explained how legal work could be both abstract and particular, self-expressive and socially controlled, and creative yet grounded in established norms. This effort, which embraces the work of Roscoe Pound and Benjamin Cardozo early in the century, of Karl Llewellyn and Henry Hart later on, and Ronald Dworkin most recently, constitutes the major preoccupation and enduring achievement of American academic lawyers.

This is not the place to try to do justice to the richness and variety of this work. For present purposes it is enough to say that a crude but accurate summary of all of it would be this: Abstraction and particularity, self-expression and social control, and creativity yet groundedness are all qualities of good contextual judgment, and contextual judgment is the defining activity of legal work in America. Contextual standards are general norms that depend on, and are typically derived from, the circumstances of particular applications. Since new and unique cases constantly arise, the answers involve creativity; yet when they are plausible, they seem to have been implicit in the pre-existing norms. To the extent that the lawyer shares the relevant public norms, she expresses her own values as she vindicates the public ones.

This jurisprudence is commonly understood to be concerned with legitimating the role of the activist judiciary in a democratic society. That is surely a prominent preoccupation. But another important concern is to demonstrate the possibility that law could manifest the virtues of meaningful work. Indeed, whatever the intentions of their authors, the classics of American jurisprudence represent the most extended illustration in all social theory of the ideal of meaningful work.

The Lost Lawyer

We now have to deal with the question of the "lost lawyer," not in Anthony Kronman's sense of the *disoriented* lawyer, but in the sense of the *missing* lawyer, the lawyer who appears so little in American theorizing about law, including Kronman's.

For it is a striking fact about this literature that the legal work it explicates so exultantly is for the most part identified with the judge. Most of the literature has been produced by academics with tenuous connections to practice and whose interests and ambitions focus on judging. When these theorists have left the academy, they have usually done so to become judges. Kronman's preoccupation with the "lawyer statesman" who occupies positions in the executive branch reminds us that the theorists' preoccupations have occasionally ranged more broadly, but this ideal is equally indifferent to the world of private practice, where the vast majority of American lawyers have always worked.

I have been arguing that the ideas developed in the mainstream of American legal theory imply a powerful criticism of the Dominant View of legal ethics and an alternative vision based on contextual judgment and the ideal of meaningful work. Yet it is a striking fact that most of the theorists did not themselves draw these implications explicitly or indeed confront the ethical issues of lawyering more than marginally.

There is, of course, an outstanding exception. Louis Brandeis is the one great American legal theorist of the century to have made a major mark in practice.[18] Although you would never know it from contemporary legal scholarship, which remains obsessed with the comparatively ineffectual Holmes, Brandeis is probably the century's most influential legal thinker. His early piece with Samuel Warren on the then emerging "right to privacy" was a classic demonstration and defense of judicial creativity in the common law. His work on banking, utility regulation, and labor gave institutional concreteness to the ideas of the Progressive movement. His defense of social legislation against constitutional challenges in court, which produced the famous "Brandeis brief," pioneered the use of statistics and data in legal argument. His opinions on the Supreme Court laid the intellectual foundations for the Legal Process school that produced the preeminent expression of liberal jurisprudence in the postwar era. And he was the foremost prewar exponent of the idea of professionalism as meaningful work.

In 1905 Brandeis spoke to a group of Harvard undergraduates. "[Y]ou wish to know," he said, "whether the legal profession would afford you special opportunities for usefulness to your fellow-men."[19] Nineteen years earlier, Holmes, speaking to another group of Harvard undergraduates, had speculated that his audience was asking a slightly different question, "[W]hat have you said to show that I can reach my spiritual possibilities through a door such as this [that is, the life of the lawyer]?"[20] The beginning of Brandeis's answer was almost identical to Holmes's: the key feature of legal work, each man suggested, is the constant cross-referencing of the general and particular. But from this point, they took different directions. As we saw, Holmes viewed the mundane particularities of practice as raw material for solitary, contemplative theorizing. For Brandeis redemption lay in the fact that the lawyer's efforts, however general, "always have reference to some practical end."[21]

In the three decades before he became a judge, Brandeis was a practicing lawyer. He took many high-profile government assignments. He largely crafted the modern idea of the public interest lawyer who represents nongovernmental clients, pursuing reforms in accordance with his conceptions of the public interest. And he was a highly successful private business lawyer. Brandeis wrote little about his private practice, and we lack detailed information about all but a few of his cases, but we do know that in word and deed he repudiated features of what he considered common features of the practice style of his day.[22]

First, Brandeis insisted that the aggressive lawyering of the Dominant View could not promote justice in situations where all interests were not evenly represented, and he saw many such situations. His main response to this problem was government and public interest work designed to level the playing field by providing representation to underorganized interests and to curb the power of big business. He supported and helped form various regulatory agencies labor unions and consumer groups. As the paradigmatic public interest lawyer, he undertook to speak before legislatures, agencies, and courts on behalf of dispersed and more or less unorganized citizens. He also argued for the idea that counsel for powerful organizations had a duty to use their influence to discourage their clients from unjust or antisocial projects, and he practiced what he preached.[23]

Second, in situations involving parties of roughly equal power, Brandeis urged lawyers to try to steer people away from wasteful squabbling and to craft new frameworks of mutually beneficial collaboration. This required lawyers to go beyond the law and understand the client's practical circumstances. It required a willingness to consider sympathetically the interests of third parties with whom the client is involved. In one famous instance, Brandeis responded to a request from a shoe manufacturer, W. H. McElwain, for assistance in negotiating a wage cut with his workers by pointing out that, while McElwain's wage rates were high, the average wages of his workers were low because their employment was irregular. He insisted that the client study the possibility of reorganizing his marketing and inventory practices with a view toward regularizing output and labor demand. The effort was successful and made possible an arrangement that left both employer and employees better off.[24]

Since third parties always have potentially conflicting (as well as potentially harmonious) interests, such efforts required a willingness to subject the client to risks of nonreciprocity and betrayal. It also required the lawyer occasionally to put himself in opposition to clients or former clients. As a result, Brandeis sometimes found himself accused of disloyalty. Having represented both the United Shoe Machinery Company and its customers, the shoe manufacturers, for years, Brandeis sided with the customers against the Machinery Company and (without taking a fee) attacked arrangements he had helped craft after he decided the company was abusing them. In the "Lennox" case, Brandeis, consulted simultaneously by a troubled debtor and a major creditor, recommended an assignment of the debtor's property for the benefit of creditors, and when they assented, arranged one with his partner as trustee. When the partner found the debtor concealing assets, the firm felt obliged to press vigorously for their disgorgement, to the debtor's outrage.[25]

This approach to private practice led Brandeis to accept assignments involving vaguely defined responsibilities to people with potentially conflicting interests. Brandeis summarized his approach when he was asked whom he thought he was representing in the Lennox case when he recommended the assignment. "I should say that I was counsel to the situation," he replied.[26] This response was in radical tension with the spirit of the mainstream bar's view of representation, which holds that the lawyer should normally assume responsibility only to a single set of unitary interests, and Brandeis was accused quite plausibly of violating the bar's conflict-of-interest rules on several occasions. These charges became a major part of the case against him at the time of his nomination to the Supreme Court.[27]

To appreciate the radicalism of Brandeis's lawyering style and the reasons it was so threatening to the bar, we should pause to consider the relation between the bar's conflict-of-interest norms and the categorical norms of client loyalty on which we have focused. The conflict-of-interest norms are premised on the loyalty norms. It is because the lawyer is expected to be aggressively loyal to a client that he cannot take on responsibilities to people with differing interests. As John Frank put it, "Lawyers are not retained by situations, and the adversary system assumes they represent one interest at a time."[28]

The conflict-of-interest prohibition reflects the Positivism and the Libertarianism that underpin the loyalty norms of the Dominant vision. Brandeis's "counsel to the situation" idea assumes that there are tacit norms of fair dealing and collaboration to which the lawyer can resort to resolve competing interests among multiple clients. But the Positivist theme questions the substantiality of such norms, and the Libertarian theme suggests it would be illegitimate for the lawyer to impose them on clients. Together, these themes encourage the belief that the only convincing indication of the legitmacy of a cooperative arrangement is that it was produced by an arm's-length negotiation in which every interest was independently represented.

The instrumental arguments for the Dominant View also underpin the conflict-of-interest norms. If, as those arguments assert, adequate preparation is precluded by duties to share information with adverse parties, then joint representation of parties with adverse interests must jeopardize adequate preparation. Joint representation also creates an impossible situation from the point of view of disclosure. The parties cannot tell whether their interests are sufficiently harmonious to permit joint representation until they all make full disclosure to each other. Yet once they have done so, they will have sacrificed an important advantage of separate representation.

Brandeis would not have denied that there were costs and risks in the type of cooperation he urged. But there were also costs and risks to separate representation, for example, the costs of duplication of effort, of more circuitous communication, and of the failure to perceive opportunities for joint gains because of fragmentation of information and bias of perspective. Functionally analyzed, the conflict-of-interests rules rested on a dogmatic insistence that the risks and costs of collaboration always outweigh the risks and costs of separate representation.

Brandeis's lawyering style thus, at least implicitly, posed a basic challenge to the Dominant View. The radicalism of the challenge seems to have been perceived by the bar's leaders at the time of his Supreme Court nomination. Six former American Bar Association presidents asserted that Brandeis's departures from client loyalty and conflict-of-interest norms made him unfit for judicial office.[29] Ironically, in losing the nomination fight, the bar gained their antagonist's retirement from the field of lawyering.

Brandeis never made his challenge explicit. In the post-World War II period, however, Henry Hart and James Willard Hurst, the only two major American legal theorists of the time to take an interest in practice, made some effort to draw out the implications of Brandeis's vision. It is surely no accident that both began their careers as law clerks to Brandeis on the Supreme Court. The works of each are full of references to Brandeis, and their understanding of practice was precisely the Brandeisian vision of meaningful work. They saw the ennobling potential of the insight that legal theory had developed in the judicial context—that law application could be both creative and grounded in established norms. They argued and demonstrated that lawyers had creative power and that this power entailed a responsibility to see that it was used consistently with the social good.[30]

In situations of unequal power, such as the Negligent Railroad case discussed in Chapter 2, the Brandeisians castigated lawyers who allowed their clients to abuse their powers. They also advocated judicial and regulatory solutions to remedy the imbalance of power or impose socially desirable outcomes. In situations of relatively equal power, they championed the "counsel to the situation" approach in which the lawyer's job was to craft frameworks of fair and mutually beneficial cooperation. For example, the third problem in the famous *Legal Process* materials Hart wrote with Albert Sacks involves the drafting of a small business lease. The central problem is the appropriate allocation of the risks and benefits of the tenant's business. The tenant wants flexibility in the event his business has to struggle to get off the ground, and security of tenure in the event he is successful. The owner wants a minimum return, protection against inflation, and additional return if the busines is successful. The solution is a long-term arrangement with the rent based on a percentage of the lessee's sales, subject to a periodically increasing fixed minimum. The authors introduce us to the now-standard features of the percentage lease, emphasizing that the device was not legislated by a Positivist sovereign but was in fact created by lawyers. And they urge that the lease should be negotiated and interpreted in the light of the same interpretive premise they portray as standard in the interpretation of statutes—that the norms were "designed to operate rationally and evenhandedly."[31]

The Brandeisian vision of lawyering thus incarnates the virtues of the nostalgic conception of the artisan's role in nineteenth-century aliena-tion theory. Like the artisan, the lawyer applies general socially defined knowledge creatively to produce an individualized product. Similarly, the lawyer expresses a commitment to social norms and purposes by adhering to standards of quality in everyday practice. The fact that the lawyer's role is freighted with a more explicit and complex normative element makes it all the more promising as a vehicle for linking concrete practical activity with encompassing values—the hallmark of "meaningful work" in the tradition we discussed above.

The Brandeisian perspective has been an enduring voice in discus-sions of lawyering. It is reflected in parts of the modern ethics codes. For example, the codes acknowledge the propriety of lawyer advice that takes account of "moral" and "social" as well as strictly "legal" considerations. The conflict-of-interest restrictions have been substan-tially loosened, and the *Model Rules* explicitly legitimate the role of the "lawyer as intermediary."[32]

The Brandeisian Evasions

The Brandeisians never developed their perspective into a full-blown challenge to the Dominant View, and they never pressed their criti-cisms with the activist vigor their mentor brought to so many other causes. The more radical implications of the Brandeisian critique have been neutralized, and this has occurred along avenues that Brandeis and his disciples themselves first marked.

One was the idea that the Brandeisian perspective may be relevant to only certain realms of practice. The basic distinction Brandeis in-augurated was that between litigation and counseling. On the basis of his own experience, Brandeis (as well as Hurst and Hart) argued that counseling, by which he meant providing nonlitigation advice and devising cooperative frameworks, was the exciting and important realm of practice. Brandeisians tended to ignore litigation, and by implication to concede that the Dominant View might still be appropriate there.

Brandeis's followers did not themselves put a lot of emphasis on this distinction. It seems likely that they wrote off litigation for the same reason other legal theorists wrote off private practice altogether—they found it distasteful. More recently, many have proposed to adopt the Brandeisian view but limit it to counseling, and indeed the codes pay lip service to this idea, though for the most part they adopt it in the counseling sphere only as exhortation rather than enforceable duty.[33] Typically, the distinction between counseling and litigation is rationalized on the ground that in litigation the parties are likely to be more or less equally represented and supervised by the judge, whereas it is less likely that either safeguard will obtain in the counseling sphere.

This approach cannot survive reflection, and its vogue seems to be coming to end. In the midst of the current sense of crisis over the court system, it seems obvious that that not all the dysfunctions of litigation arise from imbalances of power. Indeed, some of the features that compel one party to engage in expensive manoeuvers solely because the other has or will—the "arms' race"—are aggravated when both parties are well financed.

Furthermore, the sectoral approach betrays the most basic tenet of modern jurisprudence: the repudiation, not of imbalances of power, but of categorical judgment. It makes room for contextual judgment, but only at the cost of introducing a new categorical distinction between litigation and counseling. Even if it were *generally* true that the ethics of the Dominant View are well suited to litigation, the sectoral approach would be objectionable for failing to give the lawyer responsibility to modify those ethics in the exceptional litigation situations for which they are not well suited. The lawyer's responsibilities are critically determined by a classic binary, all-or-nothing decision that guarantees that her conduct will sometimes be inappropriate.

The depths of pettifogging mindlessness to which the approach can lead were illustrated by the efforts of Geoffrey Hazard, a drafter of the *Model Rules,* to defend the Kaye Scholer lawyers in the aftermath of the Lincoln Savings & Loan collapse. Hazard argued that the lawyers were subject to a lower standard of responsibility to the public because they were acting as litigators ("litigation counsel") than they would have been if they were acting as counselors ("regulatory counsel"). Recalling that the lawyers were advising and assisting Lincoln in complying with Bank Board requests for auditing information, one might ask what this has to do with litigation. Hazard's implicit response was that since the government had begun to suspect Lincoln of illegal conduct, it was likely to initiate litigation in the future![34]

Indeed, since the government's suspicions were correct, litigation was more or less certain. Under Hazard's argument, the more clearly lawless the client's conduct is, the stronger the case for a lower standard of attorney client responsibility.[35] Fortunately for the dignity of the bar, the argument was not widely accepted. Its absurd implications are merely symptoms of a fundamental defect: it allows an important ethical decision to turn on a consideration distant from the real normative stakes of the situation.

The second idea in which the subversive implications of the Brandeisian view were contained was that public regulation might eventually moot issues of professional responsibility. Hurst and Hart argued that when business lawyers failed to curb their clients abuses, government typically responded with regulatory constraints. Of course, the more likely this response, the more the argument for responsibility shaded into the argument for long-run self-interest. The ultimate implication of this line of thought was made clear by Adolph Berle's prediction that the regulatory state would ultimately liberate "the bulk of the corporate bar from the profitable but mostly undistinguished bondage in which most of it lives" because "The moment [principles of social responsibility] are infringed, the state predictably intervenes. In that case an explicit rule of law presently results. Great and powerful interests cannot afford to risk being caught in a major infringement even though the rule has not become explicit."[36] If there was one thing the Brandeisians believed in more than professional responsibility, it was the benign capacities of the regulatory state. This latter commitment tended to dull the edge of the former. If the regulatory state did its job well, then legal ethics was more a matter of prudence than of responsibility.

But hardly anyone today shares this degree of faith in the state. In retrospect, we can clearly see defects in the premise—both spectacularly illustrated by the Savings & Loan debacle. In the first place, the chastening power of anticipated intervention works only if the client has a sufficiently long-term perspective. For someone inclined to "go for broke" and pursue small chances of short-term wealth, or someone who faces near-certain failure if she plays by the rules in the short term, it is ineffectual. These were precisely the circumstances of the Savings & Loan miscreants.

Moreover, regulation is no less dependent on the responsible conduct of officials than is private ordering on the responsible conduct of lawyers. If lawyers resist or betray responsibility, why should public officials do better? The carnival of official ineptitude, cowardice, and corruption in the Savings and Loan scandal is a monument to the proposition that effective state intervention does not necessarily follow "the moment" corporate irresponsibility threatens the public interest.

I speculate that the practical developments that have made the two Brandeisian evasions untenable account for the bar's current malaise far more than the theoretical challenges to legal reasoning that Anthony Kronman blames. The sense of crisis surrounding the litigation system and the bar's profitable association with mammoth financial scandals, exacerbated by inadequacies of various regulatory systems, make clear that that issues of responsibility are not moot in any area of practice. There is still a role for professional responsibility for any lawyer who would accept it. And while that role is responsive to the deepest aspirations of many lawyers, it is also a frightening one, and the bar's institutions provide little support for it.[37]

Self-Betrayal

The frightening aspect of the meaningful-work ideal is as important as the hopeful one. For the striking fact about the history of legal professionalism is that lawyers' betrayal of the ideal has been has consistent as their espousal of it. The notion of professional redemption belongs to a class of values that includes Christian love, Freudian mature sexuality, and Marxian self-actualization that people are portrayed as naturally both striving for and turning away from.

Although this dialectic of affirmation and denial seems puzzling, there are familiar explanations for it. Sometimes people, through weakness or short-sightedness, overvalue the immediate short-term satisfactions such as material wealth or social harmony over more important but less readily accessible goals. Sometimes it seems that habituation to their fallen state has made people cynical about the possibility of something better or has induced a kind of addiction to the trivial but familiar comforts of the status quo. Sometimes people lack the courage to accept the dangers of failure that attend efforts to achieve their most exalted goals.

Of course, one might also attribute the rejection of the ideal to a person's calculation that the costs of striving for it are likely to exceed the benefits. However, such a view has rarely been asserted, at least publicly, within the legal profession. The more common response has been to defend the profession's detours with the arguments of the Dominant View that we have been examining. In the Christian, Freudian, and Marxist traditions, it is common to see the evasions, misrepresentations, and nonsequiturs of such arguments as a kind of support for the ideals they deny or qualify. The more implausible the arguments, the more strongly they signal bad faith, and the greater the homage the seem to pay to the ideal. For our purposes, it is sufficient to insist that one cannot take lawyers' consistent subversion of the professional ideal as a considered rejection of it. The record shows ambivalence, not rejection.

Conclusion

The ideal of meaningful work articulated in Progressive-Functionalist social theory and implicit in many literary treatments of professionalism lends support to the critique of the Dominant View and offers a clue to the underpinnings of the pervasive but vague expressions of moral anxiety within the profession.

The aspirations of many lawyers have resonated with the "meaningful work" ideal that suggests personal fulfillment depends on the experience of work as the vindication of general norms in particular contexts, of simultaneous social commitment and self-expression, and of groundedness conjoined with creativity. At times legal professionalism has promised to provide this experience. The key responses to this ideal have been participatory self-regulation and contextual judgment. Brandeis and his disciples articulated the promise of professional work organized around contextual judgment more ambitiously than anyone else.

But the proponents of "meaningful work" have tended to shy away from direct engagement with the Dominant View. The Brandeisians apparently hoped that social trends outside the profession would obviate the need to do so by pushing the profession in directions that would vindicate the ideal. They were wrong, however. The ideal of "meaningful work" is not a historical inevitability. It is at best a political possibility.

6

Legal Ethics as Contextual Judgment

Lawyers should take those actions that, considering the relevant circumstances of the particular case, seem likely to promote justice. This is the maxim that the Contextual View proposes to resolve the core issues of lawyers' ethics—those in which the interests of clients conflict with those of third parties or the public.

"Justice" here connotes the basic values of the legal system and subsumes many layers of more concrete norms. Decisions about justice are not assertions of personal preferences, nor are they applications of ordinary morality. They are legal judgments grounded in the methods and sources of authority of the professional culture. I use "justice" interchangeably with "legal merit." The latter has the advantage of reminding us that we are concerned with the materials of conventional legal analysis; the former has the advantage of reminding us that these materials include many vaguely specified aspirational norms.

Responsibility to justice is not incompatible with deference to the general pronouncements or enactments of authoritative institutions such as legislatures and courts. On the contrary, justice often, perhaps usually, requires such deference. Nor does such responsibility preclude deference to the adjudicatory process in the resolution of contested cases. Again, justice more often than not requires such deference. Responsibility to justice is also consistent with vigorous advocacy on behalf of client goals in a broad range of circumstances. The idea of justice invokes the lawyer's simultaneous commitments to partisan advocacy and service as an "officer of the court" to both sympathetic identification with clients and detachment from them.

A preliminary answer to the question of how the lawyer should decide questions of justice is that she should think about them as she would if she were a judge. The answer has the advantage of invoking the one sector of the legal culture in which contextual judgments about legal merit and justice are routinely viewed as possible and appropriate. But the answer needs to be qualified to emphasize that thinking like a judge does not necessarily mean reaching the same decisions that one would make as a judge. The reference is to a style of judgment, not to a particular set of decisions or substantive responsibilities. Justice is often served by a differentiation of function in which occupants of different roles assume responsibilities for different aspects of a situation.

The Structure of Legal Ethics Problems

It will be helpful to illustrate the Contextual View by considering ethical issues in terms of certain recurring tensions: Substance versus Procedure, Purpose versus Form, and Broad versus Narrow Framing. Most legal ethics problems involve all three, but usually one seems especially salient and troubling.

Substance versus Procedure

The substance-versus-procedure tension arises from the lawyer's sense, on the one hand, of the limitations of her judgment regarding the substantive merit of a matter and, on the other hand, of the limitations of the established procedures for determining the matter. We could tell the lawyer to look only to substance; we might then say that she should work to advance only the claims and goals she determined ought to prevail. The most important objection to this approach is not that the lawyer's decisions about the substantive merits would be controversial—the decisions of judges, juries, and executive officials might be controversial as well. The main objection is that judges, juries, and executive officials acting within the relevant public procedures are generally able to make more reliable determinations of the merits than are individual lawyers.

But the relative capacities of the people in these other roles depend on how the lawyer performs in her role. Moreover, even though the other actors may *generally* be better positioned than the lawyer to assess the merits, there may be important occasions when they are not. Perhaps an adverse party or official lacks information or resources needed to initiate, pursue, or determine a claim. Or perhaps an official is corrupt, or politically intimidated, or incompetent. Or perhaps the relevant procedures are ill designed to resolve the matter; maybe it is impossible to get jurisdiction over a necessary party or to decide the matter in a sufficiently short time to protect some urgent interest, or to find property against which to enforce a judgment.

The basic response of the Contextual View to the substance-procedure tension is this: the more reliable the relevant procedures and institutions, the less direct responsibility the lawyer need assume for the substantive justice of the resolution; the less reliable the procedures and institutions, the more direct responsibility she needs to assume for substantive justice.

This means, to begin with, that the lawyer needs to develop a set of practices that tend, in the settings in which she works, to contribute to just resolutions. These practices will usually be those recommended by the Public Interest View—ones that facilitate the presentation of relevant information and forego deception and manipulation. The most distinctive feature of the Contextual View is that the lawyer should treat her commitment to these practices as a set of weak presumptions. Once the lawyer formulates her general style of lawyering, she must remain alert to indications that some premise underlying her judgment that a practice it includes is a good one does not apply in the particular case, and when she finds such an indication, revise the practice accordingly.

The lawyer should respond to procedural defects by trying the mitigate them. By directing the lawyer to attempt first to improve the procedure, the Contextual approach respects the traditional premise that the strongest assurance of a just resolution is the soundness of the procedure that produced it. But to the extent that the lawyer cannot neutralize defects in the relevant procedure, she should assume direct responsibility for the substantive validity of the decision. She should form her own judgment about the proper substantive resolution and take reasonable actions to bring it about.

The Uninformed Plaintiff's Lawyer.[1] Imagine a tort case brought by an indigent plaintiff who has suffered severe injury as a result of the undisputed negligence of the defendant, but who may have contributed to his own injury. During negotiation, the insurance company lawyer conducting the defense realizes that the plaintiff's lawyer is unaware that a recent statute abolishing the contributory negligence defense would apply retroactively to this case. The plaintiff's lawyer is negotiating under the assumption that there is a substantial probability that his client's negligence will entirely preclude recovery, when in fact there is no such probability. The defense lawyer proceeds to conclude the negotiation without correcting the misimpression.

Gary Bellow and Bea Moulton, who tell this tale, incline here toward the Public Interest approach. Proponents of the Dominant View might prefer a scenario in which the victim of nondisclosure is not an indigent and the beneficiary is not an insurance company. For this purpose, we can recall Monroe Freedman's tale of a divorce lawyer opposing a "'bomber' who has no value in life other than stripping the husband of every penny and piece of property he has, at whatever cost to the personal relations and children, or anything else."[2] The Dominant and Public Interest approaches would resolve such cases through categorical rules, of nondisclosure in the case of the Dominant View or disclosure in the case of the Public Interest one.

The Contextual View requires a more complex judgment. In the personal injury case, the critical concern for the defense lawyer should be whether the settlement likely to occur in the absence of disclosure would be just. On the facts given, it seems probable that the settlement would not be. The plaintiff's lawyer probably set her bottom line well below the appropriately discounted value of the plaintiff's claims because of her mistake about the law. Here the defense counsel's responsibility is to move the case toward a just result; the best way to do that is probably to make the disclosure and resume the negotiation. This duty is triggered by the fact that, without some assistance from defense counsel, the procedure cannot be relied on to produce a just resolution. The plaintiff's counsel's mistake is an important breakdown in procedure, and with the case headed toward pretrial settlement, there will be no further opportunities for counsel, judge, or jury to remedy the breakdown.

The defense counsel should also assess the likelihood that disclosure will backfire and lead to a less just result because the plaintiff's counsel takes this information and then tries to get more than she is entitled to through some aggressive tactic of her own. But this risk seems small if, as the scenario implies, the defendant's lawyer is more experienced than the plaintiff's, the latter has not been aggressive, and the matter seems likely to be wound up before the plaintiff has an opportunity to initiate new maneuvers. In Freedman's divorce case, things may be different; disclosure of the husband's actual income to the "bomber" may prompt escalation of the already unfairly high demands. If so, then disclosure might be deferred until future developments indicate whether the case is likely to be resolved fairly without it. The lawyer's duty is not discharged, however, until she either makes the disclosure or the case is resolved justly without her doing so.[3]

Tax Avoidance. Now consider a case in which the breakdown arises from incapacity on the part of official institutions. Suppose an experienced tax practitioner has conceived a new tax avoidance device. She herself is convinced that it should not be allowed, but there is a nonfrivolous argument for its legality.[4] The lawyer might believe that the Internal Revenue Service and the courts are best situated to resolve such questions. She might reason that the agency and the courts have greater expertise than she, that they are better able to resolve issues in a way that can be uniformly applied to similar cases, and that they are subject to various democratic controls. However, such arguments are relevant only to the extent that the agency and the courts will in fact make an informed decision on the matter. The lawyer's premises would not warrant her using the device in a case in which the agency and the courts would never effectively review it. This might happen because the agency lacks sufficient resources to identify the issue or to take the matter to court.

In such a situation the lawyer should respond to the procedural failure. She can do so by trying to remedy it, for example, by bringing the issue to the attention of the IRS (say, by flagging it on the return). If that course is not possible (for example, because the client will not permit it), or if it will not be sufficient to remedy the procedural deficiencies (for example, because the agency is so strapped that it cannot even respond to such signals), then the lawyer has to assume more direct responsibility for the substantive resolution. If she thinks that the device should be held invalid, she should refuse to assist with it. In these circumstances, she is the best situated decisionmaker to pass on the matter.

In situations in which the procedure is reliable enough that the lawyer need not assume direct responsibility for the substantive merits, she retains a duty to make the procedure as effective as possible and to forego actions that would reduce its efficacy. While she need not consider the substantive merits herself, she should do what she can to facilitate the adjudicator in doing so.

The Handwriting Expert. Take an issue of deceptive impeachment tactics. Is it appropriate for a lawyer in cross-examining a handwriting expert surreptitiously to substitute a writing with a signature different from the one the witness has identified in the hope that the witness will not notice the substitution and continue to insist on what will then be a demonstrably mistaken identification? The Dominant View tends to permit such tactics; the Public Interest approach tends to condemn them.[5]

Under the Contextual View, the matter requires an inquiry into whether the tactic is likely to contribute to the adjudicator's ability to decide the case fairly. If the lawyer has no knowledge that will be witheld at the hearing, the ethical issue will not be urgent because, to the extent the tactic fails to contribute to fair understanding of the issues, the adjudicator can discount it appropriately. But if the lawyer has knowledge that cannot be formulated as admissible evidence,[6] the ethical issue may be important. Suppose the lawyer has reason to believe that the witness is competent and the identification is correct but that the tactic might work because the witness is prone to nervousness and distraction in public appearances. Here the tactic is likely to impede rather than enhance the adjudicator's ability to decide fairly. On the other hand, suppose the lawyer has extra-record information indicating that the witness is not competent and the identification is mistaken. Here she might plausibly decide that the tactic would contribute to a fair decision.[7]

In cases like this, the ethical concerns arise from the fact that, even in a relatively reliable procedure, the lawyer typically has opportunities to improve her client's chances of success in ways that do not facilitate decision on the merits by the adjudicator. The Dominant View relies on the judge to check such moves at the prompting of opposing counsel, but the judge, even after hearing from both sides, is often less well informed about specific factual issues than counsel. In such situations, counsel should not defer responsibility to the judge for tactics she does not believe contribute to a fair decision. Since she has an advantage in assessing the matter, she should exercise her own judgment and, when appropriate, self-restraint. Far from collapsing the lawyer's role into that of the judge, the Contextual View envisages one that complements the generally accepted understanding of the judge's role. The lawyer assumes responsibility for vindicating substantive merits to the extent that the judge cannot be expected to do so. In other situations, her responsibility is simply to facilitate informed judicial decision.

Of course, one can imagine a procedural context that is so reliable as to make superfluous the type of responsibility urged here: the dispute will be determined promptly, through an adjudication by a competent decisionmaker able routinely to identify and neutralize obfuscation and excessive aggression, after a hearing at which both sides are ably represented and adequately financed, governed by rules and procedures that ensure full development of the evidence and issues, and in which effective relief is available. But situations that even approximate this ideal are exceptional in the real world, not, as the Dominant View implies, the empirical norm. One of the strengths of the Contextual View is that it acknowledges and responds to procedural imperfection.

Purpose versus Form

Some instances of the Substance-versus-Procedure tension look like variations of the Purpose-versus-Form tension. When the lawyer impeaches a witness she knows to be truthful, when she objects to hearsay she knows to be accurate, when she puts the opposing party to proof on a matter the client has no legitimate reason to dispute, she takes advantage of procedural rules designed to promote accurate, efficient decisionmaking in ways that frustrate this purpose. When judges apply rules, we expect them to take account of the values (purposes or principles) underlying the rules. But the judge often lacks sufficient knowledge to determine whether the relevant values would be served by applying the rules. The lawyer, however, often does have sufficient knowledge to do so. Thus it is an important objection to the Dominant View that it imposes no responsibility on the lawyer to see that the rules she invokes are applied in a manner that takes account of their purposes.

The argument so far suggests that a lawyer's choice between a purposive or formal approach to procedural rules should depend on which approach seems better calculated to vindicate the relevant legal merits. In most contexts, considerations of merit favor a purposive approach. Yet the Contextual View also requires the lawyer to remain alert for indications that a purposive approach might not further this aim.

In many situations, especially when the lawyer must take direct responsibility for considerations of substantive merit, Purpose-versus-Form considerations are distinctively troubling. One reason for regarding law as legitimate in our culture is that it embodies the purposes adopted by authoritative lawmakers: parties to a contract, legislators enacting a statute, judges pronouncing a common law rule, the people adopting a constitution. But the legitimacy of law also depends on these purposes being embodied in the form of rules. By mediating between legislative intention and coercive application in specific cases, the rule form differentiates law from a regime of personal subordination to the legislator. The rules cannot be applied sensibly without regard to their purposes, but the purposes can only be implemented appropriately by referring to their expression in the rules.

This tension recurs where lawyers have an opportunity to shape an activity or transaction in a way that seems consistent with a plausible surface interpretation of a rule but that appears to undermine its purpose. For example, a divorced husband who agreed at separation to pay his ex-wife a percentage of his income for five years might try to save money by making arrangements with his employer to defer his income until the alimony period expires. Or the owner of a fleet of taxicabs might shield his business assets from tort liability by holding each cab through a separate corporation.

The Dominant View tends to license the manipulation of form to defeat purpose; though its pronouncements are less clear, the Public Interest View tends to forbid such manipulation. The Contextual View responds to the Purpose-versus-Form tension with the following maxim: the clearer and more fundamental the relevant purposes, the more the lawyer should consider herself bound by them; the less clear and more problematic the relevant purposes, the more justified the lawyer is in treating the relevant norms formally. Treating them formally means treating them the way the Dominant View prescribes for all legal norms—understanding them to permit any client goal not plainly precluded by their language.

The references to "fundamental" and "problematical" purposes invoke the established practice of favoring interpretations of the legal texts consistent with values to which the legal culture assigns strong importance and disfavoring interpretations that threaten such values. A "fundamental" purpose vindicates a basic value; a "problematical" purpose threatens such a value. In both contractual and statutory interpretation, it is common to favor the former and disfavor the latter by varying the burden of formal specification imposed on people trying to achieve them. Courts strain to avoid interpreting contracts to mandate unjust consequences and to avoid interpreting statutes in ways that would infringe constitutionally important interests (even when the rejected constructions would not be constitutionally prohibited).[8] Lawyers should reason analogously in deciding what weight to give ambiguously expressed purposes in the rules they deal with.

Tax Avoidance II. Here is an example involving a clear, unproblematic purpose. The client is a highly paid hotel manager. The lawyer determines that the client could save a good deal in taxes by renegotiating his contract with his employer so that in return for a reduction in cash compensation he agrees to reside on the hotel premises. The lawyer must decide whether to suggest this to the client, or if the client has suggested it, she must decide whether to implement it. Assume that some institutional limitation makes it implausible to rely on the IRS to determine the case, so that the lawyer must take direct responsibility for the substantive merits.

If there is any authorization for the arrangement in the income tax laws, it lies in a statutory provision exempting lodging furnished by the employer on its premises when the arrangement is "for the convenience of the employer" and is "required . . . as a condition of employment."[9] The rule arguably permits the contemplated arrangement—the employment contract could be drafted to impose such a "requirement."

Suppose the lawyer interprets this provision to express a belief that it is unfair to tax such in-kind benefits at full market value because they are probably worth much less to the employee, since she associates them with work and she cannot exchange them for things she may want more, as she could with cash. The in-kind benefits probably have some value to the employee, but to estimate this value in each case would be administratively impractical, and no plausible general presumption would be accurate in a large enough percentage of cases to warrant its use. Thus, on this theory, the statute exempts the income because that is the fairest practical approach.

Suppose that the lawyer decides that it would not be consistent with this statutory purpose to apply the exemption to arrangements the taxpayer has initiated. In such situations, it is more reasonable to presume that the taxpayer does value the benefits at the amount of the agreed salary reduction, or perhaps at their market value. Moreover, in such situations it may be more likely that the motivation for the transaction is purely tax savings rather than business efficiency, so that discouraging it would have little efficiency cost. Thus the lawyer concludes that the exemption should not be available for the contemplated transaction.

Suppose further, however, that courts in the relevant jurisdiction have rejected IRS challenges to in-kind arrangements initiated by taxpayers.[10] The lawyer's theory of institutional competence suggests that the court's decisions are more authoritative than her own views on the substantive merits. Accordingly, she is inclined to set aside her own views and proceed with the transaction. But the analysis is not yet complete. She still ought to consider the purposive basis of the courts' rulings.

Suppose she concludes that the rulings are not based on a judgment that such arrangements are consistent with the purposes of the statute, but on a belief that it would be too costly to determine whether each particular transaction was in fact chosen or initiated by the taxpayer. At this point the lawyer should review her theory of institutional competence. It may be impractical for the courts and the IRS to make such determinations, but quite practical for the tax lawyer to do so, especially if the lawyer came up with the idea herself and has not yet communicated it to the client. Since the lawyer believes the relevant purpose is clear and not problematic, she should not proceed with a plan that would frustrate the purpose.

Welfare Maximization. Now consider a case in which the relevant purpose is less clear and more problematic. The client is a public assistance recipient under the Aid to Families with Dependent Children program. She and her child live rent-free in a home owned by her cousin. Under the applicable regulations, their receipt of lodging "at no cost" is considered "income in kind" that requires a reduction of about $150 in the welfare grant.[11] The lawyer has to decide whether to recommend that the client make a nominal payment of, say, five dollars to the cousin so that she would no longer be receiving lodging "at no cost," and thus avoid the $150 reduction in her grant.

Again, assume that some institutional failure requires that the lawyer take some responsibility for the substantive merits. Upon examination, she is unable to come up with a sense of legislative purpose as clear and coherent as the one involved in the tax case. On the one hand, the benefit reduction seems designed to reflect the lesser needs of people with subsidized shelter, and the fact that the provision could be effectively nullified by financial planning suggests that planning was not contemplated. On the other hand, the regulation does not explicitly preclude such efforts, although it would have been simple enough to do so by providing for a benefit reduction of the difference between the rent payment and the $150 implicit shelter allowance in the grant. (Unlike the situation in the tax case, the welfare authorities have already addressed the valuation issue in a potentially administrable way.)

Suppose the background case law and legislative history suggest that the regulation is a compromise between the principle that grants should reflect the lesser needs of people with low rent expenses, and the competing "flat grant" principle that need determination should consider only the basic and easily determinable factors of cash income and family size.[12] In this situation, the lawyer has no clear sense of which course of action would be most consistent with legislative purpose. This uncertainty weighs toward treating the regulation formally.

Even if the lawyer found stronger indication of a purpose to preclude strategic planning, she might be justified in disregarding it if she thought it problematic. A purpose is problematic if it endangers fundamental values. The lawyer might decide that the claimant's interest in a minimally adequate income is a value of exceptional legal importance, that the AFDC grant levels provide considerably less than a minimally adequate income, and the plan in question might move her closer to one.

These judgments would be debatable, but there is substantial authority for all of them. Although the Supreme Court has denied that rights to minimal subsistence are "fundamental" in some contexts, it has recognized them as exceptionally important in others.[13] There are several public standards of minimal income adequacy; probably the most authoritative are the federal poverty standards. If the grant levels are below these standards in the relevant state, the federal standards would support the lawyer's judgment that the levels were inadequate.[14] The lawyer might conclude on the basis of such authority that a purpose to preclude such a rental arrangement should not be assumed without an explicit legislative statement of it.

Broad versus Narrow Framing

An important aspect of ethical reflection is the description, or framing, of the issue. If we frame the issue in terms of a small number of characteristics of the parties and their dispute, it will often look different than if we describe it more broadly.

On the one hand, legal ideals encourage narrow definition of issues in order to limit state intrusion into the lives of citizens and to simplify decisionmaking. On the other hand, making rights effectively enforceable sometimes requires broadening the issues. When issues are narrowly framed, their resolution is often influenced by factors, such as wealth and power, that, when we are forced to confront them, seem arbitrary. Lawyers tend to weigh these competing considerations differently in different areas of law. In contract, they favor relatively narrow framing; in family law, relatively broad framing. But within these and other fields, there are many controversies about framing practices.[15]

Framing questions are not often discussed directly, but they play an important role in discussions of legal ethics. For example, in arguing for the minimal duty of candor in the Dominant View, Monroe Freedman hypothesizes situations in which candor may impede the appropriate substantive resolution because of some other procedural deficiency. A famous example concerns whether a criminal defense lawyer should cross-examine a prosecution witness who accurately places the defendant near the scene of the crime about her defective vision.[16] In Freedman's scenario, although the testimony is accurate and thus the contemplated impeachment seems irrelevant, the defendant is in fact innocent but lacks an alibi and is the victim of some unlucky circumstantial evidence. So the proper resolution—acquittal—may depend on impeachment of the truthful witness. Similarly, in Freedman's divorce scenario, which we discussed earlier, for the husband to disclose hidden income would aggravate the injustice of the probable resolution, because the wife's lawyer will take advantage of the information while continuing to pursue aggressive tactics of his own.

What Freedman does in these discussions is to broaden the frame. The issue is initially framed as a matter of candor about a specific piece of information (the witness's eyesight, the husband's income). Freedman then insists the matter be viewed in the context of the entire proceeding and in terms of the likely incremental influence of the disclosure on the resolution. Nevertheless, this type of broadened framing has no place in Freedman's view of individual lawyer decision-making. At that level, he adopts the general libertarian practice of narrow framing. He favors a categorical duty of aggressive impeachment and confidentiality regardless of the surrounding circumstances. Freedman adopts the broader frame only when taking the perspective of the rule-maker deciding whether to mandate or preclude cross-examination or disclosure in such situations.

In contrast, the Contextual View gives individual lawyers substantial responsibility for determining whether broad or narrow framing is appropriate in the particular case. It suggests that lawyers should frame ethical issues in accordance with three general standards of relevance. First, a consideration is relevant if it fits the most plausible interpretation of the applicable substantive law. Ethical issues should be framed narrowly under laws that regulate narrowly. For example, traffic laws tend to regulate more narrowly than family laws.

Second, a consideration is relevant if it is likely to have a substantial practical influence on the resolution. Ethical issues can be framed more narrowly to the extent that substantively irrelevant factors are not likely to influence the resolution. Equality of resources and access to information are among the more important considerations weighing toward narrow definition under this second standard. Third, framing should take account of the lawyer's knowledge and institutional competence. Broadly framed issues tend to require more knowledge and more difficult judgments. When the lawyer lacks needed knowledge or competence, narrow framing becomes more appropriate.

The Union Representation Election.[17] Here is an extended example. A wealthy private university has a collective bargaining agreement with a local union representing its clerical and technical workers. The workers had previously been organized as a single-employer local, but they merged with a larger local representing workers from several employers shortly before the most recent contract negotiation. The merger was not a success, however, and the university workers' leaders and the officials of the big local agreed that the university workers would revert to a single employer local. Accordingly, the big local purported to delegate its representative function to the reconstituted university local and disclaimed any interest in representing the university workers. A few weeks later the reconstituted local held an election of the bargaining unit members in which the new arrangement was ratified by a five-to-one margin, though with only fifty-five percent of those eligible voting. The university local has not made or proposed any changes in internal membership rights or in the terms of the existing collective bargaining agreement.

On the advice of counsel, the university now refuses to recognize the reconstituted local or pay over dues to it under the "check-off" provisions of the collective bargaining agreement. It asserts that the big local could not transfer representative authority without an election and that, when it disclaimed the university workers, those workers ceased to be represented. Since the university local was not the lawful representative of the workers at the time of the ratifying election, it had no authority to conduct the election, and the vote was therefor invalid. The university argues further that the hiatus between the disclaimer and the election, and the change in the unit's size, officers, and internal procedures resulting from the reorganization, indicate that there is not sufficient "continuity of representation" to warrant a presumption that the workers want to be represented by the local. In the absence of such a presumption, the local must establish its status through a certification election conducted by the National Labor Relations Board.[18]

The union regards the demand for an election burdensome, not only because it duplicates the internal election already held, but because it would be considerably more expensive in terms of time, energy, and money. Unlike the internal election, an NLRB certification election would give the employer wide opportunity to campaign against the local and make it possible for other unions to compete for certification. The local would thus have to devote a lot of resources to its own campaign. Moreover, the university might be able to cause additional delay and expense by challenging the results of the certification election before the NLRB, a proceeding that could take years to resolve.[19] On the other hand, the local's only practical recourse for the University's refusal to pay over dues is to file a complaint with the NLRB, which will also definitely consume large amounts of time and money before effective relief can be obtained.

We can see the ethical issue for university counsel in terms of both Substance-versus-Procedure and Purpose-versus-Form. The delay and expense of NLRB proceedings arise from a procedural breakdown which triggers some responsibility on the part of university counsel to assess the substantive merits of the university's argument. This argument is not frivolous, but it is supported only by formal considerations that undercut the relevant statutory purposes. Most of the argument would have been mooted by an election held before the big local disclaimed interest, and it seems strongly likely that the result would have been the same then as it was in the election held later.

The clear reason for the delay in holding the election was carelessness on the part of the university local's leaders, but this carelessness does not seem to have prejudiced anyone. The internal changes accompanying disaffiliation are substantial, but they involve a return to the old pre-affiliation structure with which most workers are familiar, and there is no indication of worker dissatisfaction with it. The university's demand for a certification election does not, under the circumstances, seem strongly supported by the National Labor Relations Act's purpose to make unions genuinely representative of the bargaining unit. Moreover, it seems to frustrate another important statutory purpose—to minimize employer intervention into and disruption of union affairs.[20]

Nevertheless, describing the matter in this way ignores many of the considerations that are most important to the parties and their lawyers.

Although the lawyers have framed the issue in their briefs in terms of only the limited sequence of events described above, they and their clients understand the ethical issues in terms of broader perspectives on a complex and long-standing relationship that has become increasingly acrimonious and mistrustful.

In the view of the university and its lawyers, the local is in the hands of zealots who are out of touch with the membership. These leaders prefer rhetorical and ideological posturing to pursuing the concerns of the rank and file. They have dissipated the university's resources on a huge number of unsuccessful grievances. They have precipitated costly strikes over issues of little importance to the membership. They have generated hostility around collective bargaining that has poisoned personal relations within the university without making any practical improvement in the union's bargaining position. The members have not been able to hold the leaders accountable because they have been confused by deceptive statements of the leaders; because some members fear retaliation by the leaders; and because few of them can devote the time and energy necessary to mount a challenge to the established union power structure. From this perspective, an NLRB election would facilitate membership reconsideration of its own interest in a setting that provides the university with an opportunity to counter the deceptions of the union leaders, while the NLRB's presence would undercut intra-union intimidation.

The union leaders and their lawyers have a different perspective. They believe the university's conduct amounts to oppressively paternalistic union busting. University officials have been blinded by their biases about what workers want and by their own preferences for an informal work environment in which elite professionals have untrammeled discretion. They thus have failed to take seriously the union's nonmonetary demands (for example, for tighter job classifications and more worker control of scheduling) and have failed to recognize the need for reforms that would constrain managerial power. Their hostility toward union leadership arises from an understanding of the role of the union—one that precludes all forms of militance and limits the union to a narrowly economic and disciplinary role—that is at odds with the one held by most workers. The university has negotiated aggressively in collective bargaining and has defended grievances energetically without regard to their merits. Forcing the union to conduct a new certification election will exacerbate the effects of this prior course of conduct. The unmistakable message—that while they have a union they can expect an exhausting and expensive struggle to achieve and maintain every concession—will demoralize and demobilize many members.

If the issue is framed broadly and if the university's view is accepted, the case for the university's aggressive course of action seems stronger. The chances that the university's course will succeed on the merits are slim, and it is certain to impose a heavy burden on the union. Yet from a broader view this burden might be justified, since the threatened representative structure appears to be a legally inappropriate one.

In some respects the broader interpretation of the statute is supported by the first two of the three standards of relevance suggested above—substantive implication, practical impact, and institutional competence. To begin with, the matter is governed by a statute that regulates broadly; the labor act is designed to constitute and protect relationships. Insuring representativeness of union structures is one of its principal goals. Furthermore, the university's interpretation suggests that its aggressive tactics might neutralize the influence on the resolution of legally arbitrary factors, such as the manipulations of the local's leaders and the inability of many workers to invest much time in union politics.

Yet the third framing standard brings out serious objections to this line of thought. For the university to rely on this broader view seems inconsistent with the statute's premises about institutional competence. The applicable law accords the incumbent union a presumption of representativeness that the employer must rebut by "objective considerations." The NLRB would not consider any of the impressions on which the university bases its broad interpretation competent as rebuttal. Even if these impressions are not sufficient for the purposes of the NLRB, university counsel might think it appropriate rely on them in deciding whether to take advantage of the union's procedural lapse. The university might see an analogy between this approach and the practice of prosecutors of taking inadmissible evidence into account in deciding whether to initiate a prosecution.

However, the analogy is not strong. University counsel should recognize that she has a bias in the matter and that there are limitations on her knowledge of the union that are more severe than the comparable disadvantages of prosecutorial judgment. Moreover, the rules that make evidence inadmissible at a criminal trial are based in substantial part on factors other than a mistrust of prosecutorial judgment, such as concern about police misconduct, desire to protect confidential relations, and limited trust in juries.

By contrast, the requirement that the employer establish a basis for doubting the union's representative status by "objective considerations" seems intended to prevent the employer from causing the sort of disruption its present course creates, by precluding reliance on precisely the kind of impressions its broader view is based on. Thus, on balance, university counsel should frame the issue in relatively narrow terms that obviate judgments she is poorly situated to make. As we have seen, their aggressive tactics seem inappropriate in the narrower frame.

The question of framing seems less important for union counsel. The issues for university counsel stem from their opportunity to take advantage of the burdens that NLRB delay and expense impose on the union. For the union lawyers, regardless of whether the issue is framed narrowly or broadly, the appropriate response is to press for the quickest and cheapest possible NLRB determination. Pursuing the NLRB proceeding is the best available way for the union to protect itself against the employer's tactics, and the scenario so far suggests no reason why this course of action would threaten any legitimate interest of the employer.

To illustrate how the framing issue might become relevant to union lawyers, we could complicate matters by hypothesizing an additional concern about the reliability of the NLRB procedure. Recall that, aside from its nonfrivolous but weak claim regarding the circumstances of disaffiliation, the university cannot make the prescribed showing by "objective considerations" of reasonable grounds for doubting the majority status of the union. As we have noted, this constraint on the employer's ability to trigger an election reflects a belief that neither the employer nor the Board is reliably situated to determine when a union is no longer representative in the absence of objective evidence. However, in some situations the employer may lack this kind of evidence, but the union lawyer may be in a good position to make determinations of this sort.

A lawyer with a close, long-standing association with the union would not have an employer's bias and might have enough knowledge to conclude with confidence that the employer's claim of unrepresentativeness is in fact correct, and that the "objective considerations" requirement will preclude the NLRB from reaching this conclusion. In this situation, institutional competence weighs in favor of broad framing. The union lawyer should not be content to rely on the weakness of the employer's narrow claim regarding disaffiliation to oppose the certification election. She should push the local leaders to submit to a test of representativeness—by a certification election if that is the best way.

Positive and Substantive Authority

Each of the three sets of tensions we have discussed is related to the opposition between Positive and Substantive legal authorities discussed in Chapter 4. In general, a tendency to emphasize substance over procedure, purpose over form, and broad framing over narrow resonates with Substantivist jurisprudential perspectives. A tendency to emphasize procedure, form, and narrow framing resonates with Positivism. In the earlier chapter I suggested that in presuming a strong Positivism, the Dominant View was implausible and out of touch with mainstream jurisprudential assumptions outside the legal ethics field. The same point applies to the Dominant View's strong privileging of procedure, form, and narrow framing.

Once one abandons these dubious commitments, there may be a temptation to rush to the other side of the spectrum and embrace categorically substance, purpose, and broad framing. The Contextual View resists that move. It doesn't offer a single general or theoretical resolution of these oppositions. It merely suggests that the more reflective of the conventional approaches to legal decisionmaking will often lead us to sufficiently strong conclusions about how these competing elements should be balanced in specific contexts.

Some Objections

We can now consider three practical objections the Contextual View often prompts: that the type of decisionmaking it calls for requires more time and effort than lawyers typically have; that contextual decisions are likely to be at loggerheads with conventional practices and hence ineffectual; and that a contextual regime would threaten the interests of "unpopular clients."

Time and Effort

Some ethical issues seem vastly complex. The Contextual View has the virtue of inviting and permitting the lawyer to explore that complexity, but it does not require her to do so without regard to time and resource constraints.[21] Decisions often should be made quickly, either because of some imminent deadline or because the stakes involved don't warrant the resources that extensive analysis would require. In such circumstances, the lawyer properly relies on incomplete analysis and norms that indicate presumptive responses to broad categories of situations.

A contextual regime can conserve resources in precisely the way that a categorical one does—by using rules. Its use of rules nevertheless differs from that of a categorical regime. Under a contextual approach the lawyer does not limit herself to categorical analysis uniformly, but only after making a judgment that time and resource constraints prohibit a fuller analysis. To the extent time is available and the stakes are high, she proceeds to more extensive consideration. Moreover, even where the lawyer must decide in haste, she treats the presumptions she relies on as rebuttable, so that when she is aware of considerations that warrant an unconventional response, she remains open to taking it.

Contextual ethical decisionmaking resembles in this respect tactical decisionmaking. When time permits and the stakes are high, lawyers make subtle and elaborate analyses of tactical choices. But sometimes they have to decide quickly and summarily. For example, a cross-examiner surprised by an unfavorable answer from a witness may have to decide in a matter of seconds whether to ask for a recess (and risk signaling his distress at the answer), ask follow-up questions (and risk aggravating the effect of the first answer), or pass on to another topic (and risk losing the prime opportunity to mitigate the effect of the answer).

In making their decisions under such circumstances, lawyers fall back on a number of rules, such as "Never ask a question you don't know the answer to." Although these rules are sometimes taught to novice lawyers as categorical norms, experienced lawyers always treat them as rebuttable presumptions to be disregarded when the circumstances suggest the client's interests would be served by doing so. (A leading trial practice text gives more than a dozen examples of situations in which it might be in the client's interest for a cross-examiner to ask a question he doesn't know the answer to.)[22] One of the measures of a lawyer's technical abilities is his capacity to recognize, especially in situations of pressure, when it is best to depart from the dictates of such norms. The same point applies to ethical decisionmaking.

Convention

Some lawyers feel that in the world of practice ethical analysis is typically trumped by the force of convention. Where individual responses to an issue converge, they acquire the force of custom or institutionalized practice, and once this happens, lawyers will tend to follow the practice more or less unreflectively.

This idea is a challenge to the Dominant View as well as the Contextual one, and indeed to the entire aspirational tradition of professionalism that exalts the importance of ethical reflection. However, if convention coincides more often with the dictates of the Dominant View than with those of the Contextual View, it is perhaps a greater problem for the latter. And the strong focus on client loyalty and confidentiality in the Dominant View does overlap substantially with conventional norms.

Lawyers are drawn toward convention by both practical and normative forces. Practically, in a marketplace where lawyers compete for clients, lawyers who reject conventions that favor clients will be at a disadvantage in attracting them. (However, there may be countervailing forces, as we will see in chapter 8.) Moreover, the lawyer's refusal to do something for the client that lawyers conventionally do will often be inconsequential, since the client will be able to find another lawyer to do it. Normatively, the fact that a practice is a convention is some evidence of its soundness. The widespread use of a practice may mean that most lawyers believe it has merit. This is especially true of open, visible practices. And the more openly widespread the practice, the greater the ability of authorities to assess and police it, and hence the less need for lawyers to assume that responsibility. Finally, denying a client the benefit of a conventional practice means treating him differently from clients of other lawyers, which might be inequitable.

All these reasons warrant giving positive weight in Contextual decisionmaking to the conventional status of a practice. But it would not be plausible to see conventions as trumps that end analysis. Some of the values that underpin a conventional practice may be patently absent in some circumstances, and some may be patently outweighed by competing considerations. If a lawyer cannot earn a reasonable living without undertaking a particular service, that fact weighs in favor of his undertaking it, but it would be given no weight by a lawyer who is financially secure. If refusing a particular course of action will be inconsequential because someone else will readily do it, that again weighs in favor of going ahead, but that does not mean one should ignore countervailing considerations just because of this fact. If a racketeer asked me to arrange for the murder of the prosecution's chief witness, no one would consider me justified in going along even if I were certain she could hire someone else to do so.

Of course, murdering witnesses is not a conventionally accepted practice. But conventionality is no guarantee of normative plausibility. In administering even the most conventional of legal norms—the tort duty of "reasonable care"—we reject conventionality as a conclusive defense. As Learned Hand put it in a case holding a tugboat company liable for disdaining a safety measure routinely disdained by other such companies, "some precautions are so essential that even their universal disregard will not excuse their omission."[23]

Similarly, popular moral judgment seems to accord nothing more than presumptive legitimacy to conventional behavior. Consider, for example, the prevailing practices with respect to marijuana smoking prior the nomination of Douglas Ginsburg to the Supreme Court in 1987, or with respect to payment of employment taxes for domestic workers prior to the nomination of Zoe Baird for Attorney General in 1993. Both nominations failed because of public condemnation of conduct that was conventional at the time the nominees engaged in it. In Ginsburg's case, the convention regarding marijuana use had changed by the time of the nomination, but the public felt free to penalize previously conventional practices. In Baird's case, the convention regarding employment taxes for part-time domestics was still in place—most people didn't pay them—but the public felt free to penalize conventional behavior as a way to encourage a change in the convention.

Finally, the strong conventionalist argument exaggerates not only the moral force of convention, but its determinacy and comprehensiveness. Convention does not provide clear answers to many ethical issues. Lawyers lack good information about what other lawyers do in many situations (in part because much relevant information is subject to confidentiality norms). Practices often vary widely from one geographical area to another and from one practice area to another. Defining convention requires controversial judgments about what the geographic and substantive scope of the relevant community is.

In the Lincoln Savings & Loan case, the Kaye Scholer lawyers argued strongly that the practices for which the Office of Thrift Supervision sanctioned them were conventional, but some lawyers strongly disagreed. Some suggested that because the Kaye Scholer lawyers lacked banking experience, they thoughtlessly replicated practices conventional among New York litigators in another context—bank examination—where they weren't conventional. Their defenders responded that, since the examination was unusually adversarial, the relevant context was that of general civil litigation rather than bank examination. In fact, there simply is no clear answer as to what the relevant conventions were.

Unpopular Clients

A frequent objection to enlarging the ethical responsibility of lawyers summons up the image of the "unpopular client." Once lawyers engage in anything more than minimal scrutiny of the merits of client goals and claims, might not "unpopular people"—dissidents, nonconformists, outcasts—find themselves without representation? The argument is often accompanied by references to famous incidents in which lawyers courageously defended victims of red scares, religious persecution, and mob violence.[24]

We can get a sense of the limitations of this concern by considering two famous episodes in which it was invoked. One was the representation of Jim Fisk and Jay Gould by David Dudley Field in the Erie Railroad control contests of the late 1860s. The journalist Samuel Bowles criticized Field, arguing that his efforts injured the railroad, its stockholders, and the economy. Field replied that he had done no more for Fisk and Gould than "giving them legal opinions and arguing cases for them in court," and that he had a duty to do this so that they would "be judged according to the law of the land" rather than by "public clamor."

Field invoked Lord Erskine's defense of Tom Paine, in the face of public vilification, against charges of seditious libel in *The Rights of Man*. Erskine had responded to popular derision by proclaiming, "I will forever, at all hazards, assert the dignity, independence and integrity of the English bar, without which impartial justice . . . can have no existence." Field argued that the same principle applied to his representation of Fisk and Gould.[25]

There are distinctions between these two representations of a sort that the Dominant View tends to ignore. While the activities that prompted the public clamor against Erskine's client involved the publication of a controversial book, the activities that prompted the public clamor against Field's clients involved the looting of the Erie Railroad and the fraudulent manipulation of its stock. That, at least, is how many informed, disinterested observers have viewed it. Admittedly, Field might have viewed it differently because some of the claims he asserted on behalf of Fisk and Gould were upheld in the New York courts, and the contest was resolved substantially in favor of his clients by an act of the New York legislature. However, the judiciary that sustained these claims was highly politicized, partly corrupt, and organized in a way that made it incapable of resolving the matter effectively; and many members of the legislature had been bribed by Gould.

Field does not appear to have been involved in the bribery of the legislators,[26] but he probably knew about it, and he was the principal strategist of the notorious war of injunctions in the lower courts. Field's clients and their adversary, Commodore Vanderbilt, would each in turn apply to a friendly judge, who would promptly enter ex parte the requested order vacating prior orders entered by other judges at the behest of the adversary and newly enjoining the adversary in accordance with the wishes of the applicant. The state code of civil procedure facilitated this chaos by giving trial judges in different districts statewide venue and jurisdiction without providing an adequate method of resolving conflicting decrees.

From the Contextual viewpoint, this seems a striking case of the kind of procedural failure that triggers responsibility to assess substantive merit. It was not plausible to think that the court, given its staffing and organization, was reliably equipped to resolve the matter justly. Thus Field was wrong to think he had no duty to assess the substantive merits of his clients' claims. Those who have made such an assessment have concluded that these claims had no merit at all.[27]

The relevance of this analysis to the "unpopular client" argument is to illustrate that whether one should be concerned about a client's unpopularity depends on what the source of the unpopularity is. If the unpopularity reflects a valid assessment of the legal merits of the client's claims and goals, there should be no concern at all. Of course, the lawyer ought not to accept passively popular judgments of legal merit, but when her own judgment agrees with the public's, the client's unpopularity is no reason to assist him.[28]

Of the many distinctions between Erskine's situation and his own that Field ignored was that the claims of Erskine's client had considerably more legal merit. They were strongly grounded in legal norms of free speech. The other classic examples of civil representation of unpopular clients, such as those involving civil rights demonstrators or victims of red scares, are also compelling because the claims of the clients had strong merit, often under the First Amendment. Under the Contextual View, this merit provides strong reason to take the case.

Moreover, it seems unlikely that the Dominant View has made any practical contribution to the bar's willingness to take on "unpopular clients" in civil liberties cases. The typical "unpopular client" in the civil liberties area is unable to pay the costs of representation and thus depends on the willingness of lawyers to take such a case *pro bono*. Yet in *pro bono* cases, lawyers have always made judgments of substantive merit. Survey evidence indicates that lawyers tend to be more committed to substantive civil liberties values than the lay public.[29] This substantive commitment, and not the ethics of the Dominant View, accounts for the bar's admirable service to unpopular clients with meritorious civil liberties claims.

The Moral Terrain of Lawyering Reconsidered

We are now in a position to reconsider the three examples introduced in Chapter 1.

The Innocent Convict. The drama of the client who confesses to a murder for which a mistakenly convicted man awaits execution might be described as an extreme conflict of procedure (confidentiality) and substance (innocence).[30] Clearly, the general procedural system has failed so far, and it seems unlikely that, in the absence of some intervention by the lawyer, it is likely to correct itself. The lawyer thus has some responsibility to assess substantive merit, and it seems clear that a horrendous injustice is in prospect.

Compared to the stakes for the innocent convict, the client's legitimate interest in silence seems trivial. To be sure, he has placed his trust in the lawyer, but just as "honor among thieves" shows that not all forms of honor are especially worthy, the trust of a murderer in a lawyer's willingness to remain passive in the face of enormous injustice seems of small weight. The most important competing consideration is not the entitlement of the client to silence, but the effect of disclosure in deterring people with more legitimate interests in seeking legal advice.

In Chapter 3 I expressed skepticism about the bar's arguments that categorical confidentiality guarantees are essential to induce people to seek legal advice. The arguments seem especially weak as applied to this case. If the lawyer could make an anonymous disclosure to help the innocent convict, that would have no weakening effect on general trust in attorney confidentiality. Even a highly publicized disclosure seems unlikely to have a major effect. The most likely public interpretation of disclosure would be, not as some indiscriminate weakening of lawyers' commitment to confidentiality, but as an exception for the extreme circumstances of this case. Lay people are aware that the confidentiality norms are not absolute, and many of them already believe (incorrectly) that the norms make an exception for cases of this sort.[31] To the extent that is so, public disclosure would have no effect at all on public willingness to seek legal advice.[32]

If the disclosure would make a difference and the rules gave the lawyer discretion to disclose, then the case would be an easy one. It becomes difficult when we recognize that the bar's disciplinary rules, which have the force of law by virtue of their adoption by the courts, forbid disclosure. This case at least is not within the explicit exceptions of the rules.[33] Perhaps the rules could be interpreted to imply such an exception, but there are strong objections to such an interpretation.

The drafters' comments to the *Model Rules* discourage implied exceptions, and commentators who have considered the Innocent Convict case have tended to interpret the rules as inflexible.[34]

So the lawyer might have to consider disclosure as a form of nullification. It can be argued generally that the bar's confidentiality norms should be viewed as, at best, weakly binding. The bar's rationales for these norms are dogmatic and incoherent. The norms seem out of harmony with the treatment of confidentiality in analogous situations by legislatures and agencies and even by courts outside the realm of professional responsibility rules. The norms were enacted through a process strongly influenced by professional associations, which are both historically and structurally disposed toward more than occasional narrow self-interest.

Even if the arguments for categorical confidentiality safeguards are not strong, we have to acknowledge that many people, including people with authority over the matter, accept them. For the most part the norms have been recently enacted, often after substantial public debate. Though inconsistent with some legislation on analogous matters, the bar's rules are consistent in important respects with the attorney-client privilege in the law of evidence. Notwithstanding the influence of the bar associations, professional responsibility norms are ultimately enacted by the courts.

Yet these considerations seem outweighed by the substantive absurdity of the rules' application in the particular circumstances of the Innocent Convict. If the facts are such that disclosure would probably save an innocent life without posing a demonstrable threat to important rights of others (through limiting future access to legal advice), then it would be grotesque not to disclose them. While a rule forbidding disclosure would be degrading for any actor, it is particularly so for a lawyer, since it compels him to acquiesce in a monumental violation of a core commitment of his role. The rule should not be interpreted to require such degradation. If such an interpretation is unavoidable, then the lawyer should defy the rule, not as an act of lawlessness, but as an act of principled commitment to legal values more fundamental than those that support the rule.

Agribusiness Welfare. This case is readily framed as a conflict between form and purpose. By providing for water benefits for each farmer, the statute at least arguably permits a wealthy farmer to disperse his holdings among trusts and corporations and have each of these "farmers" get benefits up to the maximum. However, this interpretation seems inconsistent with the apparent purpose, to preclude wealthy people from claiming greater benefits than nonwealthy ones. The landowners who would make these arrangements start out wealthy, and although the transfers disperse formal control and enjoyment rights, informally the transferor retains most or all of them. The purpose to limit transfers to the wealthy is not "problematical" in the sense discussed above: it does not threaten any fundamental value. So there's no reason to be wary of it.

Of course, the conflict of form and purpose becomes troubling only if we find some defect in the public enforcement process. If the process is reliable, the lawyer contributes to the elaboration of the statute by presenting the claims in a manner that facilitates determination by the authorities. Many students of agricultural policy during the period when these transactions were popular suggest that the enforcement process was not reliable. They claim that the enforcement agencies were "captured" by the large farm organizations, which were in turn dominated by the wealthier farmers. The farm organizations controlled the flow of information to the agencies, orchestrated pressure on them both directly and through their influence on Congress, and doled out jobs to departing bureaucrats and junkets and other nonmonetary emoluments to incumbent ones in a manner well calculated to induce sensitivity to the interests of their most powerful members. These students interpret the agencies' acceptance of the transactions in question as a function, not of dispassionate judgment on the legal merits, but of their "capture" by the people who benefited from the transactions.[35] A lawyer who agreed with this conclusion would have an increased responsibility to assess the substantive merits of the transaction. In many cases, he should probably have concluded that the transactions should not proceed because they are inconsistent with the statutory purpose.

Of course, it might be costly for the lawyer to implement this conclusion. Once these transactions become more or less standard, lawyers who decline to go along with them will have a hard time attracting clients in this area and may even subject themselves to malpractice liability. Thus the lawyer has to weigh his own interest in earning a living against the wrong such transactions do. Neither the certainty nor the magnitude of the wrong seem so great that it would be unreasonable for him to decide to proceed.

The fact that economic pressures sometimes outweigh concerns of legal merit doesn't mean it isn't important to think about the merit, however. In other situations the pressures may not be so strong. For example, if the lawyer were considering the practice before it came into general use and the client had no expectation she would adopt it, she would probably be able to forego it without serious cost and probably should. Moreover, a lawyer who has not yet entered the relevant field but is considering doing so should view pressures that force her to engage in unmeritorious practices as a strong reason against entering it. Even the lawyer in the field who plausibly believes that she has an excuse for yielding to pressures to engage in the arrangement should be aware of its dubious merit. We might view this kind of self-awareness as a good in itself, as a constitutive feature of ethical autonomy. We might also think of the practice of assessing the moral costs of what one does as an important disposition and skill that needs to be maintained and cultivated. A lawyer who permits herself to become insensitive to the moral costs of actions she feels she must take risks losing her capacity to assess such costs in situations where she has greater discretion.

The Recalcitrant S & L. Much of the debate about the misleadingly incomplete disclosures of the Kaye Scholer lawyers to the Bank Board concerned framing. Kaye Scholer's defenders framed the matter as litigation, and argued that in that context counsel had no duty to avoid misleadingly incomplete (as opposed to specifically false) representations. The Office of Thrift Supervision framed the matter as bank regulation and argued that in that context a higher duty of candor was appropriate.[36]

On these issues OTS was largely right. The banking system, as the guarantor of Lincoln's debts, had a strong interest in its soundness. Moreover, when Lincoln became insolvent, the insurance system was effectively the residual claimant on Lincoln's assets and thus entitled to assume control of the bank. Hence the Bank Board at all times had a strong claim to access to the information needed to determine whether the bank was insolvent. The banking laws gave the regulators practically unlimited powers to demand information and specifically prohibited misleadingly incomplete statements. The examination of Lincoln Savings & Loan was undeniably a regulatory proceeding subject to these laws, and the mere fact that litigation was anticipated was no reason to lower the standard of candor required. Moreover, even if the matter were framed as conventional litigation, much of the alleged conduct would probably have been wrongful under the standards conventionally applied in that context.[37]

In addition to this issue of context, there was a further, largely ignored, framing issue of the kind I emphasized above, an issue about the appropriate breadth of the frame. At the time of these events, the S & L industry and its regulatory system were in crisis. The inherent flaws of the original New Deal regulatory scheme had been exacerbated by the tight money policies that began in 1979, and subsequently by the loosening of regulatory constraints in the early and mid-1980s. In effect, the system created strong incentives for operators to make high-risk investments with publicly underwritten capital, keeping the profits in the event of success but sticking the government with the losses in the event of failure. The speculative temptations for the operators—and the consequent risk to the public—intensified geometrically as the institution approached insolvency, the point at which the operators were betting solely with public money. The dangers were compounded by the systematic misconduct, and occasional outright corruption, of some members of the executive and legislative branches with responsibility over the system.

In this broader perspective, the case for strong duties of candor becomes even weightier. In the first place, the Bank Board's interest in information about Lincoln's soundness was not merely strong, but urgent. The risks to the insurance system of an unsound bank tend to magnify with delay. The deeper the bank gets into the hole, the greater the risks it needs to take in order to have any chance of gambling its way out. Moreover, arguments against high duties of candor are especially implausible in this context. Such arguments, of course, are based on the adversary-system notion that the best outcomes occur when each party concentrates on advancing interests assigned to it by division of labor. But these arguments presuppose that the people representing the other interests are performing effectively and responsibly, which manifestly was not the case here. For example, the Bank

Board was woefully understaffed, and key federal legislators, who had received electoral contributions from Keating and other operators, repeatedly intimidated the Board and staff members.

On balance, the considerations mentioned above suggest that this broader view was the right way for the Kaye Scholer lawyers to frame the ethical issues. First, the banking laws regulate broadly. Second, the surrounding institutional failures were important practical influences on the likely outcomes. The relevance of the third framing concern—expertise—is harder to assess. The Kaye Scholer litigators began representing Keating without expertise in banking, but one would have expected them to acquire some rapidly. (The firm billed Lincoln for $13 million during five years of the representation, so they should have learned a lot.) A thoughtful reader of the available literature on banking problems, even without the firm's inside vantage point, could have gained a fairly accurate impression of the system's failures.

In fact, Keating—and perhaps his lawyers as well—did frame the issues broadly, though in a different way than the one I'm suggesting here. In Keating's view, the regulators were arrogant and unreasonable, callously disregarding Lincoln's legitimate business interests, insisting on a degree of formality and caution in excess of that required by federal banking policy. This view did not seem as implausible at the time as it does in hindsight. Not long after Kaye Scholer began its representation, *Forbes* identified Lincoln as the second most profitable S & L in the country. Federal banking policy makers had been sending mixed signals for years. At times they had encouraged the banks to overstate their soundness by accounting devices that, had they not been specifically authorized, would have been fraudulent, and they denied the Bank Board the resources to close even the thrifts that were insolvent under these liberalized terms. Undoubtedly some policymakers were gambling too, forestalling intervention in the hope that the S & Ls would maneuver themselves out of insolvency and spare the government the costs and pains of closing them.

But even taking this particular broader view, it would not have been plausible for the Kaye Scholer lawyers to think they were justified in withholding material information or making misleading statements. The government benefits Lincoln was receiving from the insurance system were hardly basic rights or fundamental interests that the bank had any claim to, independent of legislative and regulatory policy. (In this respect, its situation was arguably different from that of the welfare recipients above, who might claim a stronger constitutional status for their welfare interests, though even that claim would be highly controversial.) Even if public policy was ambiguous enough to allow one to believe nonfrivolously that Keating's cavalier, high-risk activities were appropriate—itself a debatable proposition—once the examiners challenged them, it was important to clarify public policy, and doing so would require accurate material information.

Although the framing issue is not decisive, since the case for candor is strong even in the narrower frame, the broader frame adds further strength to the conclusion that the misleadingly incomplete statements alleged by OTS were improper.

7

Is Criminal Defense Different?

Some people who join me in rejecting the Dominant View make an exception for criminal defense. They think practice in this field is distinctive in ways that make the Dominant View uniquely plausible there.[1] I agree that some special features of criminal defense practice have important implications for legal ethics. These features, however, are not the ones most prominently emphasized by its apologists. Moreover, they can be accommodated more plausibly within the Contextual View than within the Dominant one.

Contested Issues

At the outset, we should focus the inquiry. I take it for granted that lawyers can appropriately plead not guilty on behalf of clients they believe in fact guilty and defend these clients in a variety of ways. One reason, of course, is that it is more desirable to have disputed questions determined by the court at trial than by the lawyer unilaterally and in private; the lawyer can contribute more by assisting the trier to make the determination than by making it herself. The law, moreover, explicitly gives many rights to criminal defendants that are independent of guilt or innocence. These "intrinsic procedural rights" include the right of a defendant who concedes guilt privately to plead not guilty and put the prosecution to proof, the right to exclude unlawfully

170

obtained evidence, and the right not to be subjected to cruel and unusual punishment.

The issues we are concerned with involve tactics that cannot plausibly be viewed either as assisting the trier in making an informed determination or as vindicating specific intrinsic procedural rights. It will be convenient to focus on tactics over which lawyers have some discretion, in the sense that these tactics are neither clearly (at least effectively) prohibited nor clearly required by current norms of effective assistance of counsel.

Strategic Delay

Defense lawyers have opportunities to draw out and delay cases by deliberately arranging their schedules to require repeated continuances. This can have the advantage of exhausting prosecution witnesses and eroding their memories.[2]

Deception

Defense lawyers are sometimes asked to present perjured testimony by defendants. They sometimes find they can benefit their clients by impeaching the testimony of prosecution witnesses they know to be truthful. And they sometimes can gain advantage by arguing to the jury that the evidence suggests factual inferences they know to be untrue. For example:

> My client Norman, and his co-respondent, Steve Thomas, were charged with receiving stolen property. The police happened upon Norman and Steve in an alley transferring a stereo and TV from a junked car into the back seat of a white Pontiac.
>
> The case hinged on whether our clients knew (or should have known) that the property was stolen. . . .
>
> When Norman borrowed his cousin's Pontiac, he told us he was given only the ignition key, not the trunk key. But when all the evidence was in, no mention had been made of that fact. At Steve Thomas's lawyer's suggestion, we made what was to me, at the time, a novel and shocking argument: obviously Steve and Norman had no idea that the property was stolen, else why would they have been

loading into the Pontiac's back seat, instead of concealing it in the trunk?[3]

Greymail

Lawyers occasionally find it advantageous to disclose or threaten to disclose information they know does not contribute to informed determination on the merits because such disclosure injures the prosecution or witnesses. Take the practice of "greymail" as pioneered in the perjury defenses of various government officials, for example, CIA director Richard Helms, who lied to Congress about the agency's involvement in the overthrow of Chilean President Salvador Allende. The defense requests discovery of large amounts of information that would be damaging or at least embarrassing to the government solely in order to pressure it to drop the prosecution. Or consider the practice of bringing out embarrassing but irrelevant information about adverse witnesses. Assume for example, that the defense lawyer threatens to cross-examine the complaining witness in a rape case on her prior sexual history, even though the defendant does not contend that she consented.[4]

We can call the policy of engaging categorically in such practices whenever they are advantageous to the client "aggressive defense." The central question here is whether there is any feature distinctive to the criminal sphere that would lead a person who disapproved of aggressive defense (and its plaintiff-side analog) in the civil sphere to approve it in criminal defense.

Before discussing the assertedly distinctive features, we should consider two objections that, if conceded, would moot further discussion. First, in each of the situations mentioned above the ethically questionable tactic is permissible only because the judge allows it. The judge grants the motions for continuance, overrules the objections to the misleading examination or argument, and grants the discovery requests for the irrelevant information. The second objection challenges the premise that the defense lawyer ever "knows" anything with sufficient certainty to create the supposed tension between truth and advocacy. Even the client's own inculpatory statements may be the product of confusion or psychopathology. It is the trier's job, not the lawyer's, to make difficult factual determinations.

The general arguments of Chapter 6 seem responsive to these objections. Deference to the judge or trier is warranted only if he has all the relevant information. The issues of aggressive defense typically arise because the lawyer has information relevant to whether the tactic is justifiable that she withholds from the trier. She knows that the purpose of her motion for continuance is delay, or that the testimony of the prosecution witness is accurate, or that the requested discovery material will not be relevant to the defense.

To conclude that she "knows" these things, it is not necessary to attribute any cosmic, pre-Heisenbergian certainty to her; we just have to conclude that, given her knowledge (and the fact that she does not fully share it with the trier), she is in a better position than the trier to make the relevant judgment. If the client has told her, credibly but confidentially, that he was at the scene of the crime, then the defense lawyer is better able than the trier to decide whether it will be helpful to a determination on the merits to know that the prosecution witness who will place her there has impaired vision or a prior perjury conviction .

Nevertheless, the objections do point to one significantly distinctive feature of criminal defense—the presumption of innocence and its corollary, the prosecution's burden of proof beyond a reasonable doubt. The criminal process is committed within a broad range to resolving factual ambiguity in favor of the defendant. This implies that the defense lawyer cannot fairly "know" facts adverse to her client until she is convinced of them to a higher degree of confidence (beyond a reasonable doubt) than would be required in a civil case.

Weak Arguments for Aggressive Defense

The reasons most commonly given for a greater tolerance of categorically aggressive lawyering in criminal defense do not hold up well on examination.

The Bogey of the State

Libertarians claim that aggressive advocacy is distinctively appropriate to the criminal sphere because it serves to check oppression by the "state." Such arguments invoke the image of the "isolated," "lone," "friendless," or "naked" individual faced with the "enormous power and resources of the state." Aggressive advocacy is supposed to level the playing field and turn the trial into a "contest of equals," or at least express the system's commitment to treat all citizens with respect.[5]

It is also supposed to protect against the inherently corrupting nature of state power and the consequent aggression and rapacity of state officials. The aggressive defense lawyer inhibits abuse by increasing the difficulty of conviction. In David Luban's rhetoric,

> We want to handicap the state in its power even legitimately to punish us, for we believe as a matter of political theory and historical experience that if the state is not handicapped or restrained *ex ante,* our political and civil liberties are jeopardized. Power holders are inevitably tempted to abuse the criminal justice system to persecute political opponents, and overzealous police will trample civil liberties in the name of crime prevention and order.[6]

This type of rhetoric has been exempt from critical reflection for so long that even a small amount should be sufficient to raise doubts. In the first place, the image of the lonely individual facing Leviathan is misleading. Let's grant the lonely part even though some defendants have lots of friends. But what about the state? Libertarian rhetoric tends to suggest that the individual defendant takes on the entire state. But of course the state has other concerns beside this defendant. From the state's point of view, the defendant may be part of an enormous class of criminal defendants and suspects with which it can hardly begin to cope.

It would be more plausible to portray the typical defendant as facing a small number of harassed, overworked bureaucrats. Of course, state agencies can focus their resources on particular defendants, and when they do so, their power can be formidable. But the state cannot possibly focus its power this way on all defendants or most of them. Yet aggressive defense would treat all defendants as if they were facing the full concentrated power of the state.[7]

Second, there are no victims in the Libertarian picture. Criminal actions are styled as claims by the state for punitive remedies. But in fact they are often initiated on behalf of particular individuals whose rights have been violated by the defendant and who have a strong personal stake in the outcome (not necessarily a claim for tangible compensation—although some criminal proceedings involve restitution remedies—but a desire for vindication/retribution or for protection that might be afforded by the defendant's punishment).

The "victims' rights" movement has worked for the past two decades to replace in the popular consciousness the defense lawyer's image of the criminal trial as a state v. defendant contest with that of a victim v. defendant contest. The movement is often naive or blind about the efficacy of criminal punishment in either deterring future wrongs or aiding victims, but its imagery seems as plausible as that of the defense lawyer.

Now consider the suggestion that it is desirable to equalize the abilities of prosecution and defense or to level the playing field. If we really wanted to do this, we could "handicap" state officials (to use Luban's word) the way we handicap horses in thoroughbred races—by requiring the stronger ones to carry weights. It would certainly slow down prosecutors and police if they had to carry around belts with, say, 40 pounds of lead weights. If we wanted to pursue equality, we would have to increase the weights in proportion to the probability of conviction. The prosecutor of a defendant caught red-handed before a crowd of witnesses might have to drag around a ball-and-chain of several hundred pounds.

The reason this sounds silly is that the premise that there is an interest in *categorically* remedying imbalances of power between prosecution and defense is itself silly. We want the prosecution to be strong in its ability to convict the guilty and weak in its ability to convict the innocent. When these goals are in conflict, we make trade-offs, more often than not in favor of the latter. But an indiscriminate weakening of state power unfocused on any of the goals of the process serves no purpose at all. The problem with aggressive defense is that it impedes the state's ability to convict the guilty without affording any significant protection to the innocent.

The state-focused arguments for aggressive defense are driven by what might be called the Libertarian dogma. The right-wing version of the Libertarian dogma is that the only important threat to liberty is the state. The left-wing version is that the only important threats are the state and powerful private organizations like business corporations. In the latter view, as David Luban puts it, the central goal of the advocate's role is "the protection of the individual against institutions."[8] The idea that informal, diffuse violence or oppression might be a threat to liberty is incomprehensible to both versions of the dogma.

The Libertarian dogma is usually accompanied by references to totalitarian regimes like Nazi Germany and Soviet Russia and absence of criminal defense rights in such regimes.[9] These examples are supposed to illustrate the danger to liberty of the overpowerful state and the value of criminal defense in checking the danger. The point has merit, but it is incomplete. It ignores the dangers to liberty of the weak state. Both Nazi Germany and Soviet Russia emerged from weak states (the Weimar Republic and the Provisional Government), in part as a consequence of illegal private terrorism and paramilitary aggression these states were unable to check. Since the end of colonialism, Latin America has seen many examples of weak states powerless to check the terroristic oppression of the paramilitary forces of landowners or narcotics traffickers.

Moreover, as an argument for defendants' rights in the criminal process, the Libertarian dogma ignores that criminal law enforcement, in addition to posing a threat of abuse of state power, is an important *protection* against such abuse. This is tragically illustrated by the inability of certain weak Latin American states to prosecute effectively the crimes of their military officers. And in the United States the conversion of the friends of Oliver North to criminal defense partisans struck many liberals as a satisfying irony, but now that the Fifth Amendment has thwarted his prosecution for one of the most egregious abuses of state power in recent years, liberals should qualify their claims about its role as a safeguard against such abuses.

The left-wing version of the Libertarian dogma at least has the virtue of recognizing the potential threat to liberty of private organizations like the Nazi party under Weimar or the Mafia in Italy. But it too makes arbitrary distinctions. Consider David Luban's effort to update the dogma to acknowledge the powerful threat to the liberty of women posed by rape and sexual battery. This point might seem hard to square with the Libertarian dogma, since rapists and batterers are not typically agents of the state or organizations. But in his argument for restraint in cross-examining complainants in rape cases, Luban solves the problem by asserting that in such cases the state opposes another menacing institution—"patriarchy"!

This tactic proves too much. Since all behavior is situated in and influenced by social structures and processes, you can reify almost any act as an institutional act. Imagine prosecutors urging moderation in the defense of drug prosecutions on the ground that the state is confronting the institution of the Drug Culture; or in the defense of muggers on the ground that the state is pitted against the Underclass, or in the defense of a small-time con artist on the ground that the defendant represents Capitalism. Carried far enough, the tactic would lead to the insight that formal institutions are not the only important threats to liberty, that a wide and unspecifiable variety of social processes that are experienced as diffuse violence can do so as well. But the whole point of the tactic is to deny this insight, to make rape look exceptional and distinctively state-like so that the liberty interests in its effective prohibition can be acknowledged without conceding the point for a broad range of criminal prosecutions.

Luban's argument that aggressive defense desirably "overprotects" liberty against its abuse by the state raises the question of why overprotection against state abuse is worth the resulting underprotection against private abuse. To the extent one can discern an answer, it is the customary Libertarian claim (typically unaccompanied by anything passing for political or historical analysis) that the dangers of totalitarianism are greater than the dangers of anarchic chaos.

If we put aside the problem noted above that these dangers are not altogether distinct, there is a further objection to this argument. It assumes that we must choose categorically between a criminal justice system that protects against one danger and a system that protects against another. But in fact the relevant choices should be made at the margin. We can all agree on a system that provides strong opportunities for the establishment of innocence and for the assertion of some intrinsic procedural rights. The question then becomes whether any net benefits are achieved by the addition of a categorically adversarial defense that includes, for example, active deception.

Although the image of the powerful, rapacious state is the most prominent one in the rhetoric of criminal defense, one occasionally finds aggressive defense rationalized in terms of an image of a weak, bumbling state. In this image, the problem is not the bad faith of public officials but their sloth and ineptitude. Aggressive defense works to keep them on their toes and enforce higher standards of practice.

In working this rhetorical vein, John Kaplan refers to a prosecution in Los Angeles of a celebrity for soliciting prostitution in a police decoy operation. As executed prior to this case, the operation involved a microphone in the decoy's purse that transmitted to officers hiding nearby but did not record the soliciting statements. Defense counsel won an acquittal by emphasizing how easily the police could have obtained more reliable evidence by tape-recording and thereby casting doubt on the officers' "uncorroborated" evidence. As a consequence of this case, the police improved their practice by routinely taping the soliciting statements.[10]

The idea here is that the defense of the guilty helps the innocent by raising the standards of police and prosecutorial practice. Police and prosecutors who know that convictions are hard to get will gather more evidence and prepare more thoroughly, and this will result in more consistent vindication of innocent suspects and defendants because the officials will discover more exculpatory evidence and better understand ambiguities and weaknesses in superficially strong cases.[11]

As an argument for aggressive defense, the argument invites several objections. To begin with, we might ask why someone cynical about the dedication of public officials would expect them to respond to acquittals resulting from aggressive defense by raising their standards of practice. Mightn't they simply slack off, rationalizing their failures on the excuse that the courts aren't cooperating? Or perhaps they would increase their efforts along less constructive lines than those contemplated by the argument, spending more time on misleading and coercive tactics of their own.[12] Or perhaps they might try get the legislature to compensate for the increased difficulty of conviction by increasing the severity of punishment, giving them more plea bargaining leverage.

Indeed, recent demagoguery around crime control issues—efforts across the political spectrum to rally the public to vindictive, ineffectual punitive measures by exploiting fears of criminal violence—suggests that the argument might be turned around to assert that reliable conviction of the guilty is a crucial safeguard of the innocent. In a world where aggressive defense is legitimate, acquittal is less a signal of probable innocence than it would be in a world without aggressive defense. It is more likely to be seen as a consequence of defense delay, deception, or intimidation, and this might tend further to demoralize officials and the public and to exacerbate official misconduct and the vindictive irrationality of voters.

In addition, the argument mistakenly assumes that *any* enlargement of the requirements of proof for the prosecution is desirable. But the kind of defense offered here increases costs. There will always be some point at which the social benefits of increased prosecutorial burdens do not warrant the costs. Someone has to make a judgment on behalf of society as to where the balance should be struck. A defense lawyer committed to aggressive defense refuses to make such a judgment, and he impairs the ability of the court (judge, jury) to do so.

In order to appraise the conduct of counsel in Kaplan's story, we need to know something he doesn't tell us: did defense counsel mislead the court? If counsel simply argued that the court should acquit because police practices were inadequate, he did nothing questionable, but neither did he engage in aggressive defense. On the other hand, if counsel suggested to the jury that the defendant had not made the solicitation, knowing that he had, then he made no contribution to an informed decision about police practices.

The argument further assumes that society responds to the increased burdens aggressive defense puts on the prosecution by increasing prosecutorial resources. This seems unlikely. Such resources are scarce and compete with many other social needs. At some point increased burdens are sure to press against constraints on expansion. At this point, the critical effect of aggressive defense is to force a reallocation of resources *among* cases. This reallocation is more likely to be harmful to innocent defendants.

Ideally, one would want prosecutorial resources focused on (aside from protecting intrinsic procedural rights) resolving doubts about the guilt of suspects or defendants. But aggressive defense forces prosecutors to reallocate resources to cases (and within cases, to issues) in which neither they nor the defense lawyers have any doubts about guilt (or to the clarification of issues that make no contribution to the reliable determination of guilt). To the extent that resources are fixed, this means that fewer resources are available for cases and issues that involve doubts about guilt. Thus, innocent defendants are harmed.

Dignity

A frequent concomitant of the idea that aggressive defense checks the rapacity of the state is the idea that it expresses respect for the "dignity of the individual."[13]

One might distinguish two ways of showing respect for individual dignity. One can show respect in a general way through rights independent of guilt and innocence—for example, rights to notice of charges and to freedom from cruel and unusual punishment. Defense lawyers respect the dignity of their clients by enforcing such rights as well as by observing civilities of polite intercourse with them. But this sense of dignity in no way implies delay, deception, and intimidation. On the contrary, this general sense of dignity, which applies regardless of the characteristics of the particular person, has to be consistent with a comparable measure of dignity for others. It seems implausible, even incoherent, to think that anyone's dignitary interests require delay, deception, and intimidation of others.

The more specific type of respect that differentiates among individuals because of who they are and what they have done seems incompatible with aggressive defense for two reasons. Most obviously, aggressive defense treats all defendants alike. It tries to thwart conviction regardless of whether or not the accused is guilty. In addition, aggressive defense pushes the defendant to present himself as someone other than who he is or think he is. Not only does it portray defendants who have committed the acts charged as not having committed them; it also leads lawyers to orchestrate their clients' behavior in court to conform to the judge's and jury's stereotypes about how a respectable law-abiding citizen looks and behaves. Of course, if this is the best way to get an acquittal, most defendants would prefer such a defense, but few experience it as an affirmation of their individuality.

The idea that individual dignity might be served by helping the accused escape substantively appropriate conviction through deception or procedural manipulation is hard to square with the legitimacy of punishment after conviction. A viable ideal of dignity has to make room for respect for the rights of others and (at least in our system) for acceptance of punishment when the individual violates such rights.

Equal Opportunity

Defense lawyers often justify Libertarian ethics as a way of equalizing the circumstances of rich and nonrich defendants. A poor defendant should have as good a defense as a rich one, they say, and since a rich person has the benefits of delay and deception, so should the poor one.[14] The specious plausibility of this argument depends largely on its conflation in the phrase "as good a defense" of *as good an opportunity to prove one's innocence* (and to vindicate one's intrinsically valuable procedural rights), and the quite different notion of *as good an opportunity to escape conviction.*

Not all inequalities are illegitimate, and more importantly, not all the illegitimate ones can be desirably mitigated by extending the advantages of the better off to the rest. Rich people have much better opportunities to murder others than the nonrich, since they can buy expensive weapons and hire skilled henchmen to help them. This, however, is not an inequality that could be desirably corrected by extending the advantage to the nonrich. Whatever gain would result from greater equality would be swamped by the loss resulting from increased criminal violation of basic substantive rights of the victims.

The greater ability of the rich to escape conviction for their crimes is morally comparable to their greater ability to commit them in the first place. It is one of a large number of arbitrary determinants of conviction. Among criminals, the dumb, the clumsy, and the neurotic are more likely to be apprehended and convicted than the smart, the swift, and the single-minded. These inequalities are injustices, but they are trivial injustices compared to the injustices of many of the crimes themselves, and remedying them would not be worth the costs.

Needless to say, this point does not apply to advantages the rich enjoy over the nonrich in establishing their innocence. Moreover, we should also distinguish between advantages the rich enjoy because of social circumstances independent of the criminal justice process, and advantages created or enhanced by the criminal justice process. An example of the latter would be the advantages created by official decisions to focus prosecutorial efforts disproportionately on nonrich defendants. I return to this point below.

Self-incrimination

The constitutional privilege against self-incrimination is an undeniably distinctive feature of the criminal process. It is not controversial that where this privilege applies and the defendant wishes to take advantage of it, the defense lawyer should assist him in doing so. The application of the privilege with respect to a broad range of defense issues is, however, ambiguous. Moreover, for many lawyers the privilege embodies a general principle which, even where it is not specifically applicable as constitutional, statutory, or common law mandate, should inform the defense lawyer's ethical decisionmaking.

The importance of the privilege to the broader question of the defense lawyer's ethical obligations depends on how we understand it in relation to the right to counsel. On the one hand, we could interpret the relation to mean no more than that the defendant is entitled to the assistance of counsel in asserting his right to remain silent in the face of official interrogation. At the other extreme, we could decide that the privilege and the right to counsel require that the defendant not suffer any adverse consequences as a result of disclosures to counsel. As we have seen, this conclusion would require the lawyer to acquiesce in many forms of deception in circumstances when she knows that a particular tactic is deceptive because of something the client has told her.[15] Choosing among the positions along this spectrum requires some interpretation of what the privilege is about, and given the entrenched position of the privilege in the legal culture, it is surprisingly difficult to find a plausible one.[16]

The privilege plays a prominent role in the history of Anglo-American liberty, most notably in the struggle against religious persecution in England in the sixteenth and seventeenth centuries and in the struggle against political persecution in America during the McCarthy era. In both periods, however, its proponents associated it with principles that now seem only indirectly related to its contemporary core meaning. Among their most basic concerns was the criminalization of belief and expression; the claim that the defendant should not be forced to incriminate himself was usually linked to a more or less explicit contention that the activity in question could not be legitimately punished. Another set of concerns was procedural; the privilege was used to support objections to "roving questioning," that is, official interrogation without specified charges and without supervision by independent judges.

The American legal system now deals with the first concern under the rubric of freedom of belief and expression; with the second under the rubric of due process. These doctrines provide a variety of direct restraints on the criminalization of belief and a variety of explicit requirements with regard to charging and judicial supervision in the criminal process. To the extent these measures seem inadequate, the plausible way to respond would be to strengthen them directly. The contemporary practices we associate with the privilege seem a round-about route to these concerns.

To advance the inquiry, we have to ask what role the privilege has to play in connection with activity that has been legitimately criminalized and in a procedure where there is fair notice and specification of charges and some preliminary judicial determination that the charges have some basis. Four defenses of the privilege are relevant to this narrower inquiry.

First, it is said that the privilege deters irresponsible prosecution. In its absence, prosecutors might proceed to trial without adequate investigation in the hope that they could prove their case through examination of the defendant. This argument could be made just as well against the subpoena power. Limiting access to evidence at trial seems an inefficient way to encourage more investigation. One would think this concern would be adequately served by requiring the prosecutor to make a sufficient prima facie showing before examining the defendant.

Second, it is often asserted that forcing someone to "admit his guilt" is an unjustifiable infringement on autonomy or liberty. The limited plausibility of this suggestion is owed entirely to the possibility that "admit guilt" could mean *concede that punishment is justified,* rather than simply *acknowledge conduct that the law defines as criminal.* To preclude the defendant from disputing the legitimacy of the proceeding or the punishment she faces would violate important First Amendment values. But precisely for that reason we don't need the privilege to protect the defendant against this danger. The real issue with the privilege is whether she may be asked to describe her conduct (to the same extent that a third party witness could indisputably be asked about it).

For some, requiring even this much participation in a process leading to punishment is an intolerable assault on individuality. The prospect moves David Luban to reach for heavy rhetorical artillery. "[M]aking me the active instrument of my own destruction signals the entire subordination of the self to the state," he writes.[17] If we put aside the questionable conflation of punishment and "destruction" here, the problem remains that the subordination of the individual to the state is signaled most strongly by the substantive criminal law itself. To most people that subordination is tolerable to the extent the law is just. A duty to provide factual information about one's crime doesn't seem to intensify subordination much beyond the prohibition of the crime itself (except to the extent it makes enforcement more effective) and ought to be similarly tolerable.

Third, the privilege is sometimes associated with privacy values. The argument seems to be that it is a violation of subjectivity to enlist a person's knowledge against her for the purposes of punishment. But let's face it, the entire criminal process is one massive invasion of privacy. (Murder is the most private act a person can commit, William Faulkner suggested.)[18] Moreover, compelled testimony about self-incriminating conduct seems a far less serious inroad on privacy than substantive rules that make liability turn on subjective intent (even where intent is established by third party testimony). For example, intent is often the critical element of many fraud and embezzlement prosecutions, and this issue entails an investigation into the defendant's subjectivity in which a broad range of his conduct and lifestyle is potentially relevant. Yet invasion of privacy has rarely been treated as a serious objection to substantive rules of this kind.[19]

A fourth argument asserts that the basis for the privilege is the unreliability of self-incriminating statements. Confessions often reflect police coercion or internal psychological pressures. The point is well taken, but it is questionable whether it supports a norm as categorical as the privilege. Other types of evidence—for example, identification evidence by eyewitnesses otherwise unacquainted with the defendant—are also unreliable, but we typically deal with the problem by assessing reliability on a case-by-case basis rather than by wholesale exclusion. Nevertheless, reliability is the most plausible rationale for the privilege, and it implies a more limited scope than the others.[20] To the extent reliability is the concern, the privilege warrants exclusion of types of self-incriminating evidence with a strong tendency to mislead. On the other hand, reliability concerns do not support the claim that the client should never suffer adverse consequences because of a self-incriminating statement. If a statement has little likelihood of being unreliable or if it leads to reliable independent evidence, the reliability rationale suggests no reason why the material cannot be used adversely to the client.

Thus, on this view, the privilege offers no support for aggressive defense. Inculpatory statements made to counsel are not likely to be induced by coercion. The attorney should be in a good position to assess whether they reflect internal psychological pressures, and the insistence that the attorney be convinced of their truth beyond a reasonable doubt before taking any action adversely affecting the client should adequately protect against such pressures. There is, of course, no question of authorizing counsel to disclose client statements themselves. But the reliability explanation suggests no reason why counsel should employ tactics that neither vindicate intrinsic rights nor contribute to adjudication on the merits, even when counsel's assessment is based on information from the client.

Burden of Proof

I conceded earlier that it is proper for a defense attorney to seek an acquittal for a substantively guilty client on the ground that the prosecution has failed to meet the burden of proof. Some defense lawyers view this concession as a slippery slope leading to active deception. In practice, there are difficulties in maintaining the line between arguing that the burden of proof has not been met and actively deceiving.

The case of Norman and the borrowed Pontiac is a good example. The defense lawyer argued that "*obviously* Steve and Norman had no idea that the property was stolen, else why would they have been loading it into the Pontiac's back seat, instead of concealing it in the trunk?"[21] In fact the lawyer knew that they had not loaded it in the trunk because they didn't have the trunk key. This sounds like deception. The lawyer at least strongly implied that they could have opened the trunk, knowing that they could not have.

But many defense lawyers feel that this argument simply amounts to pointing out an omission in the prosecution's case; it failed to produce adequate evidence that Norman could not have opened the trunk. Thus any counterfactual argument can be seen as a suggestion that the prosecution has failed to sustain its burden in negating the inference in question.

I think this goes too far. Defense lawyers who press this contention concede that the jury does not understand this sort of argument as matter of burden of proof but as a suggestion that the exculpating inference is true. Although ethics rules forbid lawyers from asserting their "personal opinion[s]" about the matters they argue to the jury,[22] lawyers often violate the prohibitions in form, and many believe that lawyers *must* violate them, at least in spirit, to be effective. As Monroe Freedman writes, "[e]ffective trial advocacy requires that the attorney's every word, action, and attitude be consistent with the conclusion that his client is innocent."[23] Thus where the defense lawyer knows the inference is false, this type of argument can only be regarded as deception. That doesn't necessarily mean that it is unjustified, however. Defense lawyers feel that jurors tend not to understand and to undervalue procedural norms; they are naturally substance-oriented. If deception is the only way to get the jury to take account of burden-of-proof considerations, it is an ethical price worth paying. The problem with this argument is that misleading juries is not the only way to take care of burden-of-proof concerns. The usual procedure where we distrust the jury with an issue is to give it to the judge. And indeed the judge now has responsibility to dismiss charges on motion of the defense when the prosecution fails to produce evidence from which the jury could reasonably infer guilt.[24]

Why isn't this practice adequate to address burden-of-proof concerns without deceptive argument? There are three relevant concerns. One is the privilege against self-incrimination, which is partly implemented by placing the burden of proof (the burden-of-going-forward dimension) on the prosecution, but which I argued above does not require aggressive defense. Another concern served by the burden of proof (risk-of-nonpersuasion dimension) is to institutionalize a social judgment about the relative harms of erroneous acquittal and erroneous conviction by encouraging the resolution of doubts in favor of acquittal.[25] But aggressive advocacy makes only the most indirect and overbroad contribution here. It decreases the likelihood of erroneous conviction only by decreasing the likelihood of any conviction. Licensing the proffer of fraudulent evidence would have the same effect, though nearly everyone concedes that this would be improper (excluding the controversial case of client perjury). As I argued above, the idea that aggressive advocacy protects the innocent through its long-run effects on standards of police and prosecutorial practice is mistaken.

Finally, putting the burden of proof (going forward) on the prosecution serves the purpose of discouraging officials from subjecting citizens to the expense and anxiety of prosecution without adequate investigation and consideration in the hope that the defendants' evidence will help them complete their cases. But this concern seems adequately served by a rule requiring the judge to dismiss the case if the prosecution fails to produce evidence warranting conviction. As we saw above, it is not obvious that aggressive defense induces higher levels of preparation or, even if it does, that the benefits of the additional preparation warrant its costs.

Punishment

Some people find the criminal process categorically different from the civil one because the former is concerned with punishment rather than compensation. When a civil litigant prevails despite the merits of the case, the result is typically injustice to another particular citizen. When a criminal defendant prevails despite the merits, the cost is more abstract and diffuse. The victim of the injustice is society at large. Moreover, the nature of the loss is harder to define. Given widespread uncertainty about the legitimacy and efficacy of punishment, one might argue that we should have a high tolerance for the costs of wrongful acquittal.[26]

As I will soon acknowledge in detail, I think there is some substance to this point, but it fails as a categorical rationale for aggressive defense. First, this point has already been taken into account in defining the substantive terms of punishment and such procedural protections of the accused as the right to counsel and the high burden of proof in criminal cases. Moreover, the criminal process is often a substitute for the civil process. In cases when defendant and victim are in continuing contact, the criminal process is often used to specifically deter wrongs that are in principle civilly actionable but for which to civil process is too expensive or the civil remedies inadequate. (In addition, some criminal processes involve victim restitution remedies that are indistinguishable from civil remedies except in their relative ease of enforcement.)

Social Work, Justice, and Nullification

So far, the arguments for a special level of partisanship in criminal defense seem weak. However, we have yet to consider an argument that is not prominent in public rationalizations of aggressive defense but in fact seems to reflect an important ethical motivation of many defense lawyers. Barbara Babcock calls it the "social worker's reason," and she illustrates it with a story about how she used a strained insanity defense to save an indigent black client from a mandatory 20-year prison sentence for possession of heroin.[27]

The "social worker's reason" focuses on the harshness of contemporary punishment practices and on the disproportionate incidence of harsh punishment on racial minorities and the poor. The practices in question seem to be both spreading and intensifying. A few years ago Texas sentenced a man convicted of three frauds involving a total of about $200 to life imprisonment.[28] In California a young three-time loser who had never been charged with a violent crime recently received life without possibility of parole for possession of 5.5 grams of crack.[29] These are not idiosyncratic instances but examples of an enormous class of insanely harsh sentences, many of them prompted by public and official hysteria over the drug problem fueled by demagogic politics. The United States now has a larger proportion of its population locked up than any country in the world; in the 1970s and 1980s its incarceration rates exceeded those of nearly all totalitarian states.[30]

The fact that such punishment is disproportionately visited on racial minorities and poor people is surely an important part of the explanation why these practices are politically supported. (Nearly a third of all black men in America aged 20–29 are locked up or on probation or parole.)[31] Moreover, at least in some jurisdictions, the punishment practices are an integral part of a system of policing that targets minority communities and people of color, especially young men, for intensive and often abusive surveillance and discipline designed in part to keep them out of areas used by privileged racial and economic groups and in part to reinforce their subservience to a local power structure that excludes them.[32] To be sure, this characterization of contemporary criminal law enforcement is controversial, but for those of us who believe it is accurate, it is worth assessing what support it could provide for aggressive defense.

Consider first that Babcock calls the argument in question "the social worker's reason." At first glance, this seems an odd way to characterize an argument about *legal* ethics. It refers to a different profession. Moreover, it eschews rhetoric that is associated with the legal profession and is appropriate here, notably "injustice." Babcock's formulation seems to reflect the fact that the argument is in tension with the Positivist strains of the legal culture.

For the most part the punishment practices in question involve the imposition of statutorily prescribed penalties and the exercise of statutorily conferred official discretion. Moreover, constitutional doctrine has long restricted the principal routes to constitutional review of these practices. It all but precludes review of the fairness or proportionality of punishment[33] under the due process or cruel and unusual punishment clauses, and it permits relief under the equal protection clause for abuse of prosecutorial discretion only in rare and extreme circumstances.[34] This was true even throughout the period in which the federal courts opened wide avenues for review of police interrogation and search-and-seizure practices.

Consequently, lawyers who would work against the practices of excessive and discriminatory punishment find they must do so for the most part indirectly, by exploiting procedural obstacles to conviction. Especially in the absence of any ample constitutional footholds, many lawyers feel bereft of direct support within their own professional culture for efforts that are in essence designed to subvert these practices. Since the legislature has authorized the punishments and conferred discretion on police, prosecutors, and judges with respect to them, the punishments have sovereign authorization and hence legal legitimacy.

However, this view reflects the extreme Positivist orientation of professional responsibility discourse. It ignores the Substantive themes in the broader legal culture that are responsive to the defense lawyers' concerns. From a Substantive perspective, the fact that the legislature has authorized and the courts have refused to condemn or provide remedies for the practices in question doesn't conclude the issue of their legal legitimacy. There may still be room for a legal actor to decide that the legislatures and courts are wrong—that they have misapplied the relevant legal norms in approving these practices—and then to proceed on the basis of what the actor believes would be the correct decisions to the extent she has the practical ability to do so. This is the practice of nullification discussed in Chapter 4.

I think that an argument based on the idea of nullification would provide better support for aggressive defense than the rationales commonly offered for it. The argument is that aggressive defense is justified because it subverts punishment which, although formally prescribed, is unjustly harsh and discriminatory in terms of the more general norms of the legal culture. Moreover, the illegitimacy of such punishment is further suggested by the fact that it seems a product of various political breakdowns, including the political disfranchisement of the poor and demagogic obfuscation in the electoral process.

However, even when one concedes the view of contemporary criminal prosecution on which this argument is premised, that is still not an adequate justification of aggressive defense. The problem is that the argument is under-inclusive as long as one concedes that there is substantial class of defendants for which punishment would be just and otherwise appropriate. Aggressive defense is a practice of categorical or wholesale nullification; it doesn't focus on subverting the prosecutorial and police practices that could plausibly be opposed as excessive and unjust.

For the "social worker's" or nullification argument to work, the practice of aggressive defense would have to be reformulated toward one of ad hoc or retail nullification. Aggressive defense should be limited only to cases that present a threat of excessive or arbitrary punishment and should be employed only to the extent it is likely to counter the threat. The practice of aggressive defense ought to be part of a larger strategy designed to focus resources and effort on cases that present the greatest threats of injustice.

The practical ability of lawyers to adopt this approach will vary with the degree of autonomy a lawyer has in her practice. Some lawyers will find it easier to continue to commit themselves categorically to aggressive defense but to apply selective criteria at the point they decide to take on clients, restricting their practice to clients at risk of excessive or discriminatory punishment. Other lawyers will have more discretion about how they handle cases than about which cases to take. Lawyers in offices that regulate ethical issues through institutional standards may be able to persuade their offices to adopt the approach and specify institutional criteria for it. Others may be unable to influence their office policies toward the approach but may retain a good deal of discretion over their own cases. It is probably better for lawyers to formulate criteria for ad hoc nullification collectively and publicly—through public defender programs or specialized bar associations. (Such criteria should take the form of general standards, not ad hoc institutional management of individual cases.) But if this is not practical, it is better to have criteria formulated and applied individually and in private than to have no criteria at all.

To varying degrees, defense lawyers are subject to pressures from bar associations and courts that regulate their practices, from referral and funding sources, and from clients. Some lawyers may have enough autonomy in these relations to adopt the ad hoc nullification approach publicly and to link it to public opposition to excessive and discriminatory punishment, perhaps allying themselves with alternative bar associations and nonlawyer groups seeking to reform the system. Other lawyers will lack the autonomy to adopt the approach publicly but will have enough discretion over their cases to apply the approach tacitly. The more practical discretion the lawyer has, the more ambitiously she can apply the approach, but very few lawyers are so lacking in discretion that they could not meaningfully apply it at all.

Of course, some people will question whether there are any plausible criteria by which lawyers could distinguish excessive and discriminatory punishment, but the "social worker's" argument presupposes such criteria, so anyone who subscribes to this argument should have some. Moreover, while legal doctrine on sentencing and discrimination does not specifically legitimate the lawyer decisionmaking proposed here, it provides ample illustration of how lawyers disposed to make judgments of proportionality and discrimination might go about doing so in a manner that takes account of social values and practical reason.

No doubt particular lawyer nullification judgments will be controversial, but that is not in itself an objection to the practice. Particular judgments by police about when to arrest, prosecutors about when to prosecute, and judges and juries about when to convict are controversial as well. In deciding whether to favor giving responsibility to these actors, we don't ask whether each decision they make will meet with universal agreement, but whether on the whole their decisions will make a positive contribution in terms of the values we believe are relevant.

It is not possible to predict that the widespread, open adoption of ad hoc nullification would improve the criminal justice system without committing ourselves to some criteria of evaluation of the system and making assumptions about what criteria defense lawyers would adopt and apply. But I think anyone who subscribes to the critique of the present system as systemically prone to excessive and discriminatory punishment should be optimistic about the potential of this approach. My guess is that most idealistically motivated defense lawyers subscribe to this critique. The ad hoc nullification approach would allow them to express it more directly in their practice. It could improve practice both by leading to advocacy decisions that better fit the values most plausibly invoked to justify aggressive defense and by easing many defense lawyers' sense of alienation from their basic normative commitments in their day-to-day practice.

Some people will be concerned that since criteria will necessarily differ within the defense bar, defendants will get different levels of defense depending on which lawyer they end up with. However, that situation already exists under current ethical regimes: we defined aggressive defense in terms of tactics that were not explicitly regulated. Moreover, this seems to be another situation in which the concerns of horizontal equity seems less weighty than concerns of substantive justice.

One standard liberal response to the legitimacy of this kind of decisionmaking by lawyers in the civil sphere is the community-controlled legal services office. It is curious that the idea of community control has not been extended as often or as enthusiastically to public defender programs. There are serious problems with the community control ideal: for example, there is no self-evident way to define and represent communities, and fairness requires that in representing their clients lawyers should be free from various forms of political interference. But many of the judgments regarding the fairness and humaneness of police and prosecutorial practices and the relative social harm and iniquity of different offenses (which any rational deployment of defense resources requires) would best be made by a body generally representative of a meaningfully defined local group. There are plenty of precedents and examples in the civil sphere, and while the record is mixed, the idea retains promise.

There may be a concern that the open adoption of ad hoc nullification would make defenders vulnerable by appearing to politicize their practice. Ad hoc nullification might simultaneously enrage the forces of crime control demagoguery and alienate libertarian liberals whose support for criminal defense rests on the fallacious but ideologically powerful views criticized above. Yet it might turn out that a substantive critique of excessive and discriminatory punishment would provide a more powerful ideological basis for opposing crime-control demagoguery than does Libertarian liberalism.

The ideological appeal of libertarian liberalism has waned, especially outside the bar, and indeed crime-control demagoguery seems to have profited from popular revulsion at its antinomian contempt for responsibility and punishment, its paranoid antistatism, its indifference to victims, and its obsession with procedural at the expense of substantive justice. Many people concerned about crime control would be far more receptive to appeals for support for criminal defense based on ideals of substantive humaneness and fairness than they would to appeals based on the preoccupations of libertarian liberalism.

The Stakes

Some criminal defense partisans respond to my critique by asserting that, overall, aggressive defense does little to impede the prosecution of guilty defendants and indeed has little practical effect at all.[35] Even under my normative assumptions, they say, the serious problem is not aggressive defense but insufficient defense. Given resource constraints and the exploding volume of criminal prosecution, most defendants do not get the attention and effort to which they are entitled even under the most limited views of the proper scope of criminal defense.

This is an important point. However, the significance of the criminal variation of the Dominant View does not lie solely in its effect on current practices. It is also relevant to how we assess the system for purposes of reform and popular legitimation. Whether we can secure support for an increase in defense resources depends in part on what people think additional resources will be used for. If the extra resources will fund efforts to substantiate good-faith factual defenses, many will feel quite differently about them than if they will fund efforts to uncover evidence to impeach truthful witnesses.

If aggressive defense is of trivial practical importance, then the arguments for it are simply a pose, but the pose has important effects on popular attitudes toward the system. The popular view that defense lawyers commonly get acquittals for guilty defendants is probably wrong, but it is a reasonable inference to draw from arguments that portray aggressive defense as a potent bulwark against the state. Another important stake in the argument concerns the moral self-conception of defense lawyers and their capacity to express their moral commitments in their work. My approach would enable defense lawyers to connect their most plausible commitments more directly to their everyday practices. This ought to be counted as an important benefit.

Conclusion

We began with the question whether criminal defense should be treated differently from civil practice for purposes of the critique of the standard conception of adversary advocacy. The reasons most commonly offered for such a distinction turn out to be implausible. Nevertheless, there are reasons that might justify the selective use of aggressive defense tactics, as opposed to the categorical use prescribed by the Dominant View. The selective or ad hoc approach is the one prescribed generally by the Contextual View. So at the most general level, the ethics of criminal defense should not be different. On the other hand, this approach looks to the context of practice, and the problem of excessive and discriminatory criminal punishment seems distinctive both in severity and scale. In that sense, criminal defense is in fact different.

8

Institutionalizing Ethics

Discussions of legal ethics have a tendency to collapse into discussions of lawyer regulation. This happens when people assume that an ethical criticism of lawyering could be plausible only if it were susceptible to formulation and enforcement as a disciplinary rule.

This tendency should be resisted. Although it is supported by many of the current practices of bar associations and examiners, it runs against the central current of the aspirational tradition of professional rhetoric. The term "ethics" has been applied to our subject precisely to suggest that it involves more than coercive rule enforcement. It is in part a collective effort to define the meaning of good lawyering and to mark out the road to personal satisfaction and social respect as a lawyer. As such, one of its most important uses is as a guide to the exercise of discretion by lawyers. And while sanctions play a role in this project, informal criticism is as important.

I have left the subject of institutionalizing legal ethics for the end because we should think about implementation only after we've thought about what we are trying to implement. I don't propose to offer a comprehensive program. The current disciplinary regimes and any alternative ones likely to be adopted leave lawyers a good deal of discretion. Without any institutional changes, the Contextual View can serve as a basis for guiding and appraising lawyers' exercise of their discretion.

Nevertheless, institutions are important. An ethical program that resists institutionalization is handicapped. So it is important that the

Contextual View be susceptible to institutionalization. In particular, it is worth responding to the objections that any ethical program such as the Contextual View, which relies on informal norms or insists on higher-than-minimal responsibilities to nonclients, will be thwarted by economic pressures. We have had occasion to consider aspects of these objections in prior chapters; I can elaborate here on the responses to them.

An enforcement structure inspired by the Contextual View would have two main features: a disciplinary regime consisting largely of contextual norms, and a set of rules designed to encourage voluntary ethical commitments and strengthen the forces that make for informal enforcement of such commitments.

Such a program could be undertaken by an inclusive bar association such as the American Bar Association and its state counterparts, but it is an important virtue that it does not require support from such an association. It could be effectively pursued as well by courts, legislatures, and public regulatory agencies, and there is an important role in it for specialized voluntary bar associations. From the Contextual perspective, the role of inclusive bar associations in professional responsibility matters has been largely regressive. The vision of professionalization we reviewed in Chapter 5 considered its twin commitments to contextual judgment and self-regulation through inclusive professional associations to be complementary. In fact, inclusive bar associations have tended to use their authority over the regulation of practice to shear off the aspirational aspects of the professional vision, to replace contextual with categorical norms, and to minimize responsibilities to nonclients.[1]

The recent developments in professional regulation most compatible with the Contextual View have been invariably undertaken by other institutions—courts, regulatory agencies, and specialized bar associations. While the courts in their roles as ethical regulators have been inclined to adopt the national bar's codes more or less wholesale, they have taken different tacks in other contexts. In applying criminal and tort norms against fraud and assisting illegal activities and in liberalizing the discovery system, several courts have enlarged (or rediscovered) lawyer duties to nonclients under relatively contextual norms. So have some regulatory agencies, notably the Securities and Exchange Commission and the Office of Thrift Supervision (the latter in the Kaye Scholer case), in applying their disclosure norms to lawyers practicing before them.[2]

Moreover, exclusive or specialized voluntary bar associations have occasionally taken promising initiatives on professional responsibility issues. To mention three examples: the Association of the Bar of the City of New York is an old organization with a long history of interest in ethics. It has occasionally encouraged commitments to nonclient interests that were considerably stronger than the minimalist standards of the ethics codes. In recent years it has urged standards that would require tax lawyers to take more responsibility for the validity of the positions they take on behalf of clients.[3] The American Academy of Matrimonial Lawyers was organized in 1988 with a declared intention to elevate the ethical standards of divorce practitioners. It has promulgated its own ethical code for members in areas such as disclosure and litigation tactics that imposes significantly stronger responsibilities to adverse parties than do the ABA codes. Three Associations of Business Trial Lawyers, recently formed in each of the major metropolitan areas of California, have also promulgated ethical rules for their members designed to moderate the strategic, counter-purposive use of litigation procedures. For the most part the new standards proposed by these organizations are only modest departures from the status quo, and they have not been accompanied by formal enforcement procedures. Nevertheless, they are suggestive.

A Contextual Disciplinary Regime: The Tort Model

A disciplinary regime inspired by the Contextual View would start with the "promote justice" maxim and develop it into a set of more definite precepts. The regime should include one or more codes or "restatements." The norms in these compilations would take the form of general standards, rebuttable presumptions, and illustrative cases. Elaboration would not occur in a single effort at promulgation but progressively through clarifications and revisions announced in the course of specific cases.

Those who doubt that a lawyer regulatory regime of contextual norms would be viable need to be reminded that we already have such a regime. It has been fully operational for decades and has been accepted with less controversy than surrounds the ABA ethics codes. I refer of course to the tort system as it applies to lawyers.

The Dominant View characterizes only one of two parallel systems of professional responsibility. This is the disciplinary system focused on bar associations and courts in their regulatory role. The other system—common law tort liability—is focused on courts in their adjudicatory role. The disciplinary system primarily administers sanctions designed to deter future misconduct, while the tort system primarily administers damage awards designed to compensate for past misconduct. Both systems, however, are centrally concerned with the elaboration of standards of professional conduct, and the substantive norms they enforce overlap substantially. (Nearly all lawyer liability in tort involves either negligence or fraud, both of which are violations of the ethics codes.)

Comparison of the two systems might be helpful in considering a range of institutional questions about the design of disciplinary regimes, such as the relative roles of public authorities and bar associations, of judicial versus administrative proceedings, of public versus private enforcement, and of punitive versus compensatory remedies. However, I will not address these issues here.[4] I simply want to invoke the negligence system to suggest that there is nothing radical about the notion of a legal ethics of contextual norms and to give some idea of how contextual norms might work in a Contextual disciplinary regime.

The core norm of the tort system is perhaps the most uncompromisingly contextual of legal norms—the negligence norm. As Roscoe Pound said, such norms "are not formulated absolutely and given an exact content, either by legislation or by judicial decision, but are relative to times and places and circumstances and are to be applied with reference to the case at hand."[5] Or as the *Restatement of Torts* says, the negligence standard "provides sufficient flexibility to permit due allowance to be made . . . for all the particular circumstances of the case." The rhetorical touchstone of the negligence norm is reasonableness, and the "qualities of [reasonableness] differ with the various circumstances in which the phrase is used."[6]

Outside the field of legal ethics, this type of norm is routinely associated with professional judgment. The Supreme Court acknowledged this association when it declined to formulate categorical standards of "effective assistance" of counsel under the Sixth Amendment: "No particular set of detailed rules for counsel's conduct can satisfactorily take account of the variety of circumstances faced by defense counsel or the range of legitimate decisions regarding how best to represent a criminal defendant."[7]

The established bar itself often speaks this way. The *Model Code,* explaining the prohibition against law practice by nonlawyers, concedes that lay people are capable of learning and following specific rules. What they lack (presumptively) that lawyers have (presumptively) is "professional judgment"; and "The essence of the professional judgment of the lawyer is his educated ability to relate the general body and philosophy of the law to a specific legal problem of the client. . . ."[8] Notwithstanding their treatment of lawyer obligations to third parties in categorical terms, the ethics codes themselves tend to treat lawyer obligations to clients in contextual terms. The key duties to clients—those concerning competence, conflicts of interest, and reasonableness of fees—take contextual forms.[9]

We do not expect norms of this type to be fully specified. In the context of ordinary torts, the actor and the jury in reviewing her conduct are expected to bring to bear a broad range of tacit knowledge accumulated through social experience. When a lay jury appraises professional conduct, we typically require that it be assisted by expert witnesses who are expected to draw on tacit, informal knowledge.

We use rules to ground and specify the standard of care. In meeting the standard, however, an actor can't simply look at a body of rules and assume that anything not specifically prohibited there will be satisfactory. We expect that often there will be no specific rules at all. And when we find rules, we rarely treat them as conclusive. Rule violation is at best "evidence" of a breach of care and can be rebutted by a showing that following the rule in the particular context would not have vindicated the more general goals of the relevant practice. And compliance with rules is rarely a conclusive defense.

Empirical regularity of practice—custom—also provides grounding, but again, we don't treat custom as conclusive. It is always open for a plaintiff or defendant to show that customary practice is out of harmony with more general norms. Another type of guidance comes in the form of exemplary cases. This is, of course, the hallmark of common law adjudication, and it has many analogues in professional practice—for example, model forms or protocols for various tasks. A key element of this type of guidance is that it requires a relatively complex judgment about the extent to which the particular circumstances in which the professional finds herself are analogous to those involved in the case or model.

Of course, courts play different roles when defining tort standards than they (or agencies or associations) do when creating a disciplinary regime. A common law court enforcing the standard of care for professional tort liability purposes draws on norms elaborated within the profession. It may decide among competing professional norms and may occasionally reject norms prevalent within the profession, but for the most part it thinks of itself as enforcing commitments established independently of its efforts. Although its powers might well be considered legislative, they are secondary legislative powers. In this role, it would not be plausible for the court to undertake a comprehensive statement of the profession's commitments even if common law traditions did not restrict it to case-by-case operation.

The intra-professional efforts on which the tort system draws, however, often take the form of codes or restatements. When a bar association, or even an agency or court with regulatory power over the bar elaborate a disciplinary regime, they are at least partly occupying an intra-professional role, speaking for the profession rather than holding it to its espoused commitments. As such they are in a better position to promulgate more general and comprehensive normative statements.

The reasonable care/negligence norm has an important relation to the notion of professional consensus pertinent to legal ethics. As we saw in Chapter 3, a frequent objection to the Contextual View is that contextual judgments about ethics are controversial, as if that precluded their use as a basis for ethical judgments.[10] Clearly, controversy is equally true of malpractice adjudication, and the response to controversy there is quite instructive for legal ethics. When we review a professional judgment for negligence purposes, we tacitly distinguish two levels of controversy.

First, professionals may disagree about whether a particular judgment is below the minimal standard of care the law should enforce. To the extent this is so, we are less likely to impose liability. But we don't consider such controversy to preclude liability. If the condemnations of the practice meet certain basic criteria of credibility and have substantial acceptance in the profession, the court is likely to consider the competing views, and when persuaded by the condemnations, to impose liability even without consensus.

Second, professionals may agree that two or more competing judgments are consistent with minimal standards and yet disagree about which is best. If that is the situation, the courts will not impose liability, and the tort system will not further consider the issue until a professional constituency of some standing asserts that one of these positions is not simply wrong but unreasonable. Until then, the tort system remains agnostic.

Within the profession, however, debate continues, and it can be passionate and intense. One would never expect, for example, doctors to say that because two alternative medical procedures were reasonable for tort purposes, there was no point in trying to figure out which would be best for the patient. On the contrary, we might expect a vigorous debate over the merits, in which each side would argue forcefully that the other's judgments were wrong, yet without any intention of subjecting it to liability. Doctors treating patients would have to read these debates and decide which seemed most persuasive before choosing which procedure to recommend. They would be unlikely to say to a patient that, because the procedures were controversial, they would withhold making a recommendation. Similarly, professional institutions whose members were convinced that one procedure was better would not hesitate to express their collective view simply because it was likely to be controversial.

When someone says the Contextual View is unworkable because the judgments it encourages are controversial, he may to refer to controversy about whether judgments meet minimal standards of care. If so, he is right in implying that such controversy weighs against liability, but he seems to have forgotten that the tort system illustrates that such controversy doesn't preclude plausible liability judgments. Sometimes, the objection refers to controversy about which of competing reasonable judgments is best in terms of the relevant values of the legal system. This would be preclusive for the Contextual regime only if it were exclusively preoccupied with liability, but it should not be.

The tort system reflects a clear division of labor in which the courts concern themselves exclusively with liability and leave noncoercive criticism and debate to institutions within the profession. Though legal ethics regimes are sometimes considered as simply liability systems, it is more plausible to think of them also as part of the noncoercive intra-professional systems of criticism and reform. This latter role is reflected in two distinctive practices of disciplinary systems not found in tort systems—the sanction of censure or "reprimand" and the advisory opinion, both of which analyze and pronounce conduct as unethical without awarding damages, enjoining conduct, or settling private disputes. The broader role of the ethics system is further evident in the fact that the same professional organizations that are active in discipline are typically involved as well in more informal ethical discussion, for example, sponsoring conferences, debate, and research.

In their disposition toward "black letter" norms, the drafters of the ABA codes seems to have been thinking in criminal rather than tort law terms. Criminal law typically requires a much higher degree of normative specification than does tort law. Legal ethics regimes have some similarities to criminal law regimes. The norms in both spheres are associated with penalties or punishment imposed by a regulatory authority, rather than with damage awards to injured parties. Furthermore, the more severe penalties under ethical regimes—suspension or disbarment—have a catastrophic quality arguably more comparable to severe criminal than to severe tort awards. And liability under both criminal and ethical norms typically carries a stronger sense of social stigma than does tort liability.

In fact, however, the analogy of professional discipline to criminal punishment is a poor one. It ignores the substantive overlap between disciplinary and tort norms; malpractice is a matter of both tort liability and professional discipline. Most importantly, the similarities between discipline and criminal punishment are dwarfed by a critical difference between them: the disciplinary process is substantially a form of occupational *self*-regulation. This means not so much regulation through participatory professional institutions as the enforcement of standards that are immanent in practice. Malpractice norms, even when determined by institutions outside the profession, are declarations of norms developed by practitioners themselves. A malpractice judgment typically must be supported by evidence that respectable practitioners generally regard the relevant standards as binding. The processes of professional education and socialization function to inculcate such norms. By contrast, howevermuch we expect the criminal law to incorporate ordinary morality, we treat criminal norms as a more remote and impersonal form of regulation than tort law.

The issue of stigma needs further comment. Many lawyers apparently believe that a judgment of unethical conduct inflicts a stronger emotional and symbolic wound that a comparable judgment of tort liability. This belief is irrational and perverse. It is irrational because, as we have noted, nearly all lawyer violations of tort duties are also violations of ethical duties. It is perverse because it fuels a resistance to the expansion of ethical duties and a demand for cumbersome safeguards, including formal specification.

The belief in the strongly stigmatic character of adverse judgments seems to be sustained by a tradition of sanctimoniousness in legal ethics rhetoric. At the same time that they have been inclined to minimize the range of ethical duties, mainstream lawyers have been inclined to speak of the ones remaining as if they had a sacred quality. This tradition has been exacerbated by the recent tendency of some ethicists to interpret professional responsibility as an expression of "character" rather than a matter of just conduct.[11] It seems to follow from this "character" perspective that an adverse ethical judgment is evidence of fundamental lack of personal worth.

The only cure for this situation is to lower the level of sanctimoniousness. Abandoning the infatuation with good "character," as opposed to good conduct, would be a good first step. The phrasing of criticism in legal ethics terms should not by itself carry greater stigma than any other adverse legal judgment on conduct. Of course, particular ethical violations can be outrageous and can carry strong connotations about a person's character. But other violations involve minor harms, or turn on close questions, or result from excusable inadvertence or understandable pressures, or represent good faith mistakes. We shouldn't be inhibited from addressing and criticizing these types of conduct in legal ethics terms by categorical rhetorical overkill.[12]

Restructuring the Market for Legal Services

Some people believe that the Contextual View, or indeed any approach to legal ethics that imposes greater duties toward nonclients than does the Dominant View, is likely to be overwhelmed by social pressures. The argument is ultimately unpersuasive, but it serves as a useful reminder that regulation, in addition to mandating conduct and penalizing deviant behavior, can influence conduct indirectly by altering the institutional structures that generate informal pressures on practice.

Begin with the Race-to-the Bottom argument. Clients, it is said, will prefer the lawyers most willing to pursue their interests aggressively. Lawyers willing to go farther than others will have a competitive advantage. They will draw clients disproportionately. In order to maintain their practices, more ethically ambitious lawyers will have to compromise their principles and imitate their more zealous competitors. When they do, the initially more aggressive lawyers will find they have lost their competitive edge and will respond by becoming still more aggressive. The cycle will continue until people settle at the lowest tolerable commitment to nonclient (third-party and public) interests. Such forces threaten to overpower the aspirational dimensions—those that rely on exhortation, example, and criticism rather than sanctions—of the Contextual project.

On reflection these pessimistic conclusions seem unwarranted. As a matter of intuition, we could just as easily hypothesize a Race to the Top. In this contest, lawyers compete, not on the basis of their willingness to assert client interests aggressively, but on the basis of their ability to induce third parties (both potential deal partners and tribunals) to trust their clients. They accomplish this by convincing third parties of their own commitment to fairness and then vouching for their clients. The more credible a lawyer's commitment to fairness, the greater his ability to induce others to trust the client and the more valuable he is to the client. Thus lawyers might try to outdo each other in at least the observable manifestations of fairness, and equilibrium would occur at a very high level of commitment to third-party interests. There is, of course, a third scenario that predicts less extreme consequences. This one suggests that lawyers will sort themselves ethically at a range of positions between the bottom (low commitment) and the top (high commitment) and attract distinct clienteles with distinct preferences for ethical commitment.

Now of the outcomes predicted by the three scenarios, the third—sorting—seems closest to the real world. Lawyers display a broad range of ethical identities. Some seem to have adopted the strategy presupposed by the Race to the Top; Brandeis is the paradigm. Some seem to have raced to the bottom; Roy Cohn is a safe example. Between these extremes there is further differentiation. Sometimes the differentiation is associated by function. For example, criminal defense lawyers who specialize in negotiating plea bargains tend to be less ethically aggressive than those who specialize in trying cases. Some differentiation exists within function. For example, some tax lawyers are much more aggressive in giving opinion letters than others. Yet it seems likely that the opinions of such lawyers are less credible, and that these lawyers trade off the reduced demand for their services by people in strong positions against the increased demand from people with weak positions who can't get opinions from lawyers with strong third-party commitments.

Thus there are more opportunities for ethically ambitious lawyers in the current scene than the Race-to-the-Bottom argument suggests. From a reform perspective, we should consider whether these opportunities might be expanded. The "Race" arguments attribute the pressures on ethical behavior simply to "the market," but there are many ways to organize a market. The current level of demand for ethically ambitious or high-commitment lawyering is in part a function of the particular organization of the market now in effect. Some features of this organization that are neither necessary concomitants of markets nor clearly efficient (in the economic sense of maximizing preference satisfaction) may inhibit demand for high-commitment lawyering.

For high-commitment ethics to work in the manner contemplated by the Race-to-the-Top scenario, lawyers need a way of making their commitments credible to third parties. Otherwise third parties have no reason to reward the lawyer and her client in the manner the scenario contemplates. One general way of establishing such credibility would be for the lawyer to negotiate a contractual commitment directly with the third party. For example, in large business deals, lawyers sometimes provide an express "10(b)-5" warranty asserting that they have not withheld material information from the third party. The negotiations can take a more subtle form when the lawyer deals repeatedly with a third party. For example, a tribunal might reward lawyers who appear to adhere to high-commitment ethics with procedural accommodation or more ready acceptance of their representations. Another way to gain credibility could be for lawyers to make commitments in a more general and public way. They might simply advertise them or they might associate themselves with an organization that holds to high-commitment ethics.

The sanctions underpinning these commitments might take a variety of forms. An explicit direct commitment might be enforceable through contract damages by the third party. Such enforcement is often cumbersome and expensive, so it is important that there are more informal mechanisms. The Race-to-the-Top argument emphasizes the importance of reputational sanctions. Current breaches reduce the future credibility of a lawyer's commitments and hence the willingness of third parties to trust and reciprocate the commitments. Such sanctions might be underwritten by organizations, for example, specialized bar associations, which might monitor their members' behavior and impose reputational sanctions such as reprimands or expulsions.

There are, however, important obstacles to such processes in a market for legal services. How the particular design of the market responds to these problems will affect the level of demand for high-commitment ethics. The present structure of the market does not seem to respond to the problems as well as it might. Consider four problems.

Psychological Bias

Behavioral psychology documents widespread cognitive biases that influence economic behavior. People tend to overestimate the likelihood of success of their projects. (For example, when interviewers ask people about to get married to estimate their own chances of divorce, nearly all estimate the chances at close to nil, even though more than half of marriages end in divorce.) They also tend to focus on the immediate, vivid, and instantiated contingencies at the expense of more remote and abstract ones. (For example, survey respondents consistently overestimate the frequency of dramatic causes of death such as homicide, and underestimate the frequency of mundane ones such as asthma.)

Speculating on the influence of such biases on contractual specification of relational duties, Melvin Eisenberg writes,

[A]t the time the contract is made, each party is likely to be unduly optimistic about the relationship's long term prospects and the willingness of the other party to avoid opportunistic behavior or unfair manipulation of the relevant contractual duties as the relationship unfolds. . . . [B]ecause of defects in capability the parties are likely to give undue weight to the state of the relationship as of the time the contract is made, which is vivid, concrete, and instantiated; to erroneously take the state of their relationship at that point as representative of the relationship's future; and to give too little thought to and put too little weight on the risk that the relationship will go bad.[13]

To the extent third parties are disposed to underfocus on the contingencies that high-commitment ethics safeguards against, they will tend not to negotiate for them directly. The same tendency would undermine informal reputational sanctions.

The emotional overload associated with ethical rhetoric may also inhibit bargaining. To doubt someone's ethics, even where people are unsure what substantive criteria the doubts presuppose, is sometimes taken as an assault on her character. Clients may fear that signaling doubts will provoke distress or indignation, and this fear may lead to an emotional, as well as cognitive, bias against recognizing issues of ethical commitment. Anxiety may lead people to screen from consciousness the contingencies that would make the issues important.

The Costs of Normative Specification

Suppose two parties negotiating a deal want to adhere to high-commitment ethics, for example, to the Contextual View. Would they be satisfied to simply add a sentence to the contract promising to bind each other to the "ethics of the Contextual View" or to "act justly"? Probably not. These terms require definition. Even parties who think they share a general sense of their meaning might feel willing to commit themselves, or to rely on the other party's commitment, only after the terms had been significantly elaborated. However, if the parties were writing on a clean slate, elaboration would involve a lot of costly time and effort. (A contextual ethic doesn't necessarily require less specification than a categorical one, just a different kind of specification—rebuttable presumptions and exemplary cases rather than formal rules.)

When publicly produced codes are available that can be incorporated by reference or that the law applies by default, the drafting task is greatly simplified. The ABA codes and the extensive case law and commentary interpreting them perform this function, but they provide only the qualified low-commitment ethic of the Dominant View. Although most elements of this ethic could be waived if the client wanted to agree to a high-commitment ethic, there is no elaboration of a high-commitment ethic as salient, as specific, or as extensively glossed as the ABA elaboration of the low-commitment one. This creates a bias in favor of low-commitment ethics. The parties might prefer the Contextual View substantively, but feel deterred by the costs of elaborating it. They might settle for low commitment because they can get it at minimal transaction costs.[14]

A lawyer who wants to market a high-commitment lawyering style to clients or convince third parties that his high commitment deserves reciprocation has to convince the clients and third parties that it is worth their while to make the effort to learn about the high-commitment style. They may have reservations about low commitment, but if it is widely mandated or incorporated, they may feel comfortable with it because they are familiar with it. By contrast, high commitment might entail costly education. Such costs give a prevalent system the benefit of an inertia independent of the substantive attractiveness of its terms.

The same point applies, though perhaps less strongly, to informal commitments and relations with tribunals. A lawyer will be less inclined to try to commit himself in a general public way to high-commitment ethics if he has to shoulder the cost of elaborating the ethic himself. A tribunal will be less inclined to impose or negotiate for high commitment with those who appear before it if it has to shoulder all these costs. A tribunal that adopts a norm widely prevalent elsewhere benefits from both past and future efforts of others who elaborate the norm. By contrast, a tribunal that adopts a distinctive norm may fear that unless others follow it, the norm will remain suboptimally elaborated.

Enforcement Information

The credibility of ethical commitments depends substantially (though not exclusively) on the availability of effective sanctions for breach. Whether the sanctions are coercive, such as contract damages or disciplinary penalties, or informal, such as loss of reputation, they require accurate information about lawyers' fidelity to their commitments.

Such information is hard to get. It is often ambiguous and closeted by confidentiality norms.[15]

Some suggest that recent institutional developments have exacerbated this problem by disrupting informal transmission networks for reputational information. When a small number of lawyers deal with each other repeatedly in a local setting, the prospects of effective informal information sharing and reputational sanctions are high. In recent decades, however, the size of the bar has grown dramatically, and practice has become more dispersed nationally and even globally. In these circumstances, information about noncomplying behavior may not be available; to that extent, lawyers have less incentive to honor their commitments and third parties less incentive to rely on them.

Asymmetric Information about Disposition

Some bargains may be inhibited by a combination of ignorance on one side and reluctance to disclose strategically valuable information on the other side. The argument is complicated, but in essence, as applied to our subject, it goes like this. Suppose that in certain deals where sharp practice (deception and abuse) occurs, it causes large losses, and that such losses could be averted if the sharpies (those disposed to sharp practice) bound themselves to high-commitment ethics. If fully informed, honest parties dealing with sharpies would insist on high commitment. In fact, however, honest parties can't distinguish sharpies from other honest parties. Sharpies want low commitment, but they do not want to have to ask for it, because doing so would signal their identities to honest parties. If, however, the default rule is low commitment, they don't need to ask for it unless the opposing party asks for high commitment.

Will an honest party who doesn't know with whom he is dealing ask for a high commitment? Perhaps not. If sharp practice is rare and the fraction of sharpies in the population is small, even though individual losses from sharp practice may be large, average losses over the whole range of deals may be small. Not knowing the disposition of her counter-party, an honest party will value a high commitment in terms of the average loss from sharp practice. It is possible that the average loss might be less than the transaction costs of high commitment (the costs of specification plus the costs of negotiating the value of the term). Thus while fully informed parties would negotiate to high commitment, if information is asymmetric and the default term is low commitment, they might end up accepting that low commitment.[16]

This is a problem that largely affects private negotiation. It is less likely to affect tribunals because the large volume of cases they deal with means that the transaction cost per case of achieving high commitment are lower; they can, for example, act through general rule. Moreover, to the extent that lawyers have definite ethical reputations, it may be possible to distinguish sharpies by their lawyers. But, as we have noted, reputational information is limited.

The four obstacles we have considered suggest that the relative strength of the forces pushing toward the ethical top and the ethical bottom are not simply matters of client preferences but also of psychological biases, contracting problems, and limited information. No market regime could eliminate these problems. But there are different ways in which market regimes can respond to them, and the balance of forces will depend on which ways are chosen. The current configuration of the market for legal services is more accommodating to low-commitment than high-commitment ethics. Thus an implementation program for the Contextual View might include various measures for the reform of the market, among which the most important involve adjustment of the contract process, elaboration of optional norms, and information provision.

Contracting Rules

One response to market defects is to eliminate contractual discretion through mandatory rules. Some ethics rules, such as those governing the more extreme forms of fraud and abuse, do and should take a mandatory form. But there are less severe responses that leave some contractual discretion.

One involves the design of the *default rules* that apply in the absence of explicit agreement. The current low-commitment default rules seem to aggravate some of the problems we've identified. First, they reinforce the effects of the psychological biases in favor of low-commitment ethics. Second, they provide no incentive for parties intending to conceal material information or engage in aggressive conduct (sharpies) to disclose information to differently disposed bargaining partners (honest parties) that would signal to the latter the risks they are undertaking.

Reversing the default rules to create a presumption of high commitment—for example, full disclosure of material information—might therefore have desirable effects. In situations where neither party is aware of or disposed to raise the issue, high-commitment ethics serves their interests. In situations where one party disproportionately wants low-commitment ethics, a high-commitment default rule would force that party to raise the issue and bargain for her preferred alternative. This would provide a counter-weight to the other party's cognitive biases against considering the issue. It would also provide the other party with a useful signal that she faces risks she would otherwise not have been aware of. In a situation where both parties wanted the low commitment, they could still obtain it by specifying it in an agreement.

A more modest reform would introduce *commitment-forcing* rules to the ethics sphere. A commitment-forcing rule requires parties to make some explicit commitment about a particular issue, regardless of the content of the commitment. An example of a commitment-forcing rule is the requirement in many states that lawyers must make an explicit agreement with clients about fees and set it forth in writing. The rule arises in part from concerns that psychological biases otherwise would discourage the client from focusing on the issue. Such rules might be extended to negotiations with third parties. Lawyers might be required in any substantial direct negotiations to set forth in writing to the other party the ethical standards they are operating under either generally or with respect to specific issues such as disclosure.

Tribunals could include such requirements in their rules of practice. A rule might specify alternative acceptable ethical standards and insist that each lawyer indicate which one she considered herself bound by. The IRS, for example, could offer a choice that included a norm under which a lawyer (or nonlawyer tax preparer) would agree to disclose all known material information and to identify all legal positions as to which there was substantial doubt. A lawyer who made the commitment and breached it would be subject to sanction. A lawyer who didn't make the commitment would subject her client to a higher likelihood that the returns would be audited.

Publicly Subsidized Optional Codes

An elaborated set of ethical commitments is a public good in the economist's sense. Once someone produces it, it is difficult to limit others' use of it, and any one person's use doesn't limit its availability to others. Economists argue that goods of this sort will tend to be underproduced through private, profit-oriented initiative. We have noted that the public subsidy for low-commitment ethics reflected in the ABA codes and related cases and commentary creates a strong bias against high-commitment ethics.

So one reform would be to subsidize production of alternative high-commitment bodies of norms that parties could adopt by incorporation. By reducing the transaction costs of high commitment, such efforts might have large impact even if their norms were optional. These alternative norms could be produced either by public agencies or private associations.

Note that the "public goods" analysis suggests reservations about the tradition of elite law reform exemplified by the American Law Institute's *Restatement of the Law Governing Lawyers*. The Institute is a philanthropic law reform association dedicated to producing "restatements" of various areas of law for the guidance of courts and practitioners. The *Restatement* approach to law reform has involved a combination of summary and clarification on the one hand and incremental reformism on the other. The governing assumptions seem to be that summary and clarification alone might rigidify or sanctify the status quo, but anything more than incremental reformism would deprive the restatements of strong influence.

If the *Restatement* norms were proposals for enactment as mandatory rules, these assumptions would be plausible. But if we think of them as optional rules available for incorporation in private agreements or public reputational commitments or rules of specialized tribunals, then the assumptions are misguided. Producing new but minor variations tends to increase ambiguity, and hence the costs of clarifying commitments by adding to stock of plausible referents of a particular standard. More importantly, by limiting reform to incremental changes, the restatements contribute little to the range of choice available for discretionary ethical commitment. The substantial resources spent to produce the legal ethics *Restatement* may make some contribution to clarifying the low-commitment ethics and may encourage a few desirable small reforms, but precisely in doing so, they exacerbate the problem of suboptimal diversity of standards and the institutional bias against high-commitment ethics. The Institute could play a far more useful role by elaborating a set of norms strongly differentiated from the prevailing low-commitment ethics and then offering it as an option for voluntary adoption.

Enforcement Information

The problem of information about lawyers' compliance with their commitments seems especially difficult, but there are some hopeful signs. At the most formal level, we have information produced by public adjudication of charges against lawyers. Such information is very expensive, but it seems likely that there has been underinvestment in it in the past. Increased efforts of agencies like the Office of Thrift Supervision and of courts in enforcing Rule 11 and discovery sanctions are thus promising.

At the most informal level, information spreads through casual communication networks and journalism. New technologies have facilitated the replacement of local networks with far-flung ones. And the emergence of a vast and aggressive legal journalism has created a wealth of information on the details of practice. Journalists have played a valuable role in raising and investigating ethical issues. (The role of the *American Lawyer* is especially notable.)

Perhaps the greatest room for development exists between these levels in the form of voluntary enforcement activity. There is a noticeable recent increase in the articulation of ethical commitments by voluntary, specialized bar associations like the American Academy of Matrimonial Lawyers. These efforts may be accompanied by casual exchange of information among members about member compliance. However, they lack explicit enforcement processes, and in the absence of such processes, they play a very limited role in transmitting enforcement information to outsiders. (Defamation law restricts casual transfer of information about occupational performance to strangers, and outsiders would have trouble evaluating casual information.)

The ultimate sanction available to voluntary association against a member is exclusion; a variety of lesser sanctions, such as reprimand, are also available. A voluntary association could enforce its commitments by inviting complaints from anyone asserting injury from a violation, adjudicating them in accordance with fair procedures, announcing its findings, and applying sanctions to violators. The procedural costs of such a system would be substantial, but probably considerably less than comparable public adjudication. The advantage would be the increased credibility of the Association's commitments and the increased value of membership as a signal of commitment. (Voluntary associations such as Underwriters Laboratories often certify commodities in an analogous manner.)

Whether public regulation would be helpful in encouraging such associational activity is not clear. Some revision of the libel laws to accommodate good faith reporting of relevant information might be a good idea. Some application of the antitrust laws to insure that the associations do not become engines for the restriction of desirable competition over price might become necessary at some point. A regulatory authority that wanted to encourage more associational activity might consider subsidizing a couple of private enforcement systems as demonstration projects, in the hope that if they proved their worth, others would emulate them without subsidy.

Conclusion

The Contextual View is susceptible to implementation both as a disciplinary regime enforced by a regulatory authority and as a set of voluntary commitments subject to private formal and informal enforcement. The role of the tort system in defining minimal standards of professional care is analogous to the role of disciplinary norms, and though there are differences in the two roles, the acceptance without controversy of contextual norms in the former sphere strongly supports their potential viability in the disciplinary sphere.

Despite their repudiation in the enacted ethical codes, perspectives similar to the Contextual View do play a role in practice through voluntary adoption and informal, reputational enforcement. That they do not play an even greater role is due at least in part to certain features of the current institutional configuration of legal services, which seem to inhibit voluntary efforts to achieve high-commitment ethics. There is no reason to think that these features are more efficient than alternatives that would better accommodate high-commitment ethics, such as the Contextual View. A variety of reforms designed to mitigate cognitive biases, information problems, and the costs of normative specification have promise to foster voluntary adoption and promotion of the Contextual View.

Notes

1. Introduction

1. For notable recent laments, see Anthony Kronman, *The Lost Lawyer* (1993); Sol Linowitz, *The Betrayed Profession* (1994); Mary Ann Glendon, *A Nation Under Lawyers* (1994); American Bar Association, Section on Legal Education and Admission to the Bar, *Legal Education and Professional Development—An Educational Continuum: Report of the Task Force on Law Schools and the Profession* (1992); American Bar Association, Commission on Professionalism, *"In the Spirit of Public Service": A Blueprint for Reviving Lawyer Professionalism* (1986). For a historical perspective on the tradition of lamentation, see Robert W. Gordon, "The Independence of Lawyers," 68 *Boston University Law Review* 63 (1988).

2. For example, consider the argument of the *Model Rules* in favor of confidentiality of information regarding planned wrongful acts discussed in Chapter 3, and the tortured confidentiality rationalizations discussed in note 9 to that Chapter.

3. Arthur Powell, *I Can Go Home Again* 287–292 (2d ed. 1943). Confirming evidence that Frank had been wrongly convicted emerged after his death. Wendell Rawls, Jr., "After 69 Years of Silence, Lynching Victim Is Cleared," *New York Times,* March 8, 1982, p. A12.

4. See Joseph Sax, "Federal Reclamation Law," in 2 *Waters and Water Rights* 111, 120–24 (Robert Clark, ed. 1967).

5. The allegations against Kaye Scholer appear in Office of Thrift Supervision, "Matter of Fishbein," AP 92–19 (March 1, 1992), reprinted in *The Attorney-Client Relationship After Kaye Scholer* 239–322 (PLI 1992). For discussion and references to the literature on the case, see William H. Simon, "The Kaye Scholer Affair," *Law and Social Inquiry* (1998).

6. Both versions of the bar's codified confidentiality norm—Model Code DR 4–101 and Model Rule 1.6—prohibit disclosure in such circumstances.

Many defenders of the Dominant View regard the case as sufficiently troubling to warrant an exception. The effort to justify an exception without trenching further on the categorical confidentiality norm has prompted tortuous analyses of a problem that most lay people would find (correctly in my view) a simple one with an obvious answer. See "Symposium: Executing the Wrong Person: The Professionals' Ethical Dilemmas," 29 *Loyola of Los Angeles Law Review* 1543 (1996).

7. General regulation of the legal profession is a state responsibility and is usually superintended by the state's highest court. The American Bar Association is a private national organization with no legislative powers. Its codes have been promulgated as models for adoption by the states. The state courts have adopted all or parts of one or the other of the ABA codes into their disciplinary systems. Discipline is typically enforced by an administrative appendage of the court system. Violations entail sanctions ranging from censure to disbarment. Courts and administrative agencies often refer to the codes in adjudicating non-disciplinary claims involving lawyers, such as malpractice or contempt of court.

8. David Luban calls the Dominant View the "Standard Conception" and shows in detail how it is presupposed by the bar's ethics codes in *Lawyers and Justice: An Ethical Study* 393–403 (1988).

9. See, for example, Marvin Frankel, "The Search for Truth: An Umpireal View," 123 *University of Pennsylvania Law Review* 1031 (1975).

10. "A Gathering of Legal Scholars to Discuss 'Professional Responsibility and the Model Rules of Professional Conduct'," 35 *University of Miami Law Review* 639, 652–654 (1981).

11. *ABA Model Rules of Professional Conduct,* Preamble, paragraph 1 (lawyers have "special responsibility for the quality of justice"); *ABA Model Code of Professional Responsibility,* Preamble, paragraph 1 ("Law . . . makes justice possible. . . .").

12. *Model Code,* EC 7–13.

13. See Geoffrey Hazard, "Legal Ethics: Legal Rules and Professional Aspirations," 30 *Cleveland State Law Review* 571, 574 (1982).

14. Jamie Heller, Letter to the Editor, *New York Times,* December 16, 1994, p. A38 (reporting advice given by New York bar review course).

15. *Model Rules,* Preamble, paragraph 1.

16. See, for example, Luban, *Lawyers and Justice*; Thomas Shaffer and Robert Cochran, *Lawyers, Clients, and Moral Responsibility* (1994).

17. *Model Rules* 1.16(G)(3); ibid. 1.6(b).

18. Charles Fried, "The Lawyer As Friend: The Moral Foundations of the Lawyer-Client Relationship," 85 *Yale Law Journal* 1060 (1976); Charles Ogletree, "Beyond Justification: Seeking Motivations to Sustain Public Defenders," 106 *Harvard Law Review* 1239 (1993).

19. Ogletree, "Beyond Justification" 1271.

20. *Model Rules* 1.5; 3.4(e).

21. Kronman, *Lost Lawyer* 283.

22. Henry M. Hart, Jr., and Albert Sacks, *The Legal Process: Basic Problems in the Making and Application of Law* ch. 1 (tent. ed. 1958).

2. A Right to Injustice

1. Karl Llewellyn, "On Reading and Using the Newer Jurisprudence," 40 *Columbia Law Review* 581, 582 (1940). Entitlement arguments are pervasive, though largely tacit, in Monroe Freedman, *Lawyers' Ethics in An Adversary System* (1975). A rare effort to give the argument sophisticated expression is Stephen Pepper, "The Lawyer's Amoral Ethical Role: A Defense, A Problem, and Some Possibilities," 1986 *American Bar Foundation Research Journal* 613.

2. For a sketch of legal Libertarianism at the height of its influence, see Duncan Kennedy, "Towards An Historical Understanding of Legal Consciousness: The Case of Classical Legal Thought in America: 1830–1940," 3 *Research in Law and Sociology* (1980). For a notable critique, see Robert Hale, "Coercion and Distribution in a Supposedly Noncoercive State," 38 *Political Science Quarterly* 470 (1923).

3. The description in the text roughly fits the older Positivism exemplified by John Austin, *The Province of Jurisprudence Determined* (H. L. A. Hart, ed., 1954). Modern Positivism retains the insistence on the differentiation of law from morality but slackens or abandons the insistence that laws must be sanctioned-backed commands or direct emanations of a sovereign. For a sample of the modern take, see Joseph Raz, *The Authority of Law* (1979).

4. James Boswell, *The Life of Samuel Johnson,* excerpted in II *The World of Law* 763 (Ephraim London, ed., 1960).

5. Henry M. Hart, Jr., and Albert Sacks, *The Legal Process: Basic Problems in the Making and Application of Law* 232–263 (tent. ed. 1958).

6. See Kennedy, "Legal Consciousness."

7. On the Libertarian conception of the Rule of Law, see Friedrich Hayek, II *Law, Legislation, and Liberty* 94–123 (1973).

8. According to Arthur Corbin, the earlier statutes primarily reflected evidentiary concerns, while the "repose" value is primary in more modern ones. *Corbin on Contracts* section 214 (1963). If we construe the statute in the modern manner, we might still want to ask whether the repose policy is relevant here. If we interpreted repose to connote a kind of reliance by the debtor, we might ask whether the creditor's delay has led him to assume that he wouldn't have to repay and to make other commitments accordingly. If the answer is no, then repose shouldn't weigh against repayment in this case.

9. Hoffman's "Resolutions in Regard to Professional Deportment" included this statement: "I will never plead the Statute of Limitations, when based on the *mere efflux of time;* for if my client is conscious he owes the debt, and has no other defense than the legal bar, he shall never make me a partner in his knavery." II David Hoffman, *A Course of Legal Study* 754 (1836).

10. See Pepper, "Amoral Ethical Role."

11. Roscoe Pound, "The Causes of Popular Dissatisfaction with the Administration of Justice," 29 *A.B.A. Rep.* 395, 404 (1906).

12. On this point see Roscoe Pound, "A Survey of Social Interests," 57 *Harvard Law Review* 1 (1943), which begins by observing, "There has been a notable shift throughout the world from thinking of the task of legal order as one of adjusting the exercise of free wills to one of satisfying wants, of which free exercise of the will is but one."

13. See, for example, Frank Easterbrook, "The Limits of Antitrust," 63 *Texas Law Review,* 1 (1984).

14. William Blackstone, I *Commentaries on the Laws of England* 59–62 (8th ed. 1778). Blackstone credits the example to Puffendorf. I've altered the wording somewhat for emphasis.

15. 490 U.S. 504 (1989).

16. See Ronald Dworkin, *Taking Rights Seriously* 14–45 (1977). My discussion of the nature of principles is indebted to Dworkin.

17. Oliver Wendell Holmes, Jr., "The Path of the Law," 10 *Harvard Law Review* 457, 462 (1897).

18. The ethics committee of the Association of the Bar of the City of New York once condemned such a practice as unethical. Opinion 722 (1948). On the other hand, the American Bar Association House of Delegates rejected a proposed Model Rule prohibiting a lawyer from preparing a document that "contains legally prohibited terms." Predictably but implausibly, the prohibition was opposed as intolerably vague. Geoffrey Hazard, Susan Koniak, and Roger Cramton, *The Law and Ethics of Lawyering* 1072–73 (2d ed. 1994).

In some jurisdictions it may be unlawful for the landlord to use a contract with an unenforceable term. See, for example, *Leardi v. Brown,* 394 Mass. 151, 474 N.E. 2d 1094 (1985). In such cases, the lawyers' preparation of the contract might constitute assistance to client fraud or illegality, which the rules condemn.

19. See Susan Koniak, "The Law Between the Bar and the State," 70 *North Carolina Law Review* 1389, 1405–07 (1992) (discussing the bar's reaction to the cash reporting rules).

Similar arguments were made by lawyers who assisted Southern officials in resisting the desegregation mandates of the federal courts in the 1950s and 1960s. They insisted that such a decision was not the "law of the land" but rather the "*law of the case* actually decided and binding on the parties to the case and no others." Pittman, "The Federal Invasion of Arkansas in the Light of the Constitution," 19 *Alabama Lawyer* 168, 169–170 (1960); quoted in Marvin Frankel, "The Alabama Lawyer, 1954–64: Has the Official Organ Atrophied?" 64 *Columbia Law Review* 1243, 1249 (1964).

20. *Model Rules* 2.1.

21. John Chipman Gray, *The Nature and Sources of the Law* 225 (1909).

22. *The Growth of American Law: The Law Makers* 349 (1950).

23. Oliver Wendell Holmes, Jr., *The Common Law* 66 (Mark Howe, ed., 1963).

24. *Buchanan v. Warley,* 245 U.S. 60.

25. 334 U.S. 1.

26. Mark Tushnet, "Dia-Tribe," 78 *Michigan Law Review* 694, 697 (1980).

27. Hart and Sacks, *Legal Process* 263. On the general theme of private legislation, see also Stewart Macaulay, "Private Government," in *Law and the Social Sciences* (Leon Lipson and Stanton Wheeler, eds., 1986).

28. Hart and Sacks, *Legal Process* 259–263.

29. Ibid. 226.

3. Justice in the Long Run

1. *Model Rules* 1.6. This rule has been adopted literally in only six states. The rules in most other states are similar, but typically slightly less protective, often permitting disclosure of future criminal acts in addition to those threatening major bodily harm. See Fred C. Zacharias, "Fact and Fiction in the Restatement of the Law Governing Lawyers: Should the Confidentiality Provisions Restate the Law?," 6 *Georgetown Journal of Legal Ethics* 903, 913–914 (1993).

2. Some Dominant View proponents believe that perjury by a criminal defendant is a special case in which the lawyer's participation is justifiable. See, for example, Monroe Freedman, *Understanding Legal Ethics* 132–141 (1990).

3. See *Model Rules,* Comments, paragraphs 3, 9. The drafters express astonishing faith in the lawyer's powers of persuasion: "Based upon experience, lawyers know that almost all clients follow the advice given, and the law is upheld" (paragraph 3).

4. See Ronald J. Allen, Mark F. Grady, Daniel D. Polsby, and Michael Yashko, "A Positive Theory of the Attorney-Client Privilege and the Work Product Doctrine," 19 *Journal of Legal Studies* 359, 363–383 (1990). These writers suggest that the danger that clients will make mistakes about what information to disclose is especially great with respect to "contingent claims"—claims that condition some advantage or mitigation on concessions

of conduct by the claimant that is otherwise wrongful. For example, the plea of self-defense presumes that the defendant has used physical force in a presumptively illegal way; the plea of contributory negligence concedes that the pleader has been negligent himself.

5. Jeremy Bentham, *Rationale of Judicial Evidence* (1827).

6. *Restatement of Agency* 2d, section 395, Comment, paragraph f.

7. Harry Subin proposes an exception for information needed "to prevent serious harm." "The Lawyer As Superego: Disclosure of Client Confidences to Prevent Serious Harm," 70 *Iowa Law Review,* 1091, 1172–81 (1985).

8. *Model Rules* 1.13.

9. Here are three further illustrations of the bar's anxiety and hypocrisy about its confidentiality norms:

(1) As originally promulgated, the *Model Code* contained a rule requiring that, when the lawyer discovered that the client had committed a fraud in a matter in which the lawyer was representing her, the lawyer make any disclosures necessary to rectify the fraud. *Model Code* DR 7–102(B)(1969). Many protested this rule as an infringement of confidentiality, and the ABA acquiesced. However, instead of explicitly rejecting the duty or simply eliminating it, the drafters retained the original language but qualified it with the phrase "except where the information is protected as a privileged communication." The ABA Committee on Ethics and Professional Responsibility then interpreted "privileged communication" to include not just information privileged under the law of evidence, but "any information gained in the professional relationship . . . the disclosure of which would be . . . detrimental to the client." ABA Formal Opinion 341 (Sept. 30, 1975). So interpreted, the relevant information is virtually always privileged, and the duty to rectify is meaningless. Although this rhetoric was often criticized as embarrassingly circuitous, virtually the same approach—a duty asserted in one pronouncement followed by its nullification in another—was adopted in the *Model Rules;* see 4.1(b).

(2) In the course of drafting the American Law Institute's *Restatement of the Law Governing Lawyers,* ALI members debated and approved a confidentiality rule resembling those of the ethics codes. In accordance with the usual *Restatement* format, the drafters had appended to the rule a series of illustrations, including one similar to the Innocent Convict case. The discussion of this case ended with the conclusion, clearly supported by the terms of the rule, that the rule precluded disclosure despite the injustice to the convict. After heated debate, the members voted to delete the illustration as "offensive" *without making any change in the rule!* 5 *Lawyer's Manual on Professional Conduct (ABA/BNA)* 1581–59 (1989).

(3) Although the exception to confidentiality in *Model Rules* 1.6 for the protection of third party interests is narrowly confined to the most extreme

situations, the exception for the protection of lawyer interests extends indiscriminately to permit the lawyer to respond to any "allegations in any proceeding concerning the lawyer's representation of the client." Although even some life-and-death interests of third parties do not warrant disclosure, the selfish interests of the lawyer always warrant disclosure, no matter how minor these interests and no matter how great the harm to the client. When allegations against the lawyer are made by the client herself, the exception might be rationalized on the grounds that confidentiality would often leave the lawyer defenseless and tempt the client to unfair allegations. But the exception applies to allegations against lawyers by nonclients as well—for example, where a third party accuses the lawyer of assisting wrongful conduct by the client. The lawyer is free to disclose client information even if the client has not behaved wrongfully and the disclosures are harmful to her. Yet there is no reason to think that, without the exception, confidentiality would leave lawyers more vulnerable to unfairness from nonclient allegations than it currently leaves third parties.

10. See Robert Weisberg and Michael Wald, "Confidentiality Laws and State Efforts to Protect Abused or Neglected Children: The Need for Statutory Reform," 18 *Family Law Quarterly* 143 (1984).

11. VII *Wigmore on Evidence,* section 2298 (John McNaughton, ed., 1961).

12. *Hickman v. Taylor,* 329 U.S. 495, 507 (1947).

13. *Federal Rules of Civil Procedure* 26(a).

14. If the client refused to permit disclosure of required discovery information, the lawyer would be precluded from unilaterally disclosing it, but she would have to resign. Since it is often costly for the client to change counsel, that threat will often induce the client to comply.

15. Moreover, it has been suggested recently in the securities context that when a client switches lawyers to keep information from the second lawyer, that lawyer may have a duty to make inquiries of the first lawyer. *FDIC v. O'Melveny & Meyers,* 969 F.2d 744 (9th Cir. 1992), reversed on other grounds, 512 U.S. 979 (1994).

16. Perhaps such assertions will be made with respect to the 1993 amendments mandating "automatic" discovery of some information. These amendments are controversial, but they represent only a marginal enlargement of the prior scope of discovery, which—cost and enforcement issues aside—was not controversial.

17. *DiLeo v. Ernst & Young,* 901 F.2d 624, 629 (7th Cir. 1990). The passage actually refers to accountants.

18. Kenneth Mann, *Defending White Collar Crime* 104–111 (1985).

19. Fred C. Zacharias, "Rethinking Confidentiality," 74 *Iowa Law Review* 351, 377–396 (1989); Jonathan Casper, *American Criminal Justice: The Defendant's Perspective* 105 (1972).

20. Fred Zacharias found that few of the 63 lawyers in his survey mentioned to clients that there were exceptions to confidentiality and only one recalled mentioning a specific exception. Zacharias, "Rethinking Confidentiality" 386.

21. David Hoffman, *A Course of Legal Study* 755 (2d ed. 1836); George Sharswood, *An Essay on Professional Ethics* 39 (2d ed. 1860).

22. See Mirjan Damaska, *The Faces of Justice and State Authority* (1986).

23. Although the party who must disclose adverse evidence incurs the costs of discovering the evidence without getting the benefit of it, this circumstance does not support a fairness objection. After all, the discovering party made her efforts out of self-interest, and *ex ante,* she might just as well have benefited from the other side's efforts. Moreover, if compensation were a concern, we could complement disclosure duties with a duty of the receiving party to share the costs of discovering the information, as indeed do the discovery provisions of the *Federal Rules of Civil Procedure.*

24. See the cases cited at Charles Alan Wright and Arthur Miller, VI *Federal Practice and Procedure,* section 2025, notes 27 and 28.

25. See John Langbein, "The German Advantage in Civil Procedure," 52 *University of Chicago Law Review* 823 (1985).

26. See Gordon Tullock, *Trials on Trial: The Pure Theory of Legal Procedure* 154–158 (1980).

27. Lon L. Fuller, "The Adversary System," in *Talks on American Law* 35, 43–45 (Harold Berman, ed., 1972). Fuller was a drafter of the *ABA Code;* a compressed statement of his argument appears in EC 7–19.

28. John Thibaut and Laurens Walker characterize the results of an experimental study as supporting the cognitive dissonance theory; see *Procedural Justice* 49–52 (1975). Their results suggest that when a *decisionmaker* has a cognitive bias, her decision is less likely to go in the direction of the bias when competing bodies of evidence are presented by different (adversary) "advocates" than when all the evidence is presented by the same person.

The study's findings on the effect of order of presentation of evidence contradict the most famous version of the cognitive dissonance theory—Lon Fuller's—which asserts that the earliest evidence will be most influential. The study purports to show that the latest evidence is most influential, and it explains this by asserting that decisionmakers treat early evidence as provisional and avoid jumping to conclusions, which is exactly what Fuller insisted they would be unable to do (see 61–65).

In any event, the conclusion about the effects of competitive advocacy on decisionmaker bias, even if accepted, has no bearing on the relative merits of the various views on legal ethics, since all these views contemplate a role for contending advocates in the presentation of evidence (as indeed do most variations of the "inquisitorial" system). From a legal ethics perspective, the critical issue is whether presentation of evidence by cognitively biased *advocates* leads to better decisions than the presentation of evidence by advocates who have greater responsibility to vindicate legal merit. The study has nothing to say about this.

29. John W. Davis, "The Argument of an Appeal," 26 *ABA Journal* 895, 896 (1940).

30. Robert Keeton, *Trial Tactics and Methods* 6–8 (1973).

31. Stephen McG. Bundy and Einer Elhauge, "Knowledge about Legal Sanctions," 92 *Michigan Law Review* 261, 313 (1993).

32. Note that the additional information that becomes relevant under the Contextual approach is less likely to involve the inefficiencies noted above in connection with trial preparation under the Dominant approach. Those inefficiencies concern what might be called "adversarial" information—information that supports presentation of one's own claims. As we saw, the competitive quest for this information is likely to be inefficient because much of it has only "strategic" value—that is, value in countering moves by the opposing party that do little to enhance adjudication on the merits—and because the expected private payoff from these claims may exceed the social value of their adjudication—that is, their contribution to compliance and clarification. By contrast, the additional information that becomes relevant under the Contextual View supports third-party and public interests. This information does not suffer from the competitive "arm's race" dynamic because the Contextual View imposes no duty to consider or develop information of purely strategic significance. And its social value is far more likely to coincide with its private value. Moreover, since producing such information is not in a party's selfish interests, there would be no incentive to produce it in excess of the standard dictated by the public interest.

33. Bundy and Elhauge, *Legal Sanctions* 313.

34. Ibid. 314, 321.

35. David Wilkins, "Legal Realism for Lawyers," 104 *Harvard Law Review* 468, 511–513 (1990), making a criticism similar to Bundy and Elhauge's about the relative indeterminacy of contextual norms, argues that the point is strengthened by the fact that many lawyer decisions occur in private and thus cannot be effectively monitored. He thinks that in these circumstances categorical norms are more conducive to "accountability." Wilkins apparently is not talking here about bad-faith lawyers, since an unmonitored lawyer acting in bad faith can violate categorical norms as readily as contextual ones. However, to the extent that we are talking about good-faith lawyers, categorical norms promote "accountability" only in the sense that Bundy and Elhauge say they promote "certainty" and "consistency": there is less often disagreement about what the norm requires. But as I argue in the text, this not the important criterion.

36. Bundy and Elhauge, *Legal Sanctions* 316.

37. Ibid. 265–266.

38. Pp. 117–118 (Everyman ed. 1968) [1862].

4. Should Lawyers Obey the Law?

1. Philip Soper, *A Theory of Law* (1984) insists on the integral connection of definition and obligation.

2. See Walter Gellhorn, *Children and Families in the Courts of New York City* 288–290 (1954).

3. See ABA *Model Code* EC 5–1 ("A lawyer . . . should refrain from all illegal . . . conduct.") ABA *Model Rules*, Preamble ("A lawyer's conduct should conform to the requirements of the law . . ."). I will argue in time that, because the terms "law" and "illegal" are ambiguous, these precepts need not be read to condemn the proposed conduct in the divorce perjury case. Nevertheless, they are invariably read to do so.

4. If there were an ongoing investigation focused on the client, advice about enforcement practices that might increase the difficulty of discovering evidence of past acts might constitute criminal obstruction of justice. For an excellent discussion of the enforcement advice issue, see Stephen Pepper, "Counseling at the Limits of the Law: An Exercise in the Jurisprudence and Ethics of Lawyering," 104 *Yale Law Journal* 1545 (1995).

5. Readers may wonder what has become of the Libertarian theme that Chapter 2 portrayed as uneasily coexisting with Positivism. For the most part, the Dominant View appeals to Libertarian notions to justify client loyalty within the "bounds" of the positive law. When the lawyer reaches these "bounds," the Dominant View treats the Libertarian theme as trumped by the Positivist one. There are some exceptions, however, especially in the area of confidentiality. For example, some lawyers and bar associations have recently urged noncompliance, on Libertarian grounds, with statutes requiring the reporting of large cash payments. This and related instances are discussed in Susan Koniak, "The Law Between the Bar and the State," 70 *North Carolina Law Review* 1389 (1992).

6. Raoul Berger, *Government by Judiciary: The Transformation of the Fourteenth Amendment* (1977).

7. It is occasionally argued that a theory that concedes any distinction between legal and moral norms has to give some priority to jurisdictional norms simply in order to distinguish legality from morality. This is wrong, however. A Substantivist could demarcate the two types of norms on the basis of ideas about the substantive differences between the two types of norms. For example, David Luban writes, "There are moral, but no legal norms against

hypocrisy, ingratitude, self-pity, and bragging." "Legal Ideals and Moral Obligations: A Comment on Simon," 38 *William and Mary Law Review* 255, 261 (1996). A Positivist would defend this statement on the ground that no such prohibitions have been enacted by institutions with law-making authority. A Substantivist could defend it by saying that such matters are best left to informal social regulation.

8. 388 U.S. 307 (1967).

9. Ronald Dworkin, *Taking Rights Seriously* 214 (1978).

10. *Shuttlesworth v. Birmingham,* 394 U.S. 147, 150–151 (1978) (holding unconstitutional the statute under which *Walker* injunction was issued).

11. See Gordon Wood, *The Creation of the American Republic 1776–1783* 319–328 (1969). Informal popular enforcement is often grounded in customary norms. For studies of the phenomenon in seventeenth- and eighteenth-century England, see E. P. Thompson, *Customs in Common* (1993); Christopher Hill, *Liberty Against the Law* (1997).

12. Indiana Constitution, Art. 1, sec. 19; Maryland Declaration of Rights, Art. 23. See generally Jeffrey Abramson, *We, The Jury* 56–95 (1994).

13. Ibid. 65.

14. See, for example, Leonard White, *The Federalists* 204 (1948): "The extent of the Secretary of the Treasury's power of superintendence was challenged by some customs collectors, who alleged that their oath of office required them to follow the law as they understood it, not as it might be explained to them by Alexander Hamilton."

15. See Mark Howe, "Juries as Judges of the Criminal Law," 52 *Harvard Law Review* 586 (1939).

16. *Welch v. Helvering,* 290 U.S. 111, 115 (1933).

17. Bruce Ackerman, "Constitutional Politics/Constitutional Law," 99 *Yale Law Journal* 453 (1989); Bruce Ackerman and Neal Katyal, "Our Unconventional Founding," 62 *University of Chicago Law Review* 475 (1995).

18. Ibid. 478.

19. *Hearings on S.26733 Before the Senate Committee on Post Office and Civil Service,* 93d Congress, 1st Session (1973), at 11 (concerning President Nixon's nomination of Senator William Saxbe as Attorney General).

20. Michael Paulsen, "Is Lloyd Bentsen Unconstitutional?" 46 *Stanford Law Review* 907, 907 (1994).

21. Guido Calabresi, *A Common Law for the Age of Statutes* (1982).

22. Ian Ayres, "Judging Close Corporations in the Age of Statutes," 70 *Washington University Law Quarterly* 365 (1992).

23. Brock Yates, "Speed Doesn't Kill, Bad Drivers Do," *New York Times,* July 24, 1995, p. A13.

24. For example, Ronald Dworkin, *Law's Empire* 266 (1986). My com-

ment ignores the jurisprudentially uninteresting fact that since Dworkin wrote the limit has been raised to 65.

25. See Dworkin, *Taking Rights* 206–222; Martha Minow, "Breaking the Law: Lawyers and Clients in Struggles for Social Change," 52 *University of Pittsburgh Law Review* 723 (1991). For an argument closer to mine, which treats the legitimacy of civil disobedience less as a function of the distinctive virtues of conscientious action and more as a function of the general weakness of the moral claims of Positivistically defined law, see David Luban, "Conscientious Lawyers for Conscientious Lawbreakers," 52 *University of Pittsburgh Law Review* 793 (1991).

26. Robert Post, "On the Popular Image of the Lawyer: Reflections in a Dark Glass," 75 *California Law Review* 379, 382 (1987). The examples of *The Talk of the Town* and *The Man Who Shot Liberty Valance* were suggested by Post's article.

27. EC 1–5.

28. Jerome Frank, *Law and the Modern Mind* (1930).

29. For example, Luban, "Legal Ideals"; Thomas Shaffer and Robert F. Cochran, Jr., *Law, Clients, and Moral Responsibility* (1994).

30. *Model Penal Code,* section 3.02(1) (1985).

31. Frederic Douglass, *The Life and Times of Frederick Douglass* 261–262 (R. Logan, ed., 1967). For an interesting discussion, see Robert Cover, "Nomos and Narrative," 97 *Harvard Law Review* 4, 35–40 (1983).

32. See David Luban, *Lawyers and Justice: An Ethical Study,* ch. 3 (1988) and the literature discussed there.

33. See Ronald Dworkin, *Law's Empire* 109–110 (1986).

34. However, recall that under a radical Substantivist view, law is absolutely, not relatively, binding because law subsumes all other relevant norms and leaves no grounds on which a rebuttal could be based.

35. For example, David Wilkins, "In Defense of Law and Morality: Why Lawyers Should Have a Prima Facie Obligation to Obey the Law," 38 *William and Mary Law Review* 269, 287–289 (1996).

36. H. L. A. Hart, *The Concept of Law* 206–207 (1961).

37. Of course, it will often be impossible to get anything close to consensus on such judgments. Consider the current situation of organizing rights under the National Labor Relations Act. Because the penalties are so small in relation to the stakes and the enforcement process so cumbersome, many employers have virtually nullified workers' rights to organize unions by treating the statute as a set of bargain prices on union-busting activities. See Paul Weiler, "Promises to Keep: Securing Workers' Rights to Self-Organization Under the NLRA," 96 *Harvard Law Review* 1769 (1979). My argument is that if such practices are defensible, they are not so as "zealous advocacy within the bounds

of the law" but as nullification. Doubtless, however, many management lawyers who reached this point would continue to argue that nullification is warranted. They believe the statute unfair and coercive, perhaps obsolete and unconstitutional. Union lawyers would passionately disagree.

The dispute raises broad social issues that will not be settled by jurisprudential analysis. But to insist that lawyers integrate substantive concerns into their ethical reflection still has a point. From the point of view of the individual lawyer deciding where and how to commit her efforts, it is sufficient that she herself finds convincing substantive reasons, even if others disagree. In addition, the debate among competing positions is much richer, the more directly substantive concerns are addressed.

38. For example, Wilkins, "In Defense" 290–291. Aside from the response in the text, one might add that the individual lawyer's profession of commitment is made under duress (as a condition of the right to practice her calling); that it seems unlikely that most lawyers benefit tangibly from entry control or other monopolistic practices; and that any such benefits are unrequested.

5. Legal Professionalism as Meaningful Work

1. Robert H. Wiebe, *The Search for Order: 1877–1920* 12 (1967).

2. Georg Lukacs, "Reification and the Consciousness of the Proletariat," in *History and Class Consciousness* 89, 99 (Rodney Livingstone, trans., 1971).

3. Max Weber, "Bureaucracy," in *From Max Weber: Essays in Sociology* 215–216 (C. Wright Mills and H. H. Gerth, trans. and ed., 1946).

4. Charles Dickens, *Bleak House* 228 (Signet ed. 1964)

5. See *The Brothers Karamazov* 547–548, 552–553 (Penguin ed. 1958); *Crime and Punishment* 350–351 (Penguin ed. 1966). Julian Sorel also makes this complaint. Stendhal, *The Red and the Black* 564, 574 (Modern Library ed. 1995).

In addition to the horrors of subordination to impersonal rules, Dickens, Dostoyevsky, Stendhal, and Kafka, in strikingly similar ways, portray the horrors of subordination to personal whim and unprincipled manipulation. All four suggest that the two kinds of experience go together. It is tempting to suggest that the idea of contextual or purposive judgment—judgment that is principled but informal—is the remedy for both pathologies. It is hard to say whether the authors would be sympathetic to this response. Jurisprudence is a very small part of the complex of sentiments, ideas, and institutions with which they are concerned.

6. Franz Kafka, *The Trial* 7 (Vintage ed. 1969)

7. Ibid. 261.

8. Ibid. 269.

9. For example, Herman Wouk's *The Caine Mutiny* (1952) is sometimes interpreted to assert that even though Captain Queeg was an incompetent and abusive commander, his subordinates should not have mutinied against him. The message is delivered with drama and irony by the chief mutineer's defense lawyer Barney Greenwald, who explains to his client that, even though he (Greenwald) believed that the mutineers had acted wrongly in refusing Queeg the deference his role demanded, Greenwald's own role as defense lawyer required him to humiliate Queeg and exonerate the mutineer. See William H. Whyte, *The Organization Man* 243–248 (1956) Note that Whyte, who popularized this interpretation of the novel as an endorsement of Greenwald's view, condemned what he took to be its conformist message.

In general, novelists seem to have opposed the notion of categorically defined role with fairly consistent vigor. Even the three biggest law-and-order men of nineteenth-century fiction—Dostoyevsky, Conrad, and Henry James—show nothing but distaste for the idea. Consider Porfiry in *Crime and Punishment*, the Board of Inquiry in *Lord Jim*, and the heroine of James's story *In the Cage*.

10. Sinclair Lewis, *Arrowsmith* 85 (1925).

11. "The Profession of Law" [1886] and "The Path of the Law" [1897] in *Collected Legal Papers* 29, 30, 32, 202 (1920).

12. George Eliot, *Middlemarch* 544 (Penguin ed. 1965).

13. Ibid. 537.

14. Ibid. 598.

15. Ibid. 174; see also the related passage at 194. Compare the following from F. H. Bradley's defense of "My Station and Its Duties" first published in 1876: "If a man is to know what is right, he should have imbibed by precept, and still more by example, the spirit of his community, its general and special beliefs as to right and wrong, and, with this whole embodied in his mind, should particularize it in any new case not by a reflective deduction, but by an intuitive subsumption, which does not know that it is a subsumption; by a carrying out of the self into a new case, wherein what is before the mind is the case and not the self to be carried out, and where it is indeed the whole that feels and sees, but all that is seen is seen in the form of this case, this point, this instance" *Ethical Studies* 196–197 (2d ed. 1927).

Note that this classically contextual style of judgment is central to the conception of role that Bradley defends. I thus think David Luban is wrong to think that Bradley's argument, if right, would be helpful to the Dominant View. See *Lawyers and Justice: An Ethical Study* ch. 6 (1988).

16. Louis Brandeis, *Business—A Profession* (1914); Talcott Parsons, "A Sociologist Looks at the Legal Profession," in *Essays in Sociological Theory* (rev. ed. 1954).

17. Wiebe, *Search for Order* 112.

18. Some might also put Thurman Arnold in this category, but he is much less important than Brandeis to both theory and practice.

19. Brandeis, *Business* 329.

20. Holmes, *Collected Legal Papers* 29.

21. Brandeis, *Business* 332.

22. See generally Alpheus Thomas Mason, *Brandeis—A Free Man's Life* (1946).

23. For example: "To one of his clients, faced at the time with labor trouble, Brandeis almost shouted: 'You say your factory cannot continue to pay the wages the employees now earn. But you don't tell me what those earnings are. How much do they lose through irregularities in their work? You don't know? Do you undertake to manage this business and say what wages it can afford to pay while you are ignorant of facts such as these? Are not these the very things you should know, and should have seen that your men knew too, before you went in this fight?" Ibid. 144.

24. Ibid. 145–146.

25. Ibid. 214–229, 232–237.

26. Ibid. 236.

27. See John Frank, "The Legal Ethics of Louis Brandeis," 17 *Stanford Law Review* 683 (1965). While Frank considers the specific charges are without merit, he calls the "counsel for the situation's" remark "one of the most unfortunate phrases he ever casually uttered." At 702.

28. Ibid.

29. Ibid. 685.

30. James Willard Hurst, *The Growth of American Law: The Law Makers* (1950); Henry M. Hart, Jr. and Albert Sacks, *The Legal Process: Basic Problems in the Making and Application of Law* (Tent. ed. 1958).

31. Hart and Sacks, *Legal Process* 230.

32. *Model Rules* 2.2.

33. For example, Rubin, "A Causerie on Lawyers' Ethics in Negotiation," 35 *Tulane Law Review* 577, 751.

34. See "Summary of the Expert Opinion of Geoffrey C. Hazard, Jr." in *The Attorney Client Relationship After Kaye, Scholer* 381, 394–397 (Practicing Law Institute, 1992).

35. Even as an interpretation of the *Model Rules,* Hazard's argument was absurd. In addition to mischaracterizing the lawyers as "litigation counsel," he mistakenly asserted that the standard applicable under that characterization would be that of *Model Rules* 3.1, which authorizes lawyers to assert any claim on behalf of a client in litigation that is not frivolous. Hazard was apparently claiming that as long as Kaye Scholer had a nonfrivolous argument that the information it held was not called for and the assertions it made were not

misleading, the firm was on safe ground. But the Rule 3.1 standard applies to litigation circumstances in which counsel is volunteering a position, not to circumstances in which counsel is obliged to produce information.

To the extent that the charges against Kaye Scholer involve withholding information, the litigation analogy is not to a closing argument, when counsel can argue any nonfrivolous characterization of the evidence, but to a response to a discovery request, the most plausible standard for which would be that counsel must comply with a reasonable interpretation of the request (a much narrower category than that of nonfrivolous interpretations). See, for example, *Washington State Physicians Insurance Exchange v. Fisons Corp.,* 122 Wash. 2d 299, 858 P.2d 1054 (1992).

To the extent that the charges involve misrepresentation, the situation is again quite different from a closing argument at trial, in which counsel's statements are supposed to refer to evidence of record only, and the trier can make its own judgment on the plausibility of the characterizations. In the regulatory context, Kaye Scholer's statements would naturally be understood to refer not just to the information they had produced but to any relevant information they were aware of. See generally William H. Simon, "The Kaye Scholer Affair," *Law and Social Inquiry* (1998).

36. Adolph Berle, Book Review, 76 *Harvard Law Review* 430 (1962).

37. Kronman and others also suggest that recent developments in the organization of private practice have narrowed the scope for Brandeis-style lawyering. Competition has eroded the leverage that lawyers once had over clients. Moreover, lawyers increasingly work on narrow, short-term tasks that give them little opportunity to gain the background understanding of the client or the respect from the client needed for the Brandeis role.

This suggestion seems plausible with respect to a broad range of firm practice. But there is a trend in the opposite direction with inside corporate counsel, whose numbers and power have been growing. In any event, these developments are too recent to explain why the Brandeisian project made so little progress to begin with.

6. *Legal Ethics as Contextual Judgment*

1. Gary Bellow and Bea Moulton, *The Lawyering Process* 586–591 (1978).

2. "A Gathering of Legal Scholars to Discuss 'Professional Responsibility and the Model Rules of Professional Conduct'," 35 *University of Miami Law Review* 639, 652–653 (1981).

3. The lawyers with the information should also consider whether their clients have any interests independent of the substantive merits of the claims that would warrant nondisclosure. In some cases there may be privacy or

proprietary reasons militating against disclosure. In the personal injury case, however, when the information concerns the status of a legal rule, it is hard to see any such interest. Legal rules are very much in the public domain. In the divorce case, the information concerns the husband's finances, in which he should have no privacy or proprietary interest as against the wife.

4. In the jargon of some tax practitioners, she believes that there is a "reasonable basis" for the device, but she does not believe that there is "substantial authority" for it or that it is "more likely than not" that the device is allowable. Cf. Special Committee on the Lawyer's Role in Tax Practice, Association of the Bar of the City of New York, "The Lawyer's Role in Tax Practice," 36 *Tax Lawyer* 865 (1983).

5. See *In Re Metzger,* 31 Haw. 929 (1931) (categorically condemning the tactic).

6. The most important reason why probative information is not offered in evidence is that it is adverse to the interests of the only party who is aware of it. However, even in situations where information is equally available to both counsel, lawyers may have significant insight into specific factual matters that cannot be formulated as admissible evidence.

First, probative information may be excluded by the rules of evidence. Some rules, such as those of privilege, are based on considerations other than probativeness. In addition, most of the rules, and especially the hearsay rules, are overbroad; they exclude some probative evidence in order to obviate ad hoc determinations of probativeness for individual items of evidence. The rules presume that such judgments would be unreliable or inefficient. Even when this is true with respect to judges and juries, however, it is often not true with respect to lawyers. For example, it has been recognized that probative but inadmissible evidence plays a valuable role in prosecutors' decisions to charge and dismiss cases. Samuel Gross, "Loss of Innocence: Eyewitness Identification and Proof of Guilt," 16 *Journal of Legal Studies* 395, 407–408, 432–440 (1987).

The second reason why lawyers sometimes have greater insight is their relative familiarity with particular items of evidence. Lawyers may spend years preparing a case that the trier must absorb in days or weeks. In the course of preparation lawyers may develop a tacit understanding or intuitive feel for some facts that cannot be fully articulated, or they may absorb many minor but relevant bits of information that cannot be effectively presented to the trier because of the trier's more limited ability to absorb information within time constraints. Despite or perhaps even because of this difference, the trier will often be in a better position to determine the entire case—she may be able to see the forest better for not being preoccupied with the trees—but the lawyers often has advantages at the level of detail.

7. In his pioneering text on trial practice, Robert Keeton offers a conclusion quite similar to mine: "[I]t is permissible to use any legally supportable ground of claim or defense, though it is a surprise move, to uphold a position you believe just, whatever the basis of your belief may be." *Trial Tactics and Methods* 4–5 (1973). Interestingly, Keeton characterizes this as the "answer implicit in prevailing practice," which suggests that some aspects of the Contextual View are less alien to mainstream views than I tend to portray them. I doubt that Keeton is right here, though it would be a good thing if he were.

8. See, for example, *Kent v. Dulles,* 357 U.S. 116 (1958); Alexander Bickel and Harry Wellington, "Legislative Purpose and the Judicial Process: The Lincoln Mills Case," 71 *Harvard Law Review* 1, 22–35 (1957); Richard Posner, "Statutory Interpretation—In the Classroom and in the Courtroom," 50 *University of Chicago Law Review* 800, 819 (1987).

When the purpose is problematic, treating the rule formally is appropriate because a problematic purpose threatens or burdens either a client goal of special significance or some more general autonomy interest to which the law gives special protection (for example, privacy). When the purpose is merely unclear, this treatment is justified by a residual background presumption that private conduct that does not offend public purposes (or private rights) is permissible. See *Papachristou v. City of Jacksonville* 405 U.S. 156 (1972) (declaring a criminal vagrancy statute void for vagueness).

9. 26 U.S.C. section 119(a) (1982). This example was suggested by Mark Kelman, *A Guide to Critical Legal Studies* 35 (1987).

10. See *Caratan v. Commissioner* 442 F.2d 606, 609–611 (9th Cir. 1971).

11. See *Code of Massachusetts Regulations* title 106, section 304.510 (1987).

12. See Arthur LaFrance, *Welfare Law: Structure and Entitlement* 351–365 (1979); Jane Hoey, "The Significance of the Money Payment in Public Assistance," *Social Security Bulletin* 3 (September 1944); Robert Rabin, "Implementation of the Cost-of-Living Adjustment for AFDC Recipients: A Case Study in Welfare Administration," 118 *University of Pennsylvania Law Review* 1143, 1148 (1970).

13. Compare *Dandridge v. Williams* 397 U.S. 471 (1970)(welfare interests are not "fundamental" for equal protection purposes) with *Goldberg v. Kelly* 397 U.S. 254 (1970) (welfare interests are fundamental for procedural due process purposes). See also Thomas Grey, "Procedural Fairness and Substantive Rights," in 18 *Nomos: Due Process* 182–202 (J. Pennock and J. Chapman, eds., 1977) (arguing that *Goldberg* makes sense only on the assumption that some welfare rights are substantively protected); Frank Michelman, "Welfare Rights in a Constitutional Democracy," 1979 *Washington University Law Quarterly* 659 (arguing that rights the Supreme Court has recognized, such as

voting rights, are not meaningfully exercisable without minimal economic subsistence and hence imply welfare rights).

Note that while *Dandridge* rejects the idea of a full-scale substantive constitutional right to welfare, it is not inconsistent with the practice of giving welfare interests sufficient weight to generate a presumption against interpretations of legislative norms that would impair them. Indeed *King v. Smith* 392 U.S. 309 (1968), in which the Court strained to adopt a statutory interpretation favoring welfare recipients, might be understood as tacitly employing such a practice.

14. The AFDC statute requires that states estimate standards of need for the purposes of the program and then permits the states to pay less than their own need determinations. Thus another possible basis for a judgment of adequacy would be a comparison of the state's own AFDC need standards with its grant levels. See, generally, United States Department of Health, Education, and Welfare, *The Measure of Poverty* 5–7, 14–17 (1976); Sar Levitan, *Programs in Aid of the Poor for the 1980s* 2–3, 29–32 (4th ed. 1980).

15. On framing in general, see Mark Kelman, "Interpretive Construction in the Substantive Criminal Law," 33 *Stanford Law Review* 591, 611–642 (1981).

16. Monroe Freedman, "Professional Responsibility of the Criminal Defense Lawyer: The Three Hardest Questions," 64 *Michigan Law Review* 1469, 1374–1375 (1966).

17. The example is inspired by events at Stanford University in 1984. Because I have altered the facts, I offer it as hypothetical.

18. See Comment, "Union Affiliations and Collective Bargaining," 128 *University of Pennsylvania Law Review* 430, 440–453 (1979) (discussing the "continuity of representation" doctrine).

19. See Paul Weiler, "Promises to Keep: Securing Workers' Rights to Self-Organization Under the NLRA," 96 *Harvard Law Review* 1769, 1795–1797 (1983) (discussing the debilitating effects of delay in the NLRA enforcement process on union organizing efforts).

20. See *NLRB v. Financial Inst. Employees* 475 U.S. 192, 203, 209 (1986).

21. For acknowledgment and critique of views that suggest that Contextual norms entail more time and effort, see Chapter 3 above.

22. Paul Berman, *Trial Advocacy in a Nutshell* 184–229 (1979).

23. *The T.J. Hooper* 60 F.2d 737 (1932).

24. See *ABA Model Code of Professional Responsibility* EC 2–27 (asserting that the "lawyer should not decline representation because a client or a cause is unpopular or community reaction is adverse").

25. See the correspondence between Bowles and Field reprinted in Andrew Kaufman, *Problems in Professional Responsibility* 424–444 (2d ed. 1984). For

general accounts of the Erie railroad struggles, see Charles Francis Adams and Henry Adams, *Chapters of Erie and Other Essays* 1–99, 135–191 (1886); M. Klein, *The Life and Legend of Jay Gould* 81–98 (1986).

26. Field was alleged to have offered $5,000 to a political crony of a judge then favoring the Vanderbilt camp to induce the judge to modify an injunction. The charge was never resolved. See Adams and Adams, *Chapters of Erie* 36–37.

27. See ibid.; Kaufman, *Problems* 431–433, 440–444 (reprinting the correspondence between Bowles and Field).

28. It is sometimes suggested that the lawyer should feel greater pressure to take on the client if the lawyer is the client's only prospect for representation, or as Murray Schwartz put it, if she is "the last lawyer in town." "The Zeal of the Civil Advocate," 1983 *American Bar Foundation Research Journal* 543, 562–563. The suggestion is wrong to the extent the ground for the lawyer's refusal is a judgment that the client's position lacks merit. In that case, representing the client would be a wasteful and potentially destructive use of scarce resources.

The situation may, however, involve a distinct problem. If the lawyer is not the "last lawyer in town" but the *only* lawyer in town (or the only one who is likely to consider the matter), then her decision involves more responsibility. This is not a reason to take the case regardless of the merits, but it is a reason to take exceptional care in assessing the merits.

29. John Heinz and Edward Laumann, *Chicago Lawyers* 145–146, 149–151 (1982); Herbert McCloskey and A. Brill, *Dimensions of Tolerance* 245–247 (1983).

30. I assume for heuristic purposes that the information came from the real murderer, though Powell's account is ambiguous on this point. Arthur Powell, *I Can Go Home Again* 289–292 (2d ed. 1943).

31. See Fred Zacharias, "Rethinking Confidentiality," 74 *Iowa Law Review* 351, 344–345 (1989), which reports a small-sample survey in which 42 percent of lay respondents indicated a belief that the rule permitted the attorney to disclose in the Innocent Convict situation, and 80 percent favored such a rule.

32. I am assuming that there is some disclosure the lawyer can make that will materially increase the chances of clearing the innocent convict. That is not necessarily the case. The lawyer would not be permitted to testify to the client's self-inculpatory statement. But reporting it to the authorities or defense counsel might make a big difference. For example, the statement might suggest the location of important evidence. To the extent that disclosure would futile, the case for making it certainly becomes less compelling.

33. Insofar as the communications involved a future criminal act, possibly including some effort to obstruct investigation of the prior one, some versions

of the disciplinary rules would permit disclosure of the intent to commit the act. Moreover, the attorney-client evidentiary privilege would not apply to many requests for information about how to evade detection or apprehension for a past criminal act.

34. *Model Rules* 1, 6, Comment, paragraph 19; Zacharias, "Rethinking Confidentiality" 390–391.

35. Paul Taylor, "Excess Land Law: Calculated Circumvention," 52 *California Law Review* 978 (1964); Grant McConnell, *The Decline of Agrarian Democracy* (1953).

36. For a discussion (focused on Kaye Scholer) of whether different norms are appropriate for different areas of practice, see David Wilkins, "Making Context Count: Regulating Lawyers After Kaye Scholer," 66 *Southern California Law Review* 1145 (1993).

37. See William H. Simon, "The Kaye Scholer Affair," *Law and Social Inquiry* (1998).

7. Is Criminal Defense Different?

1. David Luban, *Lawyers and Justice: An Ethical Study* 58–66 (1988); Richard Wasserstrom, "Lawyers as Professionals: Some Moral Issues," 5 *Human Rights* 1, 12 (1975); Deborah Rhode, "Ethical Perspectives on Law Practice," 37 *Stanford Law Review* 589, 605 (1985).

2. According to one Manhattan assistant district attorney, "By and large, defense lawyers play a game. It's called delay. The more you delay your cases, the weaker they get for the prosecution." Steven Brill, "Fighting Crime in a Crumbling System," *The American Lawyer* 3 (July-Aug. 1989).

3. James S. Kunen, *How Can You Defend Those People? The Making of a Criminal Lawyer* 117 (1983). This type of argument seems to be regarded as legitimate by most defense lawyers. By contrast, the propriety of presenting client perjury and impeaching truthful witnesses is controversial. Compare Monroe Freedman, *Lawyer's Ethics in an Adversary System* 43–58 (1975) (defending these practices) with Harry Subin, "The Criminal Defense Lawyer's 'Different Mission': Reflections on the 'Right' to Present a False Case," 1 *Georgetown Journal of Legal Ethics* 125 (1987) (criticizing them).

4. See Joe Trento, "Inside the Helms File," *National Law Journal*, December 22, 1980, p. 1 (on greymail); Subin, "Criminal Defense" 129–136 (on use of prior sexual history in rape cases).

5. See Luban, *Lawyers and Justice* 58–66; Barbara Babcock, "Defending the Guilty," 32 *Cleveland State Law Review* 175 (1983–84); Charles Fried, *An Anatomy of Values: Problems of Personal and Social Choice* 128–132 (1970).

6. Luban, *Lawyers and Justice* 60.

7. In responding to an earlier version of this Chapter, David Luban analyzed the available data on the comparative resources of prosecutors and defenders and conceded that they showed no dramatic disparity. Prosecutors have an advantage in personnel "ranging from slight to significant," but "somewhat more money is probably spent on criminal defense lawyers than on prosecutors." "Are Criminal Defenders Different?" 91 *Michigan Law Review*, 1729, 1732–33 (1993).

Luban emphasizes that this comparison leaves out the police, an enormous resource available to prosecutors in the preparation of their cases. Fair point, but I would add that the comparison also leaves out three factors that favor the defense: (1) Prosecutors have the burden of proof, and it's a high one. Arguably, fairness requires a resource advantage for the party with the burden of proof. (2) Because of the rule of *Brady v. Maryland*, 373 U.S. 83 (1963) requiring prosecutors to turn over exculpatory material to defendants, some prosecutorial investigation benefits defendants. (3) Not all activities of prosecutors involve prosecution. Some prosecutorial resources go to investigating and analyzing cases that are never filed. There is no substantial counterpart to this "screening" activity on the defense side.

8. David Luban, "Partisanship, Betrayal, and Autonomy in the Lawyer-Client Relationship: A Reply to Stephen Ellmann," 90 *Columbia Law Review* 1004, 1028 (1990).

9. Freedman, *Lawyer's Ethics* 2.

10. John Kaplan, "Defending Guilty People," 7 *University of Bridgeport Law Review* 223, 231–32 (1986)

11. The point is elaborated in John B. Mitchell, "The Ethics of the Criminal Defense Attorney: New Answers to Old Questions," 32 *Stanford Law Review* 293 (1980).

12. One apparently widespread police and prosecutorial response to strict federal court decisions on search and seizure issues has been police perjury designed to circumvent the decisions. Myron Orfield, "Deterrence, Perjury, and the Heater Factor: An Empirical Study of the Exclusionary Rule in the Chicago Criminal Courts," 63 *University of Colorado Law Review* 75 (1992).

13. Freedman, *Lawyer's Ethics* 2.

14. I have often heard this argument in conversations with defense lawyers.

15. This point is pressed by Freedman, *Lawyer's Ethics* 30. The claim that aggressive defense is important as a way of insuring adequate client disclosure to counsel is subject to the criticisms of confidentiality arguments in Chapter 3.

16. The arguments for and against the privilege are surveyed in Eugene Wigmore, VIII *Evidence* sections 2250–84 (McNaughton, rev., 1961), and David Dolinko, "Is There a Rationale for the Privilege Against Self-Incrimina-

tion?" 33 *UCLA Law Review* 1063 (1986). Dolinko's excellent article argues that the privilege lacks a plausible justification.

17. Luban, *Lawyers and Justice* 194.

18. William Faulkner, *Intruder in the Dust* 57 (1949).

19. George Fletcher, "The Metamorphosis of Larceny," 89 *Harvard Law Review* 469 (1976).

Another argument occasionally advanced for the privilege is that to require someone to give evidence that would tend to bring about his own punishment is unconscionably cruel. The cruelty lies in the psychological pain that the person suffers on two counts: from knowing that his truthful statements will bring punishment, and from fighting the temptation to lie. See, for example, Luban, *Lawyers and Justice* 194.

As David Dolinko has pointed out, this claim is inconsistent with a variety of legal practices that impose punishment on people for failing to make psychologically difficult but morally appropriate choices. People who suffer enormous psychological difficulty in refraining from sexual abuse, battery, or theft are rarely excused from failing to make the correct choices on these matters. Dolinko, "Is There a Rationale" 1090–1117.

Moreover, we usually assess the cruelty of punishment, not just in terms of the magnitude of pain to the punished, but in terms of the proportionality of the pain to the social benefits and justice of the punishment. Self-incrimination fares quite well on these latter two standards. It is often quite helpful in law enforcement, and it can be seen as a form of restitutionary justice. Both popular morality and many ethical theories see acknowledgment of one's crimes as a valuable first step in making amends to those who have been wronged. Furthermore, self-incrimination spares the public additional law enforcement expenses that would otherwise result from the crime; to the extent these additional expenses have to be incurred, they compound the initial injustice of the crime itself.

Finally, given that the dilemma affects only guilty defendants, I am unable to grasp the intuition that the type of psychological pain the argument identifies is particularly weighty in a world that accepts capital punishment and long confinement in harsh prison conditions.

20. See Akhil Amar and Renee Lettow, "Fifth Amendment First Principles," 93 *Michigan Law Review* 857 (1995).

21. See note 3 above and accompanying text.

22. ABA Model Rules of Professional Conduct 3.4(e).

23. Monroe Freedman, "Professional Responsibility of the Criminal Defense Lawyer: The Three Hardest Questions," 64 *Michigan Law Review* 1469, 1471 (1966).

24. Charles Wright, *Federal Practice and Procedure,* section 461 (1982).

25. The "burden-of-going-forward" dimension of the burden of proof involves the duty to go first and present at least a minimal case. Where the party with the burden fails to do so, the other party is entitled to a dismissal without making any showing of her own. The "risk of nonpersuasion" dimension of the burden of proof determines who loses if the trier does not find either party's case more persuasive than the other's. The person with this burden loses where the trier is left "in equipoise."

26. Wasserstrom, "Lawyers as Professionals" 12.

27. Babcock, "Defending the Guilty" 178–179.

28. *Rummel v. Estelle,* 445 U.S. 263 (1980) (rejecting the claim that the punishment was unconstitutionally cruel and unusual).

29. Mike Davis, *City of Quartz: Excavating the Future in Los Angeles* 288 (1990).

30. Fox Butterfield, "U.S. Expands the Lead in Rate of Imprisonment," *New York Times,* Feb. 11, 1992, p. 16; Elliott Currie, *Confronting Crime* 28 (1985).

31. Marc Mauer and Tracy Huling, *Young Black Americans and the Criminal Justice System: Five Years Later* (The Sentencing Project, October 1995).

32. See the chilling portrait of the Darryl Gates regime in Los Angeles in Davis, *City of Quartz* 267–322.

33. See *Rummel v. Estelle,* 445 U.S. 263 (1980); *Solem v. Helm,* 463 U.S. 277 (1983).

34. See Stephen A. Salzburg and Daniel Capra, *American Criminal Justice* 665–670 (1992).

35. See, for example, Luban, "Are Criminal Defenders Different?"

8. Institutionalizing Ethics

1. By "inclusive" bar association I refer to both mandatory or integrated bars that require membership of all lawyers in the jurisdiction—about two-thirds of the states now have them—and voluntary associations, such as the ABA, that aspire to recruit and represent the entire bar.

The disadvantage of inclusive bar associations is that, because their memberships tend to be more diverse, they have greater difficulty reaching agreement and are more subject to pressure toward the "lowest common denominator." Michael Powell, *From Patrician to Professional Elite: The Transformation of the New York City Bar Association* ch. 1 (1988).

2. See generally Geoffrey C. Hazard, Jr., Susan P. Koniak, and Roger C. Cramton, *The Law and Ethics of Lawyering* 57–153 (2d ed. 1994).

3. On the Association of the Bar of the City of New York, see Powell, *From Patrician to Professional.* For the Association's work in the area of tax

ethics, see Special Committee on the Lawyer's Role in Tax Practice, The Association of the Bar of the City of New York, "The Lawyer's Role in Tax Practice," 36 *Tax Lawyer* 865 (1983).

4. For excellent discussions of such issues, see Deborah Rhode, "Institutionalizing Ethics," 44 *Case Western Reserve Law Review* 665 (1994); David Wilkins, "Who Should Regulate Lawyers?" 105 *Harvard Law Review* 799 (1992).

5. Roscoe Pound, *An Introduction to the Philosophy of Law* 58

6. *Restatement of Torts Second* Section 283, comments c,d.

7. *Strickland v. Washington* 466 U.S. 668, 668–69 (1984).

8. *Model Code* EC 3–5.

9. *Model Rules* 1.1 (lawyer must provide skill and effort "reasonably necessary" for the representation); 1.5 (fees must be "reasonable"), 1.7 (conflicting representations permitted only with informed consent and where lawyer "reasonably believes" neither client will be adversely affected).

10. Stephen Bundy and Einer Elhauge, "Knowledge About Legal Sanctions," 92 *Michigan Law Review* 261, 313–321 (1993); David Wilkins, "Legal Realism for Lawyers," 104 *Harvard Law Review* 468, 511–513 (1990).

11. For example, Anthony Kronman, *The Lost Lawyer* (1993).

12. Moreover, character judgments are much more difficult than conduct judgments. Despite its long-standing proclivity to judge its members under categorical norms, the bar was disposed until recently to judge applicants for admission on the basis of general standards of "good moral character." The record of this practice is notoriously poor. Such judgments were more often than not erratic and frequently shields for political and social prejudice. See Deborah Rhode, "Moral Character as a Professional Credential," 94 *Yale Law Journal* 491 (1985).

13. Melvin Eisenberg, "The Limits of Cognition and the Limits of Contract, 47 *Stanford Law Review* 211, 251–252 (1995).

14. See Michael Klausner, "Corporations, Corporate Law, and Networks of Contracts," 81 *Virginia Law Review* 757 (1995).

15. See Ronald J. Gilson and Robert H. Mnookin, "Disputing Through Agents: Cooperation and Conflict Between Lawyers in Litigation," 94 *Columbia Law Review* 509 (1994).

16. See Ian Ayres and Robert Gertner, "Filling Gaps in Incomplete Contracts: An Economic Theory of Default Rules," 99 *Yale Law Journal* 87 (1989).

Further Reading

The outstanding theoretical treatment of legal ethics is David Luban's *Lawyers and Justice: An Ethical Study* (1988). Also interesting and thoughtful is Anthony Kronman's *The Lost Lawyer* (1993), though it has less to say about lawyers than you might expect. Robert Gordon's "The Independence of Lawyers," 68 *Boston University Law Review* 1 (1988), is an important effort to combine jurisprudential and institutional analysis.

Unfortunately, there are few sympathetic theoretical treatments of the Dominant View. For the most part, the Dominant View has been expounded at the level of theory by its critics, who have inferred its contours from popular and doctrinal materials. The leading theoretical defenses of the Dominant View are Stephen Pepper, "The Lawyer's Amoral Ethical Role: A Defense, a Problem, and Some Possibilities," 1986 *American Bar Foundation Research Journal* 613, and various works by Monroe Freedman, for example, *Understanding Legal Ethics* (1990).

A summary of legal ethics doctrine can be found in Charles Wolfram, *Modern Legal Ethics* (1986); an updated edition is promised for the near future. An innovative course book helpfully situates ethics rules and cases in the context of a broader set of legal doctrines that affect the lawyering role: Geoffrey Hazard, Jr., Susan Koniak, and Roger Cramton, *The Law and Ethics of Lawyering* (2d ed. 1994).

A newcomer wishing to pursue some of the general jurisprudential themes discussed in the text might begin with Elizabeth Mensch, "The History of Mainstream Legal Thought," in *The Politics of Law* (rev. ed. 1990), and Morton J. Horwitz, *The Transformation of American Law: 1870–1960* (1992). She might then go on to Ronald Dworkin, *Law's*

Empire (1986) and Duncan Kennedy, *A Theory of Adjudication* (1997).

There is a vast literature on the relative merits of categorical and contextual judgment. The best known contemporary discussion is Duncan Kennedy, "Form and Substance in Private Law Adjudication," 89 *Harvard Law Review* 1685 (1975).

Chapter 2: A Right to Injustice. For the modern critique of Positivism, see Ronald Dworkin, *Taking Rights Seriously,* chs. 2 and 3 (1977). For the modern critique of Libertarianism, see Mark Kelman, "Taking Takings Seriously: An Essay for Centrists," 74 *California Law Review* 1829 (1986), and Barbara Fried, *The Progressive Assault on Laissez-Faire* ch. 2 (1998). Positivism in the form presupposed by the Dominant View no longer has sophisticated proponents, but Libertarianism does. See, for example, Richard Epstein, *Takings* (1985). On the problem of "private legislation," see Stewart Macaulay, "Private Government," in *Law and the Social Sciences* (Leon Lipson and Stanton Wheeler, eds., 1986).

Other critiques of the Dominant View that recognize the obsolescence of some of its premises are Maura Strassberg, "Taking Ethics Seriously: Beyond Positivist Jurisprudence in Legal Ethics," 80 *Iowa Law Review* 901 (1995), and David Wilkins, "Legal Realism for Lawyers," 103 *Harvard Law Review* 468 (1990). Each includes some criticism of my argument.

Chapter 3: Justice in the Long Run. An especially elegant and influential essay that deals with some of the themes of this chapter is David Luban, "The Adversary System Excuse" in *The Good Lawyer* (David Luban, ed., 1984). The most interesting article on confidentiality is Fred Zacharias, "Rethinking Confidentiality," 74 *Iowa Law Review* 351 (1989). See also Elizabeth Thornburg, "Sanctifying Secrecy: The Mythology of the Corporate Attorney-Client Privilege," 69 *Notre Dame Law Review* 157 (1993), which usefully summarizes much of the literature. As noted above, some of the arguments of this chapter are criticized in Stephen Bundy and Einer Elhauge, "Knowledge About Legal Sanctions," 92 *Michigan Law Review* 261 (1993).

Chapter 4: Should Lawyers Obey the Law? The rich literature on principled or conscientious noncompliance is cited in the notes. More general perspectives can be found in Mortimer Kadish and Sanford Kadish, *Discretion to Disobey* (1973), and Robert Cover, "Nomos and Narrative," 97 *Harvard Law Review* 4 (1983). For sympathetic critiques of my argument see David Luban, "Legal Ideals and Moral Obligations: A Comment on Simon," 38 *William and Mary Law Review* 255 (1996), and David Wilkins, "In Defense of Law and Morality: Why Lawyers Should Have a Prima Facie Obligation to Obey the Law," 38 *William and Mary Law Review* 269 (1996), and for stronger disagreement, Selena Stier, "Legal Ethics: The Integrity Thesis," 52 *Ohio State Law Journal* 551 (1991); John DiPippa, "Lon Fuller, the Model Code, and the Model Rules," 37 *South Texas Law Review* 303, 340–343 (1996).

Chapter 5: Lawyering as Meaningful Work. David Luban deals with some of the themes of this chapter, also invoking Brandeis as a role model, in "The Noblesse Oblige Tradition in the Practice of Law," 41 *Vanderbilt Law Review* 717 (1988). So does Bryant Garth, "Independent Professional Power and the Search for a Legal Ideology With Progressive Bite," 62 *Indiana Law Journal* 214 (1986), which includes some friendly criticism of my views. The most extensive treatment of Brandeis as an ethical role model is Clyde Spillenger, "Elusive Advocate: Reconsidering Brandeis as People's Lawyer" 105 *Yale Law Journal* 1445 (1996), which takes a different, more critical view than mine or Luban's.

On meaningful work in general, see Roberto Unger, *Social Theory* 26–35 (1987), and especially, George Eliot's *Middlemarch* (1871–72) and Alpheus Mason's biography, *Brandeis: A Free Man's Life* (1946).

Chapter 6: Legal Ethics as Contextual Judgment. Other approaches that resemble the Contextual View appear in Kronman's *Lost Lawyer* and Heidi Feldman, "Can Good Lawyers Be Good Ethical Deliberators?" 69 *Southern California Law Review* 885 (1996). My approach is criticized from the perspective of variations on the "role morality" critique in Rob Atkinson, "Beyond the New Role Morality for Lawyers," 51 *Maryland Law Review* 853 (1992), and Thomas Shaffer and

Robert Cochran, *Lawyers, Clients, and Moral Responsibility* 30–39 (1994).

Chapter 7: Is Criminal Defense Different? For the most part, normative discussion of criminal defense remains a wasteland in which a "crime control" crowd attacks aggressive defense without acknowledging the systemic cruelty and injustice of current penal practices, and a "due process" crowd replies with anachronistic arguments indifferent to the distinction between substantively just and unjust punishment.

David Luban's reply to an earlier version of this chapter, though unpersuasive to me, contains many interesting factual observations and references. "Are Criminal Defenders Different?" 91 *Michigan Law Review* 1703 (1993). Paul Butler's "Racially-Based Jury Nullification: Black Power in the Criminal Justice System," 105 *Yale Law Journal* 677 (1995), though it has a more limited focus than my proposal, invokes the nullification tradition for purposes similar to mine.

Chapter 8: Institutionalizing Ethics. Comprehensive discussions of institutional issues in professional responsibility regulation can be found in David Wilkins, "Who Should Regulate Lawyers?" 105 *Harvard Law Review* 799 (1992); and Deborah Rhode, "Institutionalizing Ethics," 44 *Case Western Reserve Law Review* 665 (1994). Two studies that focus on the ethical pressures from the organization of the market for legal services are Ronald Gilson and Robert Mnookin, "Disputing Through Agents: Cooperation and Conflict Between Lawyers and Litigation," 94 *Columbia Law Review* 509 (1994), and Richard Painter, "Toward a Market for Lawyer Disclosure Services: In Search of Optimal Whistleblowing Rules," 63 *George Washington Law Review* 221 (1995).

Acknowledgments

My argument has been inspired by two broad and quite distinct bodies of jurisprudence—Critical Legal Studies and the legal liberalism of Ronald Dworkin.

In the work of my teachers and friends in Critical Legal Studies I have found the most powerful contemporary critique of libertarianism and a conception of legal doctrine as a set of structured instabilities. I have followed them in rejecting the presumption that conventional practices reflect a coherent set of normative justifications and that the practical limits on the revision of such practices are as rigid or fixed as discussion often assumes.

In Dworkin's work I have found the most powerful contemporary critique of Positivism and of radical skepticism about the possibility of grounded legal judgment. And without being completely convinced by it, I have been influenced by his phenomenological account of legal decisionmaking. Dworkin has been more successful than anyone else in suggesting what it means for a decisionmaker to take a legal issue seriously.

The ideas in this book took shape at a time when legal theorists became increasingly disengaged from practice and legal practitioners became increasingly sentimental and dogmatic. In my experience, Gary Bellow has been the outstanding exception to these unfortunate trends. He has remained dedicated to one of the most difficult and personally demanding areas of practice, while pursuing critical self-examination and speculative understanding. As example, mentor, and interlocutor, his influence has been enormous. Other theoretically engaged practitioners (and practically engaged theorists) from whom I have drawn insight and inspiration over the years include Jeanne Charn, Teresa Nelson, Louise Trubek, and Lucie White.

I owe debts of gratitude to many legal ethics scholars, but four are especially large. David Luban has done more than anyone else to bring depth to the field. He has also pioneered the critique of what I have called the Dominant View. Although I have learned much and borrowed heavily from him in private, I have tended in public—and indeed in this book—to focus on the relatively few matters on which we disagree. This perversity on my part has never impeded Luban's generosity and friendliness, for which I am enormously grateful. I am especially thankful for a detailed critique of the manuscript that led to many improvements and corrections.

Deborah Rhode has encouraged and supported me for many years in more ways than I could begin to name. She has read every word of this book, some of them more than once, and offered voluminous suggestions that have improved the argument. She also organized and presided over a seminar at Stanford that discussed a large part of the manuscript. The scant efforts I've made to suggest how my ideas might be institutionalized and implemented are largely due to her prodding and assistance.

During his years at Stanford, Bob Gordon was my closest intellectual ally. There are many points in the book where I would be unable to say whether the ideas are mine or his or our joint product. I miss him.

The last member of this remarkable quartet is David Wilkins, who has offered many forms of moral, intellectual, and epicurean support. I have drawn freely on his work, on many discussions with him, and on his extensive comments on the manuscript.

At Stanford, I also benefited from help and encouragement from Bill Rubenstein, George Fisher, Barbara Babcock, Tom Nolan, and Janet Halley. I have had valuable long-standing episodic dialogues with Steve Pepper of the University of Denver, Tony Alfieri of the University of Miami, Fred Zacharias of the University of San Diego, Robert Post of Berkeley, Rob Atkinson of Florida State University, Guyora Binder of the State University of New York at Buffalo, and Steve Bundy of Berkeley.

The Guggenheim Foundation and the Keck Foundation provided generous financial support.

I'm grateful to Pat Adan and Carol Crane for superb secretarial and administrative assistance. Stanford Law School's amazing library staff, especially Andy Eisenberg and Paul Lomio, has been invaluable. Michael Aronson and Anita Safran of Harvard University Press skillfully superintended the editing and production of the book.

I have depended on the love and emotional support of Carmen Chang, Mike Simon, and K. C. Simon. Mike and K. C. deserve credit for the patience they have shown in waiting such a very long time to see their names in print.

I have drawn freely, especially in chapters 4, 6, and 7, on the following previously published work: "Should Lawyers Obey the Law?" 38 *William and Mary Law Review* 217 (1996); "Ethical Discretion in Lawyering," 101 *Harvard Law Review* 1083 (1988); "The Ethics of Criminal Defense," 91 *Michigan Law Review* 1703 (1993).

Index